the balance of power in society

Books by Frank Tannenbaum

The Labor Movement

Wall Shadows

Darker Phases of the South

The Mexican Agrarian Revolution

Peace by Revolution: *An Interpretation of Mexico*

Osborne of Sing Sing

Whither Latin America

Crime and the Community

Slave and Citizen: *The Negro in the Americas*

Mexico: *The Struggle for Peace and Bread*

A Philosophy of Labor

The American Tradition in Foreign Policy

Ten Keys to Latin America

(ED.) *A Community of Scholars*

the balance
of power
in society
and other essays

by Frank Tannenbaum

introduction by *John Herman Randall*

the macmillan company
an arkville press book

The Macmillan Company
Collier-Macmillan Limited, London

To Armand G. Erpf

friend, philosopher, financier

preface

IT IS LOGICAL, I think, to bring these papers together under the title of *The Balance of Power in Society*, for the first essay does contain an overall view of the nature of society and man's relation to it. I would suspect that everything I have ever written would somehow find its place within this generalized statement of the institutional embodiment of human life, of man's relation to his fellows, and of the implicit proposition that freedom and responsibility are two sides of the same coin. Man can, after all, only find freedom inside an institution in which he also finds the resources and the occasion for a responsible relationship. To be free the individual must face different and often contradictory choices none of which he can decline absolutely. His freedom lies in his ability to select the order and degree in which he will attend to their varied claims. He can not in the nature of things satisfy them all in the full. Therein lies his freedom. The greater the number of choices he can make the wider the range of his responsibilities and the fuller the life he can live. This is a shorthand note of a philosophy of life—a life that man can only live in an institutional setting just as fish can only live in water.

The essays were written over many years and under some specific need to respond to a given situation—some new views, some unexpected experience, some idea I had not had before. The earlier and more ebullient pieces go back to the 'twenties. All but three have been previously published. *The International Corporation and World Order* and *Implications of an Educational Movement*—were specifically written for inclusion in this collection. *Play and Society* was prepared for a recent conference held in Mexico on the social aspects of the Olympics.

A number of the individual essays have either become books or are meant to do so. "The Professional Criminal" became in time *Crime and the Community*, with an introduction by Professor Robert MacIver. "Destiny of the Negro in the Western Hemisphere" became *Slave and Citizen;* the essay on "The Social Function of Trade Unions" became *A Philosophy of Labor;* "The American Tradition in Foreign Policy" and "The Balance of Power Versus the Coordinate State" became *The American Tradition in Foreign Policy.* "The Prospects of a Violent Revolution in the United States," "Political Stability," and "The Balance of Power in Society" are meant to become books. Two of the essays, "The Implications of an Educational Movement" and "The University Seminar Movement," are an effort to generalize about an ongoing enterprise to which I have given much time. Instead of foreshadowing a book they tell inadequately an unfolding story in higher education the future outcome of which is not fully visible at present.

Richard Eells, who is both friend and critic, saw to it that this volume got through the press, for which I am more than grateful. And I am grateful to my life-long friend John Herman Randall for his introduction.

F. T.

Columbia University
May 1968

introduction

FRANK TANNENBAUM is a man of many and varied experiences. He has always been able to feel vividly and sympathetically, to talk about, and hence to learn from, these experiences. Consequently he is a man of many and varied ideas. Since he is profoundly conservative, he is convinced men come to maturity looking out on the world through their own distinctive windows. However much they may learn, men never come to look out of different windows. Frank is a determined advocate of the American tradition, its democratic ethos, its profoundly moral conception of the proper international policy. He hopes, through a maturing trade unionism, to bring industrial society back to the world of status that antedated the rise of the individualistic national state. He wants, through developing the international corporation and other such functional organizations, like the church or professional activity in general, to bypass and relegate to innocuous desuetude the sovereign state, with its paranoiac fixation on security and expansion, and to return to a modern form of the medieval world, where sovereignty had not emerged and its place was taken by transnational functional organizations like the Church. He is so radical that he wants to revolutionize higher education through bypassing departments and disciplines in his interdisciplinary program of university seminars.

The concrete meaning of all these ideas the reader can discover from the present collection of essays. Some of the essays Frank has developed into volumes. He has written well-known books on criminology, on the labor movement, on the Mexican agrarian revolution, on slavery and the Negro's experience, on Latin America, on foreign policy, on the reform of higher education. In many senses of the term, Frank is a pluralist. The one thing he has never produced is a system that will bring all his wealth of ideas together. That is just not his window. Hence he is a contemporary philosopher, one who in the present fashion is exploring the implications of many particular problems and areas of human experience.

Frank grew up on a farm in the Berkshires, and ever since he has tended to see the world in terms of the experience of a face-to-face community. His intellectual power is revealed by the fact that when traveling through Mexico on a burro he was soon able to come to think just like that burro. Or so he maintains. This gift for the *Verstehen* of his immediate companions runs through all his reports on the diverse groups he has lived with, from professors to convicts and other regimented minds. Such a power of descriptive psychology underlies most of his studies. He can think himself into the attitudes and feelings of professional criminals and professors, of Mexican Indians and New York trade unionists, with equal ease. It is in terms of such concrete experiences that he actually thinks, not in terms of intellectual abstractions.

Running away from his parents on the farm, he came to New York and fell in with the IWW. That experience reinforced his rural parochialism; he has never had the slightest temptation toward a centralized state socialism. He came into prominence just before World War I by leading a group of homeless unemployed into a church to sleep—he took literally the Biblical injunction "Come unto me all ye who labor and are heavy laden and I will give you rest." A year's prison term on Blackwell's Island resulted, an experience that led him to make many friends among criminals, including the prison reformer Thomas Mott Osborne of Sing Sing, and aroused his interest in prison reform and criminology. The episode led Dean Frederick P. Keppel to admit him to Columbia College where he met the stimulus of the social scientists then adorning the campus. He used to visit E. R. A. Seligman, Henry Seager, and John Dewey in their offices before their classes, talk over the theme of the coming hour, and tell them what to teach. Dewey's own bent of mind—and patient tolerance—made him amenable to Frank's instruction, and together they gave a most suggestive course in institutional functional pluralism. This course is best known through Dewey's *The Public and Its Problems.*

Frank went for graduate work to the Brookings Institution. His interest in criminology led him to study Southern prisons, and the South aroused his enduring concern with the plight of American Negroes as well as poor whites, whom, with Myrdal, he judged to be worse off. His identification and contact with organized labor was a continuing concern: he sees the labor movement as a social revolution, not merely an economic drive. A visit to Mexican labor leaders directed him to the Mexican revolution and led to his doctoral thesis and eventually to his succeeding W. R. Shepherd in the chair of Latin-American history at Columbia. The Latin-American experience led him on to American foreign policy in general, where he has vigorously defended the American moral concern with the equality of coordinate states against the newer "science" of international relations based on national interest, the balance of power, and *Realpolitik;* the reader will detect (essays 4 and 5) an imperfect sympathy with Hans J. Morgenthau and George F. Kennan. Association with professors led Frank naturally to promote plans to get them together on a face-to-face basis, and to create the university seminars, the latest of his continuing concerns to take active form.

The essays range from the early 1920's to the present— covering a period of nearly fifty years. Most of them date from shortly after World War II. In substance they range from vivid reporting and descriptive psychology (15, 16, and 17) to social philosophy (1, 2, 3, and 11), foreign policy (4 and 5), and educational reform (13 and 14).

The title essay, "The Balance of Power in Society" (1946), is Frank's fundamental social analysis. It finds four basic social institutions in society, each struggling to become supreme and take over the functions of the others: the family, the church, the economy, and the state. When a precarious balance is achieved between them, human freedom is measurably assured: men can choose the obligations due to each institution. Each is inevitably frustrated in its extreme claims: society is far from malleable by any group. In the social sphere there is no discernible progress, such as is exhibited in the growth of science and technology. There is only a recurrent rise of each institution in turn. Today the state has long been absorbing the functions of the others. But Frank has come to think that the economy, in the shape of the emerging international corporation, will expand until the state, in its sovereign and nationalistic functions, will wither away and come to serve only as the preserver of local order. Frank's syndicalism has always distrusted the state. The functions he assigns it during the dominance of the national and technological state he has always granted grudgingly: and he has emphasized the military rather than the economic role of the state. Its regulatory power over the large-scale economy, and its role as the balance-wheel over the other institutions, he probably underemphasizes. Even the economy, he hopes, will with abundant power become decentralized (11).

"On Political Stability" is a statement of Frank's argument for parochialism, the preference for the power of the local community as opposed to centralization of power. There, Frank holds, is preserved more of the sense of the limitations of human power, so salutary for man's overweening arrogance, a sense lost with the Great Society (of Graham Wallas, not of Lyndon B. Johnson). Frank also argues against granting too great importance to the inevitable struggles within each institution. Thus he sees capital and labor merging together within the maturing economy, which hence seems to be approaching the syndicalistic ideal of a functional industrial democracy. He doubtless underemphasizes the effect of a technological economy on the other institutions—such fruits as the secularization of the Church, for example. One shortcoming of his analysis is his failing to take account of the extent to which the Church in the modern world, and especially in the United States, has itself become fundamentally pluralized. And one can only wonder whether, just as the national state emerged in the late Middle Ages, the University, or the "intellectual establishment," is not already emerging as a fifth institution. Education in general Frank treats as a service activity that the others struggle to dominate.

Everywhere Frank finds salutary struggle, competition for men's allegiance within and between institutions. The only friction Frank wants to abolish completely is that between sovereign states, as too dangerous given our demonic power. Essay 3, the most recent, on "The International Corporation and World Order," foresees a diminution and eventual disappearance of this friction, as corporations—which seem to him never to compete—take over the functions of sovereign states.

Frank Tannenbaum has been expressing basic ideas of American social science and philosophy as they emerged as a distinctive body of thought between 1900 and 1945. He thus belongs with such seminal figures as Charles Horton Cooley, Walton Hamilton, and John Dewey. Since 1945 the arrogance of power has greatly strengthened the state, and tended to submerge such a pluralistic analysis. One can hope that this volume of essays of a distinguished American social philosopher may help to stem the tide, and bring American thought back to its best and most stimulating tradition.

John Herman Randall
COLUMBIA UNIVERSITY

contents

the balance of power
in society   *1*

IN THEIR ZEAL for bedeviling the world, the Communists are
confounding the traditional democrats by taking over their
slogans and insisting that they (the Communists) are more
"democratic" than the traditional democrats. They promise
the individual a higher standard of living, a greater share of
the goods of this world, a true "people's peace," and a surer
felicity. The democrats of the older tradition can only answer
that the Communists' offer is spurious and the promise false,
that under the new dispensation the individual would be
poorer in worldly goods and lose his freedom in the bargain.
But if the argument seems to put the traditional democrats on
the defensive, it is because they and the Communists as well
draw their inspiration from a common source of ideas and
beliefs—only that the Communists insist that the traditional
democrats are betraying the faith. The difficulty lies in the
fact that they both aspire to felicity, both believe in continuous progress, both have the perfectibility of man as an inherent assumption, and both assume that the perfect world is
identical with a static one. The economists' ideal of "perfect
competition" and the Communists' ideal of a "classless   1

Reprinted, with permission, from *Political Science Quarterly*, LXI
(December 1946), pp. 481–504.

society" are bastard children of the same aspiration for an immutable social order. The hope of the perfect state and the perfect man lies in both traditional democratic and Communist prescription, for in both there is the assumption of a completely malleable universe, so pliable to the human will that it can be forced to yield to the design men have framed for it. The traditional democrats would achieve their ends by individual, the Communists by collective, action. But such an assumption of a world completely malleable to the will of man is neither consonant with the nature of society nor an adequate accounting of the role man plays within it.

Society is not completely malleable to the hand of man. On the contrary, society is possessed by a series of irreducible institutions, perennial through time, that in effect both describe man and define the basic role he plays. Even in his most primitive state man is always and only found in a community. We do not know him in isolation. More than that, we always find him possessed of a language, for without it he could not symbolize the universe about him, and if he could not do that he would not be a man. But he is not merely a member of a community. The antithesis between man and society is, like so many other intellectual constructions, a delusive and, in fact, a mischievous simplification; for every society, even the most primitive, is always possessed of a number of institutions, organic to the society itself. The family, the church, and the state, to mention only the most obvious, are inherent in the pattern, inclusive in their claim upon the individual, and each in turn the visible structuring of an incommensurable experience. Man, as we know him, is therefore not merely the product of society, he is the very child of a complex institutional system that conditions his survival and sets the stage for the drama of life itself. These institutions, prevailing through time, manifest themselves in almost infinitely variable forms, but always fulfill the same role—the structuring of incommensurable human experiences and needs, and giving them a visible role in the culture. The family, in all of its innumerable designs and complexities, has always fulfilled the task of rearing the children, educating and preparing them for incorporation into the larger community. The community may have been savage, primitive or civilized, simple or complex, sedentary or wandering, organized into small villages or great nations; but always a well-defined series of relationships, responsibilities, commitments, and expectancies defined how and by whom the children were to be cared for, brought up, and instructed. The family may have varied in form and size, but it always fulfilled the same function in relation to the society. The very survival of the society itself was conditioned by the performance of these responsibilities.

If the family has persisted through time, so has the church. The church is here defined as that series of experiences, beliefs, attitudes, taboos, and practices that, taken together, give man a sense of identity within the universe, for he has always had an implicit or explicit description of the world and of his place in it and has always had a pattern of behavior that symbolized that relationship. The religious, like the family, experience is incommensurable with any other. The mystical Chichicastanango Indian, who ascends the church steps, sometimes on his knees, swinging an incense burner, and once inside, bows before his special saint, spends an hour talking to him, arguing with him, pleading, begging, or, in angry gesticulation, almost shouting, and sometimes in excitement throwing the rose petals he has brought, up at the saint as if in defiance, then humbly kissing the saint's feet, lighting a number of candles in front of him, and, as if that were not enough, asking permission from one or another group of Indians, who are kneeling and praying in some specially sacred spot, to join them in their devotion—that Indian can find only in the church the embodiment of his faith. This sense of humility, isolation, and loneliness in the world can find strength and peace only through a constant series of acts and practices that make for a sense of continuous contact between man and the unknown. The church has fulfilled this role in the life of man from the beginning, and,

4   in the nature of the case, this function could be fulfilled by no other institutions. Like the family, it has survived a thousand different cultures, and in each of them in varying form fulfilled the same inevitable and organic need—of giving life meaning by making man a part of the universe.

If the family and the church have proved perennial in the experience of man, so has the state. In one or another of a thousand variables, the state has performed the same basic function—the defense of the community against outside enemies, and the maintenance of a semblance of peace internally. The effectiveness of the state has varied, but the expectancy, the habit, and the implicit or explicit structuring of society to perform these ends have been conditions of social survival. The inner patterning that defined the responsibility for the fulfillment of these necessary tasks has called into being a great variety of types of state, but, regardless of the structure, the essential need and experience which it embodied have remained the same.

If the institutions have always been multiple and proved irreducible, it is because the experiences they embody are incommensurable. They have been, however, not merely multiple and irreducible, but also competitive. Each of the institutions in its own inner logic tends to be all-embracing, laying claim to the entire man, and showing an impelling tendency to assume all responsibility for the governance of society. A glance at the role of any one of these institutions under conditions that favored its full development will illustrate the issue in hand. If we take the European church at the height of its power, how vast is its role, and how varied its responsibilities. What was there that did not fall within the province of the church? From the time the child was born—or even before that, because marriage could take place only within the church—to the time the man was buried, because he could be buried only by the church and in a cemetery sanctified by the church, the individual lived within the orbit it prescribed. His beliefs were inculcated by the church; his morals, ethics, politics, law, theology, and philosophy came to him at the hands of the church. In his social life, the church defined his holidays, saints' days, and prescribed the form and character of the festivals; it influenced the games he played, the dress he wore, the food he ate. In his economic life, it imposed a tax (one-tenth) upon his income, it defined the permissible and nonpermissible in business activity—such as limiting the rate of interest—it influenced property distribution by abstracting part of the property from the ordinary tax laws, by accumulating property and removing it from private ownership and from the market, by collecting money for the building of churches, monasteries, cathedrals, and convents. In law, it claimed through the development of the canon law an increasing role in defining and punishing a great variety of civil and criminal acts. In politics it took on the role of crowning kings and freeing subjects of their allegiance to the crown—thus actually playing the part performed by a revolution. It was the great patron of the arts—painting and music were influenced by the church and performed for its greater glory. The church set the style in architecture. Its many cloisters, monasteries, and colleges became the centers of learning, and all learned men were beholden to it and lived their scholarly life within its folds, both physically and spiritually. The church, too, was the great source of social welfare: the hospitals were under its control and staffed by special groups of trained nurses organized in religious orders; it supported orphan asylums and homes for the aged; the unfortunate—the weak, the blind, the lame, and the poor—found refuge under its roof and succor in its establishments. Nothing in the society went on outside the orbit of the church.

If we turn now to examine the contemporary state, it is clear that it lays claim to all the mundane responsibilities, prerogatives, and powers once exercised by the church. The state, like the church, casts a protective mantle over the individual before he is born by insisting that it alone can legitimatize a child by marriage, and by imposing, normally, very serious handicaps upon the illegitimate. Marriage can be performed only by persons licensed by the state and upon the payment of a fee legally prescribed. The child can be attended at his birth only by a midwife, nurse, or doctor licensed by the state; and the state assumes powers over the child in case of neglect or incompetence of the parents. In certain extreme cases it can take the child from its parents and raise it at public expense, farm it out, or permit its adoption by foster parents. At a tender age the state compels the child's attendance in school, prescribes the course of study, trains, licenses, and pays the teachers, provides the buildings where the instruction is given, chooses the textbooks the child may read, maintains a clinic to guard the child's health, and may even provide food, not to mention transportation to and from the school. It specifies and attempts to control the ideas in which the child may be reared and the essential loyalties with which he is to be endowed.

The state, like the church in an older day, influences what the individual may or may not do, the amount he can earn, the profession he may follow. The range, number, and variety of rules by which the state shapes the economic activities of the individual are almost beyond enumeration. They include the kinds of vocational, professional, and cultural training offered in schools, the multiple systems of licensing, degrees, and examinations which determine competence for the earning of a living as a doctor, teacher, lawyer, engineer, or chauffeur—for one cannot even drive a car without an examination and a special license. The state licenses the butcher, baker, and candlestick maker; and the beggar must have his official tag before he can exhort the passer-by to remember the virtue of Christian charity. The state influences and limits what a man may earn by open and hidden systems of taxation, such as tariffs, quotas, income, and consumers' taxes. It limits or encourages production, it grants patents, it controls prices, it prescribes the rate of interest, it withholds or grants credit, and it interferes in the commercial relations between men by prescribing forms of contracts and by forcing upon the banks specified policies intimately affecting the economic relations between men. It sets limits to the transfer of property from parents to children by inheritance taxes, fixes wages and hours of labor, directly or indirectly influences prices, prescribes the permissible in food distribution, thus affecting the diet by a whole scheme of regulations governing the production, sale, and distribution of foods and drugs.

So, too, in the social life of the individual, it sets limits to the permissible in styles and behavior by laws prescribing what is or is not decent; it censors movies, plays and the printed word; it licenses public halls and amusement places; it watches over family relations, interferes between parents and children, and between man and wife; it attempts to control gambling, drinking, and extra-legal sex relations. The universities have fallen to the state; so have the hospitals, infirmaries, orphan asylums, and homes for the aged. Even charity has become a function of the state on a large scale, and the poor, the weak, the halt, and the blind, once the concern of the church, have now become a special province for the exercise of those efficiencies and skills that come under the heading of a "Department of Public Welfare."

The state, too, like the church of old, has become a patron of the arts; and public buildings are decorated, sometimes with surprising results, by artists hired at public expense. The state provides public concerts, supports the opera, and finances national, state, or city orchestras. In many places, the entire range of aesthetic and artistic education is in the hands of the state.

This cataloguing could go on indefinitely, for there is nothing in the life of man upon which the sovereign state does not lay a claim, or with which it does not in effect interfere. It is perfectly clear that what the church took for its province in the past, the state has now taken for its own; and modern means of communication and control have probably increased the "efficiency" and minuteness of the state's interferences.

But these supervisory and all-embracing claims upon man have been, and in places still are, exercised by the family, where the family is powerful enough. When conditions have been propitious, the family, as in China, in certain parts of Brazil, in Scotland, or even in Kentucky, has had an inclusive influence in shaping the destiny of the individual. The powerful family, as we know it, in a hundred different places and at different times has claimed for itself a complete control of the individual. Such a family is always large, possessed of innumerable relatives, associates, and dependents. Through intermarriage the family name is spread over an entire province, and none there are who dispute it in its own territory. If the state is strong enough to name a governor for the province, he is always a member of the family. The local militia is in the hands of the family, the judge is a relative, and the tax gatherer, if he dare show his face, [is] closely related. All of the economic activity of the region is in the family's hands. The priest is some promising and likely son purposely trained to fill that post to the family's great honor. The church is built on family ground, at family expense, and the priest receives his stipend at the family's hands. The stranger is an outsider, an itinerant soul who lives in the area or passes through the family's domain by special sufferance. The law, justice, order, and social disciplines are within the hands of the family, and younger children are sent to school, married, put to vocations, and allotted their places as a matter of course. The more distant relatives and retainers find their role within the pattern and accept it as part of the immutable rule of life itself. In innumerable instances, in many parts of the world, membership in such a family was all the honor a man needed, and it exacted and received a devotion as great as that ever received by church or state. There was a time, and not so very long ago, when one would rather be a member of one of the great Scottish clans—a Douglas, for instance—than a native of Scotland itself. Just as the church and state have at different times encompassed the individual from cradle to the grave, and prescribed his spiritual as well as his material destiny, so the family, too, in its turn has played the same historical role.

These perennial institutions, structured about the incommensurable experiences of man, all in their turn claim him as their own. He is a member of each of them and cannot escape them. The very content of life is found within their framework, and their claim upon it is in each case a total claim. Quite without deliberate intent, these institutions in turn, in the unplanned insistence to fulfill the need represented by the unique experience around which they are structured, tend to embrace all of the life of man. They compete not merely for his loyalty, but also for the exercise of the innumerable responsibilities and functions, and the satisfaction of the innumerable needs and aspirations that the life of man generates in a living world. The difficulty lies in the fact that the field, though it be complex, is limited, and that whatever one institution performs, and takes upon itself to perform, is at the expense of another. When the state takes over the educational system, it takes it away from the church; and when it takes upon itself the right to compel the schooling of the children, it takes the power of decision away from the family. What is true of education is true of marriage, what is true of sumptuary rules is true of the care of the young and the old. Every time the state assumes a new responsibility previously exercised by another institution, it is at the expense of that other institution in a material as well as a spiritual sense. As the state grows strong, the church and the family grow relatively weak; and as the church or family is strong, the other institutions are relatively weak.

These institutions, all at the service of man, are competitive with each other, and the conflict between them is, in fact, irremediable. Institutional friction and instability are, therefore, the normal state of society, and the hope of peace and quietude is an idle dream. Competition, imbalance, and friction are not merely continuous phenomena in society, but in fact are evidences of vitality and "normality." They reveal a healthy competitive institutional relationship in which no one is permitted completely to dominate the scene; for, in the circumstances, the peace represented by the dominion of one institution over all of the others is unhealthy, is evidence of

10   lack of resilience on the part of the other institutions, and is
a sure sign of a spreading tyranny. The formal peace represented by the power of one institution over all of the others
is synonymous with death. It is no accident that Hitler under-
mined the family and the church, and stripped them of all
those functions that described them as family or church. It
is no accident, because tyranny is the child of the preponderance of one institution over all of the others. Complete sup-
pression and destruction of the other institutions have never
occurred, and, in the nature of the case, cannot occur, for the
experiences these institutions represent are both irreducible
and incommensurable. But if these institutions cannot be
completely suppressed, there is ample historical evidence
that one or another can be so weakened that resulting imbalance manifests itself as tyranny, and ends—as it always has
—in violence, convulsion, revolution, and . . . war between
nations. The weakening of the other institutions normal to a
healthy society seems to be accompanied by a series of political passions and moral perversions that distort the simple
values consistent with a balanced social order, and the consequent disorder seems to become all-embracing.

But if instability, competition and friction between the
institutions are inevitable and continuous, what happens to
the theory of progress? It is evident that the state progresses
at the expense of the church and the family, the church at
the expense of the state and the family, and the family at the
expense of the other two institutions here under consideration. There is no way in which all of the institutions can grow
—that is, increase the range of their activities and influences—
at the same time. The contemporary "progress" of the state
and its increasing absorption of the activities and the functions of the other institutions natural to man and society are
steadily reducing the role of these other institutions in society.

What is now said about the state could in times past have
been said about either the church or the family. The balance
between these institutions is always uneasy and always

changing. Social "progress" as an all-embracing concept becomes a snare and a delusion. The easy self-delusion men indulge in—the happy tendency to assume that what men do now is better than what they did before, that contemporary slogans have some peculiar excellencies in them denied to slogans of yesteryear—makes it almost impossible for men whose heads have been filled from childhood with the gospel of "progress" to face the possibility that the "progress" they are making is at the expense of other institutions equally important to social well-being, and equally dear to the hearts of men.

The difficulty lies even deeper than this: it lies in the fact that for many generations men have assumed that "progress" is linear, is always going up, and is in its very nature all-inclusive and endless in time. It is another instance of the taking over of a seemingly acceptable description of what seems to occur in the sciences—the progressive accumulation of knowledge, skills, and insight into the ways of nature, and the cumulative competence to do better today the task done yesterday. The increasing effectiveness of weapons of war from the wooden club through the bow and arrow, the pike, the gun, the cannon, the machine gun, and the atomic bomb, each more efficient and more destructive, up to a point where the use of the atomic bomb might "progress" the very race of men from the face of the earth, can be spoken of as linear progress in an endless chain toward infinite success. So too, perhaps, it can be said of the course of invention in transportation, where men began on foot, tamed and mounted a beast of burden, invented a wheel and constructed a carriage, a bicycle, an automobile, and more recently an airplane, each in turn increasing the distance he could span and reducing the time required to span it, until contemporary speeds are such that there is a possibility that a projectile hurled into space will travel with such speed that it will have reached its destination in a time span so small that its arrival and departure will seem simultaneous. This, too, may perhaps be

described as linear progress, infinitely cumulative. The natural and comprehensible carrying over of these notions has
obscured the issue that, material changes apart, institutional
growth occurs only in a competitive institutional setting, and
takes place only at the expense of other equally important
social institutions. The concept, if it is to be used at all—and,
in the Western world it would seem almost impossible not to
use it—can only be made to mean movement toward equilibrium among social institutions. If each of the basic institutions is structured about an essential and noncommensurable
experience, then the good life is possible only in a world
where men can live at peace within all of the institutions
organic to society, and progress could then come to mean
progress in the method of reducing the area of imbalance
that is always present. Though perfect equilibrium is not
achievable, a working equilibrium is possible; and attainment
of that might well be considered the great task of statesmanship, the true purpose of government, and the major problem
of political theory and social ethics.

If the idea of progress becomes subject to profound modifications in the light of the irreducible friction between the
basic social institutions, the nature of the role of property,
so closely identified with the idea of social progress, is similarly subject to reconsideration. When the church is strong
and growing stronger, then it accumulates, and has to accumulate, an increasing share of the wealth and income of
the community. The building of churches, monasteries, hospitals, universities, orphanages, and homes for the aged, their
support and their staffing, and the hundred other obligations
and functions which naturally fall to the church, when the
church is a great and growing institution, call of necessity
for a cumulative control of the available capital and income
of the community. When the state grows powerful, it pro-
ceeds to absorb an increasing share of the property and takes
it away from the other institutions. It takes it away from the
church—by force if necessary—by diverting income from

church sources, by siphoning off, through licensing and other means, of income that might and would have gone to the church, and, finally, it acquires it from the family, by taxation in a thousand ways—from a tax on cigarettes to inheritance taxes. If the state is going to support the schools, universities, hospitals, orphanages, old-age pensions and many other activities, it can do it only by securing for itself an increasing proportion of both the property and the income of the community. There is, in fact, no alternative to the process except not to assume such multiple responsibilities.

This process is, of course, also visible in the history of the family. Where the family is powerful and preponderant, it is rich and holds for itself all of the property that it can. There is seldom such a thing as a powerful and poor family. Power goes with responsibility, and responsibility with the exercise of infinitely variable functions; and that rule is conditioned by the possession of property and income. Property is instrumental to the institution. It is not a thing in itself. But if the major historical role of property is instrumental to the institution, then the economic interpretation of history, the theory of the class struggle, and the concept of dialectical materialism are all subject to reconsideration.

The continuous technological changes are important in their bearing upon the relative role of the various institutions, facilitating their growth or decline. While technology is not the only source of social change in the sense of enhancing the powers of growth of one institution against another—as, for instance, communication has clearly facilitated the growth of the power of the modern state—it is still a very important source of such change. To that extent, at least, it would seem true to say that a changing technology, leading to a changing position of the institutions in regard to each other, also affects the transfer of property from one institution to another; for the exercise of responsibility involves the accumulation of property, and the accumulation of property facilitates the increasing exercise of responsibility. This is, however, a very

14   different thing from saying that a changing technology induces a changing class structure and a new kind of class struggle.

The very idea of the class struggle is subject to revision; for the concept is a verbal formula derived from older ideas inherent in European theology and has nothing to do with the description of industrial society, though it may have some reference to a more static agricultural community. It is a verbal construct fitting a preconceived notion of the nature of "progress," and has within it the commitment to historical inevitability. It is really a part of European theology translated into mundane terms.

If the idea of horizontal division of society into classes is an inadequate description of social conflict, this does not deny that conflict exists both between the institutions and within them. Between the institutions the conflict is moral, psychological, and political, for the guidance and governance of the whole man. Internally, within the institutions there is a many-sided contention which might be considered a conflict of numerous interests. But these conflicts are continuous and irreducible. There is the difference in the family between the old and the young, the well and the sick, the children and the parents, and the strife embraces all of the issues that life presents. Nor is there any way of writing finis to this internal strain. In the church the laity and the clergy, the upper hierarchy and the parish priesthood, and the different orders of the church as well are continuously warring with each other. Here again the conflict is philosophical, moral, and political, and not merely economic. There is always the question of how much and what kind of responsibility different individuals and groups within the institution should exercise, and on what moral ground their power can be justified.

What is true of the family and the church is also evident within the state. The citizens are critical of the government, oppose its tax policies, resent conscription, and flout price control. The friction between the citizens and the state is

continuous. Within the government itself, the civil servants
are resentful of the elected officials, the younger bureaucrats
condemn the older ones, and the departments compete for
power, for an increasing share of the budget and for public
influence. No department ever feels that it can fulfill its
proper task with the money and personnel available to it.
But the conflict here is not merely economic. It is also moral,
political, and ideological. Strife is within the institutions,
but it is in the nature of a family quarrel.

In great part, this is the case in the contemporary struggle
between labor and capital. The habit derived from Christian
theology of stating differences in absolute terms has obscured
the issues involved, and what is in effect an internal institutional conflict has been defined as a class war, predestined in
its outcome. An internal institutional quarrel has been endowed with the qualities of a battle between good and evil,
and the end of the drama has been so weighted that the good
must win in the end as it does in fact in the Christian theology
from which the original concept is derived in the first instance. The perennial quarrel, however, is really between
both labor and capital within the larger institutions of the
economy and the other institutions, that is, the family (parents and children), the church (laity and clergy) and the
state (citizens and government). As the institution of the
economy (labor and capital) has grown strong in recent times,
it has been at the expense of the state, the family, and the
church. The issue has been obscured because the economy
(labor and capital), unlike the family, the church and the
state, has come to the fore as a separate institution rather
late in human experience.

That fact, explicable historically, does not modify the basic
character of the social structure or the inherent frictions. It
merely adds another institution to the conflict, and by that
much complicates the existing competition among them. The
economy as an institution has achieved an independent role
only in recent times because for untold centuries the activi-

ties which characterize it were immersed within the other institutions. From the very beginning—that is, from what we know of savage and primitive peoples—we find a complex body of accepted rules defining both the ownership of property and the performance of specified tasks. One might speak of an entire body of social legislation embodied in taboos denying the rights and duties of the members of the community, but the fulfillment of these obligations took place within the family structure, within the church, or within the state. It required many centuries, in most instances, before labor, ownership, commerce, and industry were divorced from the other institutions and become separate activities governed by rules apart from those that governed the other institutions. Even in highly organized societies, like those of Greece and Rome, and the European cultures before the sixteenth century, and even later, the economy, if recognized as a separate and going concern, was but a fraction of the total economic activity of the society; for the greater part of labor, commerce, industry and ownership was still within the ordinary operational behavior of the other institutions.

The precipitation of the economy as a going concern, separate and apart, on a scale so broad as to enable it to mature into an institution in its own right, is largely the cumulative outcome of the Industrial Revolution, and it accomplished that by gradually taking from the other institutions functions which had hitherto been carried out within their orbit, and by increasing the number of men and women who lived a greater proportion of their lives, either as laborers, business men, industrialists, or capitalists, outside of the other institutions, and beyond the rules natural to the other institutions. In fact, the mores of the other institutions in many instances did not apply to the activities of this new institution, and they did not apply partly, at least, because of the speed with which men and women were being loosened from their older moorings.

As it developed, this institution soon displayed all of the

characteristics of the older ones. It began to apply sanctions and to demand loyalties all of its own. It developed a new series of motives for human activity. It took over, as far as it could, the education of men, women, and children. It exacted special obligations and introduced new rules. It challenged the state, the family, and the church, wherever these interfered with its own activities, and claimed for itself, as it grew stronger, rights and prerogatives inconsistent with the other institutions. Long before labor unions became powerful, it exacted from the individual and from the other institutions very much the same kind of moral commitments that labor is exacting from them at present. The large industry, corporation, trust, and cartel, when they felt themselves powerful enough, challenged the other institutions to a point where it became a matter of self-defense on their part to find some means of controlling and confining the prerogatives which were now being insisted upon and exercised by this newcomer in the field of institutional structure. Long before labor unions became strong within the new institutions, the state, the church, and the family waged a campaign and placed numerous restrictions upon it. The nineteenth and early part of the twentieth century are replete with the record of the agitation and resulting legislation in the name of the other institutions to restrict and put limits upon the now self-conscious and imperious economy.

The rise of the trade unions is in its essence an internal movement within the economy, just as much as [is] a rebellion of the citizens against the state, or the laity against the church. From the point of view of the other institutions, their only concern with the economy as an institution is that production shall continue at an acceptable price and quality, and that in the process the economy shall not attempt to absorb the powers and activities essential to their ministration to man as a moral and psychological being. In the nature of the case, however, the quarrel continues today when the unions are strong, as it did yesterday when the industry

18   was strong and the unions were weak; for the new institution makes the same claims against the others in the name of labor that it did previously in the name of capital. The unions now exact loyalty from their members as the employers did yesterday; the unions challenge the state; they expel members (just as the employers discharged them) with the same dire effect upon the individual where the union has a monopoly. The unions participate in politics, interfere with the family in numerous ways, attack the church if it does not support them (as the employers did yesterday), control income by setting wages, influence promotion through seniority (as did the employers), impose a tax upon their members, regulate the members' holidays and vacations, and influence their politics, ideas and ethics. The unions have become the patrons of "proletarian" art, literature, and music, and, as in the other institutions, they have a whole process of supplying the reading materials and the ideas that their members are expected to acquire.

It will be said that the quarrel between capital and labor is chiefly economic. That is not really the basic quarrel, for the standard of living is ultimately determined by production, and if production is great enough it must, in an industrial economy, be distributed. If it is not distributed there is no market, if there is no market there can be no demand, and if there is no demand there can be no production. The quarrel between capital and labor within the economy is not primarily over production; it is over control. It is a conflict to determine what elements within the institution are to have the greatest influence in shaping the direction of the institution—a struggle that is characteristic of the other institutions, notably both the state and the church. The internal quarrel within the economy will go on for a long time; forever, in fact, even if the intensity of the passions that have been generated dies down, and even if the issues over which the quarrel rages will change. The real conflict is not between capital and labor. It is between the economy (capital and labor) and the other institutions, especially the state; for, if the economy continues as it has in recent years, it may take upon itself an increasing number of the powers, responsibilities and prerogatives now exercised by the state, and, if it does, it will behave toward all of the other institutions with the same arbitrariness and tyranny that both the church and the state have shown, when they were preponderant, against the other institutions.

The social conflict is not the result of a dichotomy, as the traditional class-conflict theory would have it, between two forces that have an inevitable battle to fight, with a given side predestined to win and, in the process, to destroy the other. It is rather a conflict between multiple forces in which none can really win the battle—a battle to which no finis can be written—for conflict is part of the process of institutional life itself, and the end of the conflict would really signify the end of life itself.

That these broad issues in human society should have been reduced to the simple formula of a dichotomy between good and evil is one of the strange and remarkable chapters in the intellectual history of western Europe in recent times. The Marxian formula is a European product, steeped in European theology, that probably could not have originated in any culture except one in which there was acceptance, implicit or explicit, of the belief that between God and the Devil there is an eternal war, that God is destined to win the battle in the end, that no compromise with evil is possible, that the end can be achieved only by a cataclysm, and that, when the battle is finally over, history itself will terminate, for in a classless society, as in heaven, there can be no conflict and therefore no history. This quite unconscious commitment to a division of the universe into absolutes—labor and capital—with no basis of compromise between them, with labor as the predestined victor, as if destiny itself had conspired for that very purpose, with the revolution taking the place of the cataclysm, and with Communist societies living in eternal felicity forever—progress itself seemingly coming to an end, except as continuous felicity—is really a translation to the mundane world of the underlying theology of the Christian doctrine, and calling it economics and science.

If this cultural setting conditioned the very theme, the Hegelian dialectic supplied an important intellectual tool to dialectical materialism. But dialectical materialism is only dialectical nonsense. The average Marxian adapting dialectical materialism to the use of the class war has assumed a universe in which any idea or force can have only one consequence, and that consequence its opposite—that is, assumed that all of the rest of nature is a vacuum, and only the thesis and the antithesis exist, waiting for the synthesis—the synthesis which in Marxian terms became the classless society. What is this but the transfer of the social sciences of such dichotomies from the moral field as right and wrong, good and evil, and from the physical sciences such notions as night and day, black and white, hot and cold, and the assumption that, in like fashion, just two opposites rule in all social phenomena? But the facts are completely different.

The consequences of any movement, idea, or invention are beyond present conjecture or measurement, nor is there any way of deciding which of the many influences are likely to prove most significant. It would, for instance, be impossible either to enumerate or to describe with any certainty all the consequences of even so recent and innocent an invention as the automobile.

A universe in which there are only two opposite forces, one the product of the other, waiting for the synthesis, is a figment of the imagination, has no base in reality, and falsifies the nature of the world it would describe. The facts are completely the reverse. The forces of the world are numerous, complex, and intertwined, and none there are so wise as to be able to untangle the one force that will reshape all of life. There is, in fact, no one force, process, or movement. Each item is but a thread in a complex weave, tied in with all of the others. The synthesis need not be waited for, since it occurs each day, and the world is different with every sunrise—that is, the balance between the basic institutions is always shifting, and every event has its part in the changing process. In addition to its fallacy of assuming a vacuum wherein the thesis and the antithesis can work out their destiny, this notion suffers from the implicit idea that the synthesis, when it occurs, produces a state of perpetual rest. Like the doctrine of the class struggle which leans so heavily upon it, dialectical materialism is weighted with the wish for eternal rest—that is, death.

If, then, an institutional analysis of society is incompatible with the concepts of dialectical materialism, and the idea of the class struggle, it also calls [into] question a whole series of political doctrines resting upon the antithesis of man and society that has for so long a time bedeviled political theory. There is need, in view of the above, for reconsideration of the doctrine of evolution as applied to society, of the concept of the harmony of interests, of the philosophy of inherent rights, of the principle of utility, and of the current belief that the nation is the great organizing principle. Instead, it follows that the great desideratum is the achievement of an approximate, even if ever-changing, equilibrium among the conflicting institutions. Strife is accepted as normal and as an evidence of social health, and, therefore, as a social good. It denies to any institution the power completely to destroy the other institutions, therefore putting a limit upon its ambitions to secure absolute dominion and absolute peace, which is here identified with tyranny. If the impossible should happen and one institution destroyed the others, it would have to assume their role, for they are structured about an incommensurable experience, and, therefore, willy-nilly re-create the divisions and strains which it sought to eliminate. Compromise becomes the true rule of politics. No interest can be absolutely denied, no victory can be absolutely complete. All majorities become temporary, all reforms become conditional upon the survival of active opposition, and, by the nature of the case, all government comes to be concerned with the details of the relationships among institutions.

Revolution is therefore the result of the excessive power of one institution. In a well-balanced society, where the institutions keep each other in check, man lives in comparative peace. His great problems are relative, his conflicts are over details, and the opponents live together as friends, belong to the same club, go to the same church, and marry into the same families. But as soon as one of the institutions, be it the state, the church, the family, or the economy, becomes so strong as seemingly to threaten the very survival of the others, then the issues cease to be petty, capable of compromise, and the arguments become preludes to civil wars and revolutions. The contentions between the partisans of one or another institution take on an ideological character, the contrasts between them seem absolute, and the petty quarrels become symbolic of the greater conflict. People begin to talk as if the end were in sight, as if doom were awaiting them at the next turn, and hope of peace—the older peace—fades, and with it tolerance, gentleness, and human sympathy. Life ceases to seem important or to have any special value. The cause, whatever it may be, or whatever its name, takes precedence over all else, and men make ready for death—either their own or that of their enemies—as if the earth were not sufficiently broad to contain them both.

Civil war and revolution come almost as a relief, for now it seems that the issues will be finally settled, for all time. In that situation there is no compromise, and rebellion, revolution, and civil war are a logical, inevitable, and supposedly necessary consequence of the claims to absolutism in the name of one of these institutional interests. Some sort of equilibrium is ultimately re-established among the various forces at play, and life can go on again in a normal way—with petty quarrels over immediate issues, and nothing seems so profoundly tragic as to require the destruction of those who disagree with you.

It is, of course, true that all of the institutions have this germ of over-all sovereignty in them; but, if the opposition is effective, then society can live on indefinitely in peaceful friction, in a world which seems to be going nowhere, and which seems to have no all-dominant philosophy or faith, no impassioned ideal that drives it beyond human reason and beyond human frailty, and gives some of its leaders the assumption of acting like gods, of acting for eternity, of being moved by voices and intuition to compel men to accept the new faith in the state or the church or the economy at any cost, at any sacrifice.

The road to social peace is the balance of the social institutions, and a wise statesman would strengthen those institutions that seemed to be losing ground, even if he were not addicted to them; for the only way to peace in this world of fallible human nature is to keep all human institutions relatively strong, but none too strong, relatively weak, but not so weak as to despair of their survival. It is thus only that peaceful irritation and strife, so essential to social and individual sanity, can be maintained.

For this purpose democracy is the natural vehicle, for it is essentially a process rather than a doctrine. It is a way of evaluating human experience and bringing it to bear upon the issues at hand. The sense of meaning and insight each man's life represents reflects a unique view of the universe. The sum of these views becomes the source determining government policy. The fact that the individual experiences are frequently contradictory and their sense of meaning incompatible with that derived from other experiences gives the democratic process its proper role. The process is, in fact, the patterning together of all the contradictions of life's experience, and by trial and error discovering what meaning and direction the basic conflict reveals. The government is, therefore, the funnel for all of these values, that is, the sense of direction implicit in the total social experience. The lack of certainty that may be revealed is but an evidence of the inner contradictions, and the changing policy resulting from changing experience is both the necessary and essential method of democracy. The chief function of government is to help keep the balance. At best, it would be a neutral instrumentality representing all of the institutions and their total impact upon society. It would effectuate a daily compromise between them.

Society, however, is not merely composed of a number of separate institutions in constant conflict with each other. It also consists of men who are members of all of these institutions, each of whom reflects in his character, beliefs, and ambitions the variable imprint that life's experience has given him. He does not merely live in a number of institutions, he really lives in a society made up of these institutions. But the institutions themselves contain innumerable groups and individuals whose experience is variable, whose needs are private, and whose ends are particular. Society is, therefore, the framework for all their effort, and they, each in turn, seek to mold the social structure to their private, group, or institutional ends. The individual, the group, or the institution may be assertive and purposeful, but society is neither one nor the other. It is the sum of all the past and present forces at play, of the ambitions in operation, of all the movements in conflict. Society is the recipient as well as the mold, but the mold gives the content a sort of inner cohesion. It is not just a vacuum. It contains the residue of all the past experience. This residue is the ethos, and every society has a distinguishable ethos of its own. Society is, therefore, not something formless, rootless, and uncrystallized, or just put together of a number of institutions. On the contrary, while it has no purpose or direction of itself, it does have a content derived from the past labors of uncounted human strivings, of hopes achieved, and of failures. This content, this ethos, becomes the frame for the present and future activities of all

its members, all its groups, all its institutions; for, without
attempting to define the ethos of the time, it does in its turn
define the objectives and gives direction to the will and labors
of all the men and institutions composing the society.

Neither men nor institutions labor in a moral vacuum. If
they did, they would labor to no purpose at all. Life in a world
without an ethos would be completely futile. The ethos is
neither the law nor the written word, it is neither the faith
nor the prophecy: it is the underlying sense of proportion and
propriety that gives the law, the written word, the faith, and
the prophecy what cogency they may have. The ethos is,
therefore, larger than any specific doctrine or formula, than
all of the unconsciously asserted formulae taken together.
This is an instance where the whole is greater than the sum
of its parts.

It is not true that men are cognizant of the good end to
be served by society as is implicit in Aristotle's dictum. If it
had a recognizable end it would have a sense of direction,
but the only sense of direction in any society is represented
by the conflicting ends of its component members. To speak,
therefore, of society as established for, or as possessed of,
purpose, or as aiming at any objective, is to impute to a going
concern, with special emphasis, values that are already there.
But the implicit value system, the ethos, is a result of an infinitely variable experience. The true well-being of a society,
therefore, lies in diversity rather than in identity of interests.
The greater the variety of groups, the richer is the community and the more certain of continuous harmony. The harmony best suited to a society is one which comes from many-
sided inner tensions, strains, conflicts, and disagreements.
Where disagreement is universal, men can agree only on
particulars, and where men can really quarrel only about
particulars they have too many things in common to tear the
community apart. Divergence of interests within the community, in as many-sided and conflicting forces as possible,
is the condition of healthy controversy and social peace. It

26   is a fundamental error to attempt to secure unanimity in all things, or even in many things. Agreement by a working majority, yes, but even here that agreement is best which is only temporary and which is achieved for varying reasons. In society, unanimity and death are synonymous. Conflict, strife, divergence, difference of interest and opinion over many things for many reasons, and in varying degrees of intensity, are the conditions of social peace. The conflicting processes of democracy are consistent with and essentially a part of the stresses and strains of life itself.

on political stability 2

THE FRENCH AND RUSSIAN REVOLUTIONS seemed cataclysmic to their contemporaries. They appeared like the end of the world to some, like the beginning of the millennium to others. Each was heralded by a long line of Messianic prophets who, in the name of reason and science, promised to remodel this stubborn earth of ours into a paradise, and to fit man to inhabit it.

Each of these destructive spasms took place in an agricultural country governed by an all-powerful monarchy, hoary with age, and exalted by tradition. The King of France and the Tsar of all the Russias had no rivals inside of their own dominions, and admitted no superiors beyond their borders. Their power was as absolute as centuries of unrestrained rule could make it. The power and munificence of the King and the splendor of his entourage attracted all men's eyes. Mortal man's chief ambition was to get as close as possible to the King, the center from which all visible good derived. That was where the power lay. The rest was a void—barren even in the more delicate graces; for art, literature, philosophy, music, architecture, and religion found sustenance and nourishment

27

Reprinted, with permission, from *Political Science Quarterly*, LXXV (June 1960), pp. 161–180.

in the environs of the King and his court. The grand ministers lived by the will of the King, while writers, poets, artists, and musicians got their living by flattering the powerful ministers or their minions. Churchmen, great and small, found promotion and good living by the same route.

Viewed from the outside, these two monarchies seemed stable and secure. They had lasted for centuries. The wills of most men seemed entwined in loyalty and devotion to the reigning monarch. Yet when the crisis came the power of the crowns of France and Russia vanished overnight. The mighty King of France and his beautiful wife were dragged to the guillotine and publicly beheaded to the delight of a howling mob. The Little Father of all the Russias and his immediate family were murdered one early dawn by a firing squad at the command of a handful of unknown men. In each instance the court vanished, the men and women who had crowded it in their pomp and pride and who had filled its halls with their vanities and foppery fled, if they could, to strange lands to save their lives, or suffered like their masters an inglorious and sudden death. The King's castles, so strong, so old, so well adorned, toppled down as if in a dream, and crushed all that were in them.

The collapse of these mighty monarchies revealed what all men should have known: that the power they wielded rested upon a vacuum, and that the stronger they seemed, the more fragile they were. What these monarchial tragedies set forth for the world to see was that centralized government is its own greatest enemy, that the more absolute it becomes the less resiliency it possesses, and that its very power is its final undoing. The steps by which a government becomes all-mighty mark the path toward its own destruction.

IN CONTRAST to France and Russia no convulsive revolution has transformed the governments of England and the United States. Since the Tudors, England has changed from a little nation to a great empire, from a poor agricultural country to become for more than a century the industrial leader of the world, from a government with a narrow suffrage to one based on the mass of the people, from an administration dominated by an aristocracy to one ruled by the middle and working classes. Every possible fortune, good and evil, has crowded those years and yet its political constitution—a King in Parliament—has absorbed all of these changes without convulsion.

Similarly the United States has, since the eighteenth century, grown from a slim agricultural colony to the leading industrial power of our time, from a population mainly British in origin to one compounded by forty million immigrants from all parts of the globe. In its short history it has spanned the continent, fought a bitter Civil War, two world wars that imposed great strain on American institutions and yet the government devised at the beginning has survived without revolution.

The explanation for this political miracle in England and the United States is to be found in the strength of local parish and township government and in the representative and federative principles which they imposed [1]—in fact even if not always in law. Self-government in little places has provided England and the United States with the habits that have sustained political stability and institutional plasticity at the same time.

In England the continuance of Parliament prevented the break between the people and crown which proved fatal to the French monarch and the Russian Tsar, for Parliament provided a continuing identity between the officers of local and central government. Parliament could praise the King and at the same time criticize and punish his ministers. In an extreme case it brought the King himself to boot without in the end, as seen by the Restoration and the revolution of 1688, changing the monarchial principle. Even during the

---

[1] The social mobility so important in English political and social history is itself a by-product of its local government and its impact upon social structure.

30   Commonwealth, Cromwell tried repeatedly to reproduce the
similitude of the traditional model, "the King in Parliament,"
an executive bound by an elected House of Commons and a
House of Lords.

Important is the continuance of the principle of community representation, for what was represented in Parliament
was the community—that is, the communities of England.
Parliament evidenced the vitality of local government. Members locally known and respected were sent up by localities.
Even if a "carpetbagger" intruded he required the good will
of locally influential families. In the end, Parliament preserved the British crown. It could do so only because it
rested upon the local community. The House of Commons
consisted of members chosen by shire and borough and usually experienced in local government. The shire as well as the
borough was a sort of federation of smaller autonomous governments ruled by juries in a court of justice in which most
people found some participation—including bishops, earls,
barons, knights, yeomen, copyholders and householders. Representation in Parliament proved effective through the centuries because Parliament stood to the nation much as
Quarter Sessions stood to the county.

If the survival of the county court, the borough corporation, the parish, and many other autonomous units of local
administration saved Parliament, the Parliament in turn preserved the crown. In time, the crown as a symbol of authority
sanctioned the competition between the political factions
loosely identified as Whigs and Tories for the privilege to be
first to serve the King, for they would all serve him. But for
the King to act as umpire, to recognize the new servants of
the crown picked by an uncoerced Parliament, to receive the
Prime Minister chosen by a majority, he first had to achieve
a place above the political battle. The King could consciously
play the role of umpire only after he ceased to have the controlling influence in shaping the outcome of a dispute between
the factions in Parliament for the organization of the King's
government. The crown became increasingly secure as the

King ceased to have a choice over his own most faithful first servant. His Prime Minister was selected by the majority in the House of Commons. But the House of Commons was but part of a system which contained the House of Lords and the King as well. There could be no government except as there was a "King in Parliament." The King became the symbol of the political stability represented by Parliament whose members were sent up by autonomous local governments organized as communities through their own Quarter Sessions, justices of the peace and innumerable juries.

In England, therefore, the crown became symbolic and decorative, while effective power had long been with Parliament. The control of Parliament has, at least since Queen Anne's time, been divided between opposing factions coalesced as parties, and the ability of one to govern was always precarious and limited by the reluctant consent of the other. The notable feature of the English parliamentary system is Her Majesty's loyal opposition. The opposition was loyal, but none the less real, for it would take over the government, while the party in office was equally bent to carry on with the administration. The ultimate arbiter was not the monarch but a possible election. The election, even in the unreformed Parliament, illustrated where the real political strength lay—in the borough, the county, with their multiple and complex forms of autonomous governments.

The power to decide which party would take over the government was in the hands of great and lesser lords, the barons, gentlemen, yeomen, and the corporation of the parliamentary boroughs. The electorate determined the choice of members to Parliament even in the corrupt days of George III and the faction in power had to use the government's money, the prospect of pensions, sinecures, and contracts, to keep its parliamentary majority, which in a crisis might shift from one faction to another. The real threat to the administration in power lay with the electorate.

The crown was the ruling symbol of all factions, and the King sanctioned the transfer of office after it had been de-

32 cided upon. The King was safe and secure because he had great influence but no strength. He could give legal sanction to the new government but had not the strength to change the decision once it had been made.[2]

Parliament was strong because the faction in office was weak—too weak to destroy its opposition. The opposition was strong only as long as it was out of office; for, once in office, it might lose its place at the behest of those who had made it strong for the moment—the county and the borough.

Enduring political power needs to be built upon the locality as the prime unit, and it matters relatively little whether it is controlled by a great lord, a little lord, a knight, many yeomen, or a few burghers in a town. It matters relatively little in the political destiny of nations whether the suffrage is wide or restricted or whether the knights and lords of the shire are such by inheritance and tradition rather than by formal constitutional sanction. What does matter is that the shires and boroughs are competent to assert their views and maintain them through their own chosen leaders. If the locality is not strong enough to maintain its leaders against the King, the central government, or the dominant party, it has no political influence in the end. This is the substance of political power.

But the grounds for this loyalty to the local leaders—the

---

[2] The distinction between power and strength is important; strength is structural, power is functional, and they are not necessarily related to, dependent upon, or derived from one another. A grown man is much stronger than a small boy, but his power over the boy is not equal to his strength. His power is limited by restraints over which he has no control—the opinion of his friends, the police, his own ethical and religious beliefs, his affections, and his own bringing up. Another illustration might be drawn from the international field. The United States is very much stronger than Canada, but American power to control Canadian policy is limited by public opinion at home and abroad, by the non-imperialist sentiments of the American people, by the existence of the Commonwealth, the United Nations, and so on. An institution may have great strength but little power. A modern insurance company, for example, has great strength but no power; or a nation may have great power and little strength: Egypt at the present instance in relation to England and France, or in an individual case Gandhi in comparison with the British Empire.

Hampdens, for instance—is that they are known as true
spokesmen of the community. How they are chosen is of little
importance. If they cease to be genuine spokesmen of their
district, the right to representation as well as local political
strength will pass away in time.

The English crown, therefore, was stable when the other
crowns of Europe were toppled from their thrones because
the King had influence but no strength, because the administration was temporary and the opposition was ready to replace it in office. But the opposition was certain of its own
strength only before it became the government, for as soon
as it took office it was forced to meet the challenge of the
faction it had replaced. The real political strength of the
nation lay not in the King, the group in power or the opposition. It was in the borough and in the county and these
would, when the crisis came, decide where they would temporarily deposit their support. This made the crown secure
and honorable, the group in office competent to govern as
long as the rules of the game kept the opposition from over-
throwing it and the next election could be staved off.

IF IN the United States the system seems different, it is only
a varying example of the same instance: that the central government is secure as long as it is weak, that the party in
power is unified as long as it has a strong opposition, and the
opposition is strong only as long as it can count upon the
consent in township, county, city, and state.

Obviously the basic source of political power in the United
States does not rest in the presidency. Nor is it to be found
in Congress, or in the political parties, Democratic or Republican. The power is now and has long been in the hands of
the local political machine. It is the local Republican or Democratic machines in their different cities, counties, and town-
ships that decide who the members of Congress are to be,
and whom they will nominate for the presidency. The Republican and Democratic parties in convention are gatherings

34   of local chieftains, each sovereign in his own domain, and they must all be reconciled, flattered, pleased, and propitiated by the promise of patronage, favor, and place. For they decide whom they will nominate for the presidency and for Congress.

If the President is to have a peaceful administration he must conciliate the local machine. The Hague machine can be independent of the White House, but the President requires its support for a re-election, for continuing party control in Congress, and for the vote which will write his program into law. The President has never been able to count upon a pliant Congress because he does not control it. Congress is not his creature. It is the creature of the local machine, and even if the machine is noticeably fallible, the fact that it is local has saved the United States from such growth of executive power as would have made it possible for the President to change the government and impose his will upon the nation.

What has saved the presidency from a possible conversion to a tyranny has been its weakness. The battle over the enlargement of the Supreme Court, the struggle under Wilson over the League of Nations, the present argument over foreign policy, all illustrate the point. The presidency is dependent upon Congress and Congress upon the locality, and that has made the American government one of the stablest in the modern world. The presidency is stable because there are always enough Democrats to help the Republicans defeat a Republican president, and there are always enough Republicans to help the Democrats defeat a Democratic president. But the Republican and Democratic parties have survival value just because they too are weak, because they are not centralized, efficient, integrated bodies. They are coagulations of unstable loyalties, depending upon the whim and need of the local machine. And the city or county machine must measurably represent local needs, or in the end succumb to its rivals inside or outside the party. That is the brunt of the matter.

The vigilance we are admonished to exercise for our liberties is to be read primarily at the parish and township level so that the local interest may be represented and listened to at every step above it, for political stability depends upon the parish making itself heard. The United States, like Great Britain, escaped revolution during the last two centuries because the central government has been politically weak and local government politically strong. The weak political party has given stability to the government becuse it has periodically to fall back upon a renewal of consent at the ward and township level. The municipal and county political machine has protected the United States against both "efficiency" and dictatorship.

This machine is local, particular, practical, unbothered by doctrinal issues, and immersed in its own ends. It is not even integrated on a state basis, not to speak of a national level. It can survive national defeat and can flourish during long years of exclusion from national or even state patronage. If it can control the locality—even a small one—it is in the long run stronger than the national administration. The local political machine in Mississippi can repudiate the Democratic party presidential candidate—as in the case of President Harry Truman in the 1948 campaign—nominate an opposition presidential aspirant, and survive as a part of the Democratic party.

American democracy has remained effective just in the degree that local government has been decentralized and uncontrolled. It has muddled and confused the political scene. By the same token it has given American democracy its strength and vitality. The party system has remained strong because the central party organization has been weak. No president has been stronger than his party except in moments of crisis, and then only with the support of his political opponents.

If we have been governed by fallible human beings, both they and the rest of us knew they were fallible. They could claim no absolute virtues and, therefore, no complete obedience. And lacking the power as well as the illusion that they could do certain good, they also lacked the power of doing unqualified evil. In American politics no one can unalterably win; therefore, no one can inevitably lose. What made revolution impossible in both England and the United States has been the contradictory ends of innumerable groups, each armed with an immediate program of its own. They all gain because they all contribute to shaping public opinion and public policy. They all win only partially, however; they do not dominate or control absolutely, and, in the nature of the case, cannot.

American democracy has been strong to the extent to which the national parties have been torn by internal dissension. The resiliency of American democracy has rested upon strong—even if at times corrupt—local parties. The inability of the state government to dictate to the counties has given vitality to American political life. The failure of either the national Democratic or Republican party to rule the state and city machines has made them effective instruments for keeping the central government democratic by keeping it weak. The administration could never surely count on congressional support for all its policies because neither party could dictate to its own members. The lack of unity within the two major parties made it impossible for the President to control Congress, and made the division of powers a reality in the American government. Continuing political dissidence is the essential condition of both political stability and democracy, and the contention feeds the common law and the traditional values. Political disagreement is the essence of continuing political freedom.

IF ANYTHING definitive can be said about political revolutions, it is that they do not and cannot take place in countries where political strength is dispersed in a thousand places, and where myriads of men feel personally involved in the continuing problems of a self-governing parish or township and participate in making the rules for the larger unit, county, state, or nation. The failure of the Stuarts to subvert local institutions saved England from following the path of France; while in the United States political power has from the beginning been based on the support and participation of the smaller units—it has always gone from township to county to state and nation. France and Russia, on the other hand, illustrate the way to absolutism and cataclysm.

In France and in Russia the undermining of local responsibility had gone on for centuries. In both countries there was the gradual withering away of the powers of the local nobility, the abolition or weakening of provincial representative assemblies, the wiping out of or subordination of autonomous municipal, county, and provincial government. The crown took to itself many of the functions hitherto locally exercised. The local police, the local judiciary, powers of taxation, control over schools, roads, militia, and public improvements, and regulation of trade and manufacture were all gradually absorbed by the crown. In both countries laws were issued by decree and taxes imposed by arbitrary fiat. In France the intendants regulated the minutest affairs of the smallest communities. The town could not repair its decayed church tower without special permission from the King's ministers in Paris. In Russia all church steeples look alike because they were all built on the same plan approved by the Tsar's ministry.

The crown in both countries was in effect unrestrained by any other agency. Government came to be exercised by the kings and tsars, with the ministers dependent upon their will. The government might be bad or good—capricious, expensive, and cruel, or generous, constructive, and well-intentioned— but in either case it was responsible only to the will of the ruler. The people could not be consulted through any parliamentary body and their consent was not required. There was neither a local nobility whose power, responsibility, good will, and self-interest could restrain the crown, nor a locally autonomous municipal or county administration whose wishes required consideration.

38   Local leadership had been replaced by a bureaucracy which, like a spider's web, covered every nook and corner of the land. It aimed to record every event, enforce every rule and consult its superiors upon every decision. The community, large and small, lived in suspense upon the will of even the pettiest police sergeant, while the lower bureaucracy waited upon the will of their superiors. The crown and people had come to live in different spheres with a widening gap which no one could span. There was no longer any basis or any means of political communiaction between them.

POLITICALLY, this is the point of no return. When the communities' natural leaders have been replaced by appointed officials responsive to a distant ministry, an irrevocable step will have been taken. From this time forward the communities can no longer make themselves heard politically because they have no basis of legal opposition, and no means of saying "No" to king and minister because they no longer have any political strength. And political strength cannot ever be returned to them without a revolution, and perhaps not even then.

Under such circumstances the government has come to live above the people and their communities with no basis for political communication. Reports by secret agents or police officials merely reflect the writer's interest and his desire to flatter his immediate superior.

Effective political communication *has to be political and cannot be administrative.* The bureaucracy may be a machine; it cannot be a community or a party. A political party must possess the strength to be in open opposition. If there is no prospect of influencing the policy of the government, no way in which the opposition can come to power, or come sufficiently close to it to compel the administration to consider its counsel, then there can be no political party and no political communication. For political communication is an alternate proposal and an implied future prospect of writing it into law. In the absence of such a possibility, only opinions favorable to the government can make themselves heard, and no matter how large the bureaucracy, the government remains politically uninformed and the separation between the rulers and the people continues. The communities are almost forgotten and the government is led to assume that it is the country and that the king speaks as the people. The isolation of the government becomes irremediable and a permanent feature of the political life of the nation.

The country is now ruled rather than governed and the power of the king runs through the land without restraint. The victory of the crown is complete, its power absolute. So, too, is its weakness. Self-delusion and pride have blinded the governors into thinking that their power is now secure and endless. But what has really taken place is something very different. The nation is ruled without allowing the people or their natural leaders to get morally involved in the affairs of government. They have therefore no grounds for loyalty or effective support in a crisis. Neither Louis XVI nor Nicholas II could fall back upon the masses, the localities, or the nobility. The crown, in undermining the ability of the localities to oppose it, had also destroyed their ability to come to its defense.

The strength of a government is equal to the strength of the opposition. If the opposition is strong enough it need not destroy the crown to influence or change the policy of the government—for the opposition is then a government in being and takes over the administration without the needed convulsion of a revolution seemingly inevitable in a political vacuum. When the opposition is strong, policy modifications are effected gradually, the communities remain politically in contact with the center, and the activities of local leaders provide the means of consensus for the government's policies.

Once autonomous local government has disappeared,

40   there is little prospect of re-establishing an effective political bond between the communities and the crown. The crown has become so habituated to having its own way *that any complaint—not to say opposition—is taken as a challenge to its powers rather than as a protest against its policies.* Even where the government seeks to return some participation to the communities, the bureaucracy soon discovers that administrative autonomy is really not tolerable.

The resort to local tradition, so natural to self-governing communities, is taken as a source of opposition and an effort is set on foot to wipe out the variable, to reduce all parts of the nation to the official design. Efforts by the tsars to Russify the many nationalities of Russia aimed at destroying the basis of local pride. Regional traditions make for local resistance. Uniformity is the ideal; it makes government easy, interchangeable, and provides for a single loyalty where it can be generated. The wiping out of the idiosyncratic makes for weakness at the local level and for pliability. How otherwise build a great centralized monarchy? If it is to come into being, it must reform manners, customs, dress, language, and ideas. Identical systems of taxation, administration, justice, police education, and army recruitment are made to apply everywhere. No wonder Catherine the Great considered herself a child of the Enlightenment. The "enlightened" monarchy cannot suffer an uncontrolled religious order, a self-sufficient craftsman guild, an independent university. It can tolerate no special privilege, liberty, insight, or loyalty. There can be no private judgment, almost no privacy, for the enlightened crown will attempt to register, educate, marry, and bury all of its subjects, and keep a record of all private events. But to survive, the corporate group, in whatever sphere, must be unique and uniqueness requires much room and political autonomy, something centralized government cannot tolerate.

The king in the prevailing doctrine of the enlightened monarchy was the father of his people and a good king

would treat all subjects equally. There must be no special   *41*
privilege, no unique order that gives the individual a particular sense of identity. They must all be alike. In the end,
if all men are equal to each other, the question will arise as
to who made the king unequal. Why is he alone above the
people? The inevitable answer to that is that the king too is
equal. When they caught Louis XVI while trying to escape
they dubbed him "Monsieur Capet." He, too, must be a
sans-culotte and to prove his identity with themselves they
put a cap on him.

All men, including the king, are now equal—equally helpless—and the tyranny of Louis XVI and the Tsar would in
due time be succeeded by the greater tyranny of the Committee of Public Safety and Stalin. There is no defense against
tyranny in constitution or doctrine. It can be kept in bounds
only by autonomous orders, corporate bodies, local governments, because they have a life of their own. When their
vitality has been sapped, the individual has no institutional
foothold and no protection.

THE blight of centralized government is the tendency to concentrate more and more political power in one agency. It
matters little whether this agency calls itself king, tsar, Fuehrer, secretary of a party, president, committee, republic, or
whatever. The evil is the location of power in one place. It
matters not at all whether this power is accumulated in the
name of equality, liberty, reform, or revolution. The purpose
for which the power is gathered is irrelevant to its ultimate
use. For, once gathered, political power possesses a drive of
its own—to perpetuate itself and increase. This must sound
as if "power" were an animate being. What it really attempts
to say is that the individuals who find themselves at the point
where the power is concentrated always behave the same
way. The individuals in possession of this power may have
acquired it for reasons good or bad, honest or dishonest, or

because they are efficient, energetic, shrewd, ambitious, endowed with a reformer's zeal, moved by an evil design, or because they were born where the power is located, as the heir to the crown. Whoever they may be, they will keep all the power that has come their way and attempt to increase it because it is never sufficient.

The gathered power will have been institutionalized in a series of bureaucratic agencies, each with its own standards of efficiency, methods, and prerogatives. In due time all of these separate institutions, with their special insights, responsibilities, competencies, and loyalties come to be at the disposal of the same one individual—secretary, Fuehrer, king, or tsar. The power of these many institutions is his—they are each separately aware of an inadequacy and they transmit that to him. Like the separate institutions, the crown at the center feels the need for greater power. It therefore always seeks to increase it and when successful stifles all those gathered within its folds. Like an ideal parasite, centralized power first drains the vitality of its victims and then perishes for lack of nourishment.

If one examines the means by which centralized political power grows until it accomplishes its logical end—self-annihilation—it is possible to identify the [following] steps taken along the way—at least in the two instances with which we are concerned, France and Russia:

a] By destroying or weakening the local (feudal) nobility.
b] By gradually degrading the church to an instrument of the central government.
c] By weakening the local community and undermining or abolishing local government.
d] By placing the central government's courts (the king's law) over all local justice.
e] By enforcing uniform systems of taxation collected by or under the control of central government agents.
f] By the growth of a centrally controlled secret police at the service of the crown.

g] By the establishment of a national army, the abolition of local militia, and finally by compulsory military service.

h] By limiting or abolishing the autonomy of educational institutions.

i] By censorship and control of the press.

j] By the gradual replacement of local officers by members of a centrally controlled bureaucracy.

k] By making service in the bureaucracy the conspicuous form of honorific activity.

l] By suppressing all opposition and difference.

m] By making loyalty and obedience to the central government the leading political virtue.

n] By contriving to make all personal ambition and hope depend upon the favor of the central government—the king, the tsar.

o] By so elaborating the presence of the central figure as to make it inconceivable that there could be any other figure on the public stage—the Tsar, Louis XIV.

p] By narrowing the distinction between private and public property, so that the central government can at will occupy or expropriate—through taxation, forced gift, forced loan—or in individual cases by special decree, take what part of the public wealth it requires (Louis XIV told his heir that all the property of France was at the disposal of the crown).

q] By acquiring the power to distribute the public treasure at will and without an accounting.

r] By being free to declare war or make peace.

s] And finally by being able to take human life without due process.

By these means the road to absolute power was cleared of all obstacles and it was a prophetic eye that led Setrone to observe, "France is much more happily situated than England, for here reforms that will change the whole state of the country can be accomplished in a moment, whereas in

44 England similar measures are always exposed to be defeated by party strife."[3] What he failed to see was that the King who could efficiently do these things could not insure his own survival.

CLEARLY, tyranny first and, later, social revolution follow in the path of uniformity and political "efficiency." Without uniformity centralization is impossible. Without "efficiency" tyranny is not manageable. In the name of efficiency local variables and local traditions and their ability to resist are overridden. When local autonomy has been destroyed the only alternative is chaos or tyranny, and, historically speaking, each has its turn.

Centralized administration does not understand the essence of a healthy political life or the meaning of freedom. Unless people are free to group themselves about their local and immediate interests, they are not free at all. Political freedom requires the existence of a multiplicity of groups contradictory and overlapping in their activities, having their "constitution" or their common law, playing a special role in the life of their members and enjoying a unique loyalty from those encompassed within their fold. The group may be a church, a college, a guild, a township. Each of these endows its associates with separate privileges, rights, and duties. The aspiration of the bureaucratic servant of the centralized state for uniformity is a yearning for heavenly peace, the peace after death. If the freedom and vitality which men find only in some group are denied them, they cease to have a political life. They have nothing to defend, protect, or promote and have no source of strength with which to do it. Politically, man can stand inside of some special interest—a music school, a university, a trade union, a corporation, a religious fellowship. If he is denied this group, he can no longer promote

[3] Quoted in Alexis de Tocqueville, *The Old Regime and the Revolution,* translated by John Bonner (New York, 1856), p. 196.

either a special or a general interest; he no longer has any
political influence.

POLITICAL stability requires that the government derive its
ultimate strength from the adhesion of these small societies
which in their totality contain the nation itself. The little society makes possible a busy creative life for the individual. It
involves him with his fellows in a common concern. It gives
him a place among his neighbors and allows him to take his
part in a recognized drama. It makes for the voluntary accepted rule applicable to all members. It gives a meaning to
the daily activities of humble folk. It makes for emotional
stability by involving the individual in the manifold activities
of local government. In a degree the cellular fellowship becomes the government for the little things that trouble men
in their daily lives. Each little society, such as a township, a
parish, a rod and gun club, a musical society, or a chamber
of commerce, is a code-forming and tradition-generating
body. Each of these multiplies the ways of men with each
other, and sets limits upon arbitrary power; for each in its
own realm has authority and commands the support of its
adherents. Rules grow up—unwritten and sometimes unde-
fined—wherever men associate over a period of time. This is
true in the army, in prisons, and among slaves. A society in
being, no matter how small or how informal—a boys' baseball club for instance—instructs, disciplines, and protects its
own within the rules of the game. There must be no violation
of an unwritten but recognized rule defining the separate dig-
nities of prisoners and their guards. By its mere existence, the
group sets limits to arbitrary authority.

More significant perhaps than any of these considerations
is the group's impact upon the political process. A community with numerous corporate cells is one with many centers
of autonomous strength. Each group separately stakes out a
jurisdictional area inherent in its special role and develops
objectives that bear upon the community at large. The activi-

ties of each of these groups impinge upon all the others. There are many areas of cooperation and opposition between the Red Cross, the Rod and Gun Club, the Athletic Union, and the Women's Church Union. The community is a compound of overlapping and contradictory policy-making bodies, each with its own variant of good and right. The relations among these little societies are like the possible moves in a game of chess—there is no end to them. To add to the complexity of the pattern, the local societies have their regional and national bodies which in their turn play similar roles on a broader stage. Public policy is a distillation, more or less acceptable, of the aims of these separate autonomous groups that would pattern the world to fit their particular definition of good and right. To complicate this scene still further, individual citizens may belong to a number of these little societies, so that contact runs formally between groups and informally through individuals who may have contradictory loyalties.

In this kind of society a political party is the sum of all of these corporate entities, for the active workers in any local political party are usually involved in one or more of these autonomous bodies and represent—unconsciously, if you like —the groups to which they belong. The political party is the vehicle of these contradictory interests. They, not the individuals, make up the body politic; they determine public opinion, influence elections, strengthen or weaken party and candidate. These many corporate groups are each in their way political cells that nourish the roots of the body politic. A government that has its roots thus spread over the land and deeply imbedded in the interests and passions of the communities and their many groups has a thousand sources of political strength. It is like a pyramid with a very broad base. It cannot be toppled. Centralization as exemplified by France and Russia stood the pyramid upon its head, so that any wind could blow it down. It destroyed the local cells essential to a healthy political society, the political roots dried up, and the government, blinded by its ever expanding bureaucracy, failed to recognize that the strength it needed had ebbed away and the power it exercised would prove a withered reed.

In the path of increasing centralization great harm is done to the individual by depriving him of responsibility at the local level in the little societies. Absence of responsibility strips him of meaningful activity and takes from him the zest for daily involvement. Inevitably the centralized government makes men and communities discontented by making them dependent upon a distant power. By depriving the individual of the enjoyable expenditure of energy and enthusiasm in remedial efforts for local ills, it makes him both apathetic and resentful. What he would have enjoyed doing himself he now expects a beneficent power to accomplish, and if his interest is stirred, it takes the form of seeking a formula to attract the attention of the all-powerful minister in the faraway capital. His means of compelling attention are limited —flattery, cajoling, begging—and when these fail him, as they must, he resorts to some form of magic: "pull," influence, bribery, conspiracy, revolution. Energy previously devoted to playing a part in a community drama with other actors similarly engaged toward some common end is now expended in futile gestures meant to attract the notice of what seems an indifferent or callous government. The local communities have now become incapable of doing the simplest things. They can no longer gather the enthusiasm or possess the means to build a church, or punish a criminal. They turn to the central government and wait for the benefits to come as grace from above. And end in disillusionment, as they must.

In politics it is more important to air the differences that divide men than to find the remedies they seek. Some difficulties are by their nature irremediable; others dissolve themselves into multiple questions of varying degrees of importance, and few need to have an immediate answer. But if there is no way of presenting a grievance, no means of seeking a remedy, then the smallest complaint becomes a challenge to the political system. Every difficulty seems to lead in one direction—to the overthrow of the government. It does not have to be oppressive. It need merely be impervious to popular feeling and indifferent to complaint. All that is called for is that it have what it must have to succeed—sufficient insulation from the stresses and strains of ordinary living to acquire the reputation of an insensitive monster ruling the lives of men for its own selfish ends.

WHERE there are no effective political parties, that is, where there is no opposition and therefore no two-way political communication, the ideologists take over the role of critics and prophets and they, instead of experienced participants in public affairs, shape the minds of men and define the political issues.

This is what happened in France. The ideologists became the political leaders by default, and their bold reform projects were equal to their lack of experience in public affairs. They knew the answer just because they did not understand the question. The question was, as it always has been, how to arrange the infinite details of human association so as to give a modicum of satisfaction to all who are involved. In reply to any question—whether of taxation or justice or economy in government—they said the answer was equality, liberty, fraternity. The model they held before them was in the primitive world—where all men are free. Abolish the artificialities, the false pride, the useless prerogatives, give power to the people, enthrone reason, and all will be well—so well that liberty will reign and felicity will be the portion of every man. In Russia it was abolish capitalism and all men will be free and happy. These are ingratiating doctrines but irrelevant in a real world; for in a real world the criminal has to be caught, tried, sentenced, and punished; the tax must be levied, collected, appropriated, and expended—and these are complex matters of infinite detail for which no completely satisfactory solution has ever been found. But to the ideologist, all of these harassments are a matter of indifference because he is so little aware of their existence that he can deal with them by a simple formula and remain for a time blissfully indifferent to the consequences of his policy.

The tragedy which the centralized government will have brought upon itself will be compounded by the ideologist turned politician. He will attempt to remake everything except the centralized government. He will guillotine the king, destroy the church, expropriate the property owners, and deny the privacy of the family. He will do all of this and more but keep the centralized state and strengthen it. The one thing he will not attempt will be the re-establishment of local self-government, the absence of which was the cause of the revolution itself. The revolutionist cannot think of the little parish as a source of strength to the state and as a natural way for dealing with the daily troubles of the local society. He is so taken with the power of centralized government to reconstruct everything and so full of general ideas that he remains oblivious to the political energy hidden in the small corporate towns and villages. He would not re-create this essential source of political stability even if he could because a vigorous local community would undermine the power and nullify the ambition of the new leader come to save the nation. The loss of experience in local government is the major deprivation of the people and the revolution cannot bring it back to life.

the international corporation
3 and world order

EFFORTS TO ORGANIZE the world for peace, past and present, have always broken down in the end. This is a simple statement of the historical record. One cannot argue lack of good will or honesty of purpose or a genuine desire to achieve an effective international organ that would take on itself the role of peace-keeping with the support of the nations of the earth. But, as the whole world knows, the effort has been frustrated. The League of Nations was the latest great failure. The United Nations seems headed in the same direction.

There are many reasons why this may happen. Human affairs are complicated matters shaped and influenced by a myriad of "causes" that, taken together, have given us our present heritage—the threat of human annihilation and the inability to stem the drift toward an imminent convulsion from which there would be no return. A casual evaluation of the daily record suggests that the human being has no instrumentality at hand that can reverse the armaments race or stop man from the last decision he would probably ever be

This essay was originally written for this collection. It has also been published in another form, under the title of "Survival of the Fittest," in *Columbia Journal of World Business*, III (March–April 1968), pp. 13–20.

called upon to make—to give the signal that would release thermonuclear warfare. Such a possibility would only seem consistent with a world gone mad, or held in the grip of individuals who lack reason, conscience, Christian charity, or ordinary common sense. In fact there have been worried people in the United States who are prepared to put the 200 million Americans underground as a security measure against such a war, and there have been others who seem to accept the prospects of a loss of twenty to thirty million American lives in an effort to defeat the enemy—as if in the complex effects of nuclear warfare one could calculate in advance the number of dead to be expected with any kind of precision. Such a view also assumes that in so interwoven a social system as ours it is possible to foresee what the disruption of services and communication and the physical impossibility of dealing with the dead and the injured might lead to. The dead by unexpected starvation, thirst, and exhaustion might well be greater than were set down in the calculation projection.

The mere statement of these matters as possibilities that reasonable and prudent men are trying to encompass, to plan for, so as to mitigate what seems to them even greater horrors, raises fundamental questions of why this prospect is upon us. It will not do to blame the scientists who learned how to split the atom and manufacture the atomic bomb. The problem is not a scientific one; it is political. It is not even primarily military. It is political because it involves the nature and function of the state itself.

The modern national state is of relatively recent origin. Some historians consider its emergence a result of the Reformation; others place its beginnings at about the time of the French Revolution, or as one of its major consequences. In any case, the primary function of the modern national state is to protect its citizens from external attack and maintain internal order. The emphasis upon protection from external aggression has set the tone and defined the character of the modern state more fully than any other single function that may characterize it. In fact, nationalism and all that goes with it requires the ability to keep the state absolutely sovereign, which in essence means the ability to impede any intrusion upon its territory, interests, or dignity.

In a world of competitive nation-states such as Europe represented after the Reformation, when states like France and Spain were expanding at the expense of their neighbors, and after the French Revolution, when France was trying to impose its sovereignty upon the rest of Europe, the question of national security became the prime consideration. The First and the Second World Wars are logical by-products of this state; so is the Cold War; so is the armaments race; so are the struggles in various parts of the world that have followed the Second World War. In each case the attack is against a sovereign nation to subjugate it, to impose upon it another loyalty and even another system. Though that is secondary—it is fear of conquest that governs the political attitude toward the rest of the world. The many alliances, treaties, understandings, mutual defense pacts, disarmament meetings, peace congresses, and international courts have all failed in the end. The history of the national state is a bloody one, and it could not be otherwise. As states absolutely sovereign, confined within a geographic boundary, and accepting no infringements on their absolute rights, as states beset by enemies equally sovereign, equally ambitious, and presumably equally well armed, their behavior to each other could only be that of active or potential enemies. It is seemingly inherent in the national state to expand its boundaries by force if necessary. The state is as aggressive as the weakness of its neighbors will allow and is voracious to a point that it would be difficult to say that it may reach a point where all its ambitions can be satisfied absolutely and forever.

The national state system is intrinsically unstable and the prospect of war is ever present. This system has found no means of eliminating the threat of war and its occurrence.

The improved weapons that have been placed in its hands have merely increased the size and the human and material costs of warfare. Nor have the attempts to form international organizations seriously changed the nature of the system or the relations of the states to each other. The League of Nations witnessed Mussolini's attack upon Ethiopia, Japan's invasion of China, the Chaco War in South America, and other conflicts as well. The United Nations have seen numerous small wars: the blockade of Berlin, the Korean War, the confrontation between the United States and Russia over Cuba, the war in Vietnam, the bloody strife over Cyprus and the concurrent danger of a war between Greece and Turkey, and the conflagration in the Middle East—to mention only a few as the more evident examples of the failure of the United Nations to bring peace to the world.

Whether the United Nations survives or disappears there appears to be no prospect that these wars big and small will come to an end. The state system is not capable of building an effective international order and is not capable of endowing the United Nations with the needed power to maintain the peace between the nations. An organization made up of sovereign states is not a satisfactory base for maintaining international stability. Each state in any real crisis, or even in lesser matters, behaves as a national state, and when it takes a position in the United Nations on any subject it does so in accord with its conception of its own interests. Every debate, every vote, every speech reflects this stubborn fact. Anyone who listened to the debate over the recent war in the Middle East will testify that not a single state put the international order before its own national interest. Nor could it do so. The state system by its very nature, by its overriding involvement in the question of national security, cannot act otherwise. It would seem, therefore, that an international order cannot be built on the sovereign states.

If we are going to have an international order, then, it will have to rest upon some other base, preferably upon one that is extranational by its very nature. Such a possible base does exist and is constantly growing stronger and more inclusive. What is more, its growth and continuing expansion cannot be halted for it involves the nature of the industrial system itself. This proposed base is the international corporation. It is by nature supranational; its servants are literally indifferent to the national state except as an impediment to the growth of the basis for international concurrence. Its present role contains its potential as an international poliitcal force.

A glance at the alternatives inherent in the present state system will expose their impotence in dealing with the political impasse. All of these possible alternatives are in the end unacceptable because they are self-defeating. The first possibility is that Russia and the United States will arrive at an understanding to keep the peace of the world either directly or by lending their military support to the United Nations. This would reduce the United Nations to a tool of these two powers and make a mockery of all the machinery of voting, committees, conferences, and so on, now in existence. In a measure this has already happened: when these two nations agree, the United Nations can function realistically; when they disagree, the wars go on to exhaustion—Korea, Vietnam, the Middle East, and so on. There is, however, no good ground to assume that such an agreement would be permanent. Historically, a bilateral agreement between two nations is built on sand. The adherents of each side manage because of changing conditions to erode the basis of the alliance. So it was in the past. So it would be in the future. And the world would be as unstable at the end of the period as it is at present.

The second possibility is that Europe will become a world power comparable to either the United States or Russia and thus be able to keep the peace between them by threatening to align itself with one side or the other. The history of Europe does not encourage belief either that a united Europe will arise within a reasonable time or that if it did arise, it would exhibit the wisdom and restraint required to keep the alliance between the great powers and prevent a war. The present posture of De Gaulle and the past behavior of Hitler and Stalin tax the credulity of even the most stubborn optimist.

A third possibility is an alliance between Russia and China for the imposition of their notion of peace upon mankind. Although this is possible, it is not likely because there are no grounds for lasting peace between these powers. Russia has a million or more square miles of territory claimed by China. That does not provide a basis for a permanent alliance, and what is assumed to be in store for an alliance between the United States and Russia would repeat itself in the case of Russia and China, as it would if such an agreement developed between the United States and China.

The fourth possibility is a nuclear war between the major atomic powers, leading to the virtual annihilation of each other and most of the rest of the population of the earth. There are people in both East and West who speculate that one of these powers would come off best and not only recover from the losses and the destruction but also assume the direction of the affairs of the world.

The fifth possibility is a continuation of the balance of terror that now exists until such time as—? No one knows or can predict the answer to this question. How long can it go on? How will it terminate? In the meantime, nuclear weapons are being researched and produced. One day it is announced that Russia has a satellite capable of dropping atomic bombs on American cities. A few weeks later we announce that the United States has a missile capable of carrying multiple bombs, each tuned to a special Russian city and more difficult to destroy than earlier weapons. The assumption is that these powers will somehow balance each other in capabilities to do harm. What happens if by some bit of luck or human misfortune one or the other upsets the present balance by quite suddenly acquiring the ability both to strike its opponent and detonate the nuclear weapon sent against him in response to the first blow? How long would the balance of terror last? Or, a purely political question, what if a Hitler should come to power either in Russia or in the United States, a man incapable of staying still and driven by some inner compulsion to adventure in the world, regardless of the danger? Then what?

This is the present situation in a world of nationalism where the state, great or small, can no longer protect its own from annihilation, where all of the songs, myths, and boasts that go with the idea of political nationalism have lost their meaning. This national impotence is especially true of the little nations—Belgium, The Netherlands, Poland, Bulgaria. It is also true of the large nuclear powers. They at least believe that they have the power to inflict such damage as to make the attack too expensive—a belief based upon a balance of terror and upon the presupposition of there being men of reason in control of the instrument that could speed the deadly bomb into space. As a basis for *permanent* international peace both of these assumptions reflect almost a naive optimism—an optimism that has proven a snare and a delusion in innumerable instances in the past, and will most likely do so in the future.

The history and manner of men and nations of the last five hundred years underlies the present situation, and the horror that the current impasse implies for human destiny is the obliteration of mankind by incineration. Surely, not even the vision of the Apocalypse was more convulsive than the horror hidden in the balance of terror between the great powers. And all of this is upon us because of the state's search for absolute security, which it is still pursuing and has to pursue while it exists.

How much longer will the national political state survive (if it is not destroyed by the atomic bomb)—another five hundred years? Probably not. If it can*not* supply protection for its citizens from external attack, it has lost one of its major reasons for being. This applies to both the little and the big nation. Nor, as we have seen, can the state build a viable international order. Its nationalism stands in the way. If, as some assume, the movement toward European unity suggests a decline of nationalism, then in the present state of affairs it would be replaced by a larger nationalism. De Gaulle's attitude toward the admission of Great Britain into the Common Market is an early hint of what is probably in store for the future. A European nationalism would not advance the development of an international organization; it might even make it more difficult to approve the surrender of sovereignty that would be involved. The point really is that an international organization cannot be built of nations; it must have a different genesis and composition.

An international political organization must have its source in international rather than national bodies. It must be organized upon the basis of on-going institutions that are by nature supranational, whose governors think in international terms, whose personnel are indifferent to, and almost unaware of, the nation. It must have its origin in a fountainhead that is supranational by its very existence, function, plan, and purpose. If such a base could be found upon which to build an international political institution, then indeed the *external* role of the national state would decline and gradually disappear and the problem of security—national security —would become meaningless because they would no longer serve any purpose. Security for the nation would exist because no one would be interested in challenging it. This may sound like the wildest sort of dream, like the emanations of some Utopian prophet with no sense of the real world, and therefore irrelevant. Would that the idea were irrelevant. Then the problem it tries to deal with would no longer exist. But it does exist. The threat to the security of the national state must first be by-passed, become meaningless, before the present danger of atomic weapons can come to seem irrelevant to the needs of mankind. The arms cannot be destroyed as long as there is danger to the state. The threat to national security must become meaningless before the weapons will be beaten into plowshares.

The seemingly impossible idea of the disappearance of security problems because the national state can no longer provide security for its people, is a growing daily phenomenon that is going unnoticed. If the national state can no longer protect its own against annihilation from the outside, it becomes functionless. But that would not create the international order. Such an order can come only from the existence of an expanding body of international organizations multiplying daily in function and number. These bodies are growing with the increasing speed of travel and transactions; the earth has become smaller for purposes of international communication than was the smallest nation in the days of the oxcart.

This international body is the corporation, or, preferably, the international corporate body. It is a natural body because it has its origin in the performing of a needed function; International Telephone and Telegraph is an example. It is by nature indifferent to the boundary and unconcerned about security. It only becomes aware of the national state as an impediment, an obstruction. The members of the international corporate body are only involved in fulfilling the service wherever it needs to be satisfied—in the Sahara, Switzerland, Vietnam, or Paraguay. This is true of the international airplane company. Its pilots, mechanics, ticket agents, financiers, passengers may come from any and all places. Its concern is with speed, safety, schedule, costs, landing fields, trained pilots, weather control, absolutely effective communication. The questions that bother the national state—security, national interest, customs, tariffs, fear of invasions, danger of violations of the border—are in this instance matters of indifference. Those same considerations apply to international banks, to some of the large commercial and distributing companies like Standard Oil of New Jersey, Shell, and others, and to religious bodies like the Roman Catholic Church and Islam, to scientific bodies, the International Red Cross, and a thousand other corporate bodies that exercise jurisdiction over property, have thousands of employees, have contractual relations in a hundred different countries, have their own internal systems of discipline and their own police force, make rules and regulations that affect the lives, comfort, convenience, and fortune of thousands of people in many parts of the earth. These bodies govern the enterprise under their control and in doing so exercise powers almost sovereign. When an international airplane company decides to establish a field in a nation for the first time, it has performed an act of greater import to the body politic of that nation than most acts of the government. When an international bank decides to make a loan, it exercises a judgment the political consequence of which may prove great indeed—it may save a government from being overthrown, or it might stimulate an industry that will provide employment for many, increase the national income, and raise the standard of living of all. When an international oil company opens up an oil field, as it did in Venezuela or Aden, it may change the face of the nation and lay the foundations of a modern society. In doing so it exercises authority equal to or, in some instances, greater than the local government. It makes contracts, acquires land, lays pipeline, brings in shipping, develops communication, builds schools and roads. It brings in a great variety of skills, which are gradually passed on to the local population, thus changing the social structure of the body politic. It stimulates a labor movement, a skilled working class, a middle class of distributors, a wealthy class of lawyers, politicians, and local participants. By the royalty and taxes it pays, the government is able, perhaps for the first time in its history, to perform those services expected of it in a modern society—to build schools, expand its universities, develop a national road system, and so on. The powers of the international corporate body are very great, and its influence upon the society in which it operates may also be great. The acts of an international corporate body have in effect the characteristics of a sovereign state; they may be unavoidable—such as those that arise from the need for the right of way for a pipeline that has to be provided so that the corporate body can function in this place, just as the government cannot build a highway unless its legislature will authorize the funds and the courts uphold the rights of eminent domain.

The international oil corporation, the international communications corporation, the international bank are natural bodies. They are called into being by the need for the service that they and they alone can perform. The modern world is their presence. They are the essence of the international system that has grown and expanded at a rate faster than the population explosion. In that sense they play a role more essential than that of sovereignty—or, better perhaps, they perform a unique service without which the modern state would be seriously crippled. These are services that have to be performed by an international corporate body and cannot be supplied by any other agency. The nationalist state cannot run the international telecommunication system, or the international airplane system, or the international distributing system.

These are presumably private institutions operating for a profit. The profit is the wage that keeps the system going. The function is public; it is essential and indispensable if the citizens living in the nation are to share the growing exchange of goods, ideas, and people. The picture is obscured by the presence of a few large powers like the United States or Russia. They seemingly could do all these things for themselves (they too are dependent on international exchange, services, and communication), but the smaller political bodies in Latin America, Europe, Africa, and Asia are completely dependent upon the "sovereign" corporate body—the international banking system, the international oil industry, the

international communications systems—for their participation
in the world. And when an international corporate body such
as Pan American Airways decides to build an airfield in a
small African or Asian country, it in fact exercises an act of
sovereignty—no one can compel it to do so and the local government can only stop it to its own disadvantage and increasing isolation in the modern world. Such an act would in the
long run be equivalent to a defeat in a war.

This corporate body of which we have been speaking is
increasing in numbers and size, in power and prestige, and
in the areas of modern enterprise that it embraces. It is international in its very essence. Its purpose is service, in response
to manifest needs, and it has a life span of as long as the
service needs to be performed. Its ownership is irrelevant,
for the owner neither manages nor controls it except in legal
fiction and it can, and in due course will, be owned by people all over the world. Its management can be drawn from
wherever competence is to be found; its profits may be distributed among owners in all nations; its technical personnel
and labor force can be, and often are, completely international. Perhaps more significant, the international corporate
body is devoted to the performance of an international function. Its total commitment is extranational. It has no concern
with boundaries, national interest, local cultural pride, and
regional idiosyncrasies, except as they favor or hinder the
performance of the function for which the corporate body has
come into existence. This international corporate body is thus
autonomous within the state where it operates. It draws its
capital, finance, skill, material from wherever it finds it. It is
at the service of the nation but is not of it. Its life will go on
when the present government has fallen, even when the
state has changed its character by merging, annexation, defeat
or whatever. The international communication corporations
will go on no matter what the political map of Africa or Asia
looks like fifty years from now. The functional service is more
durable than the political form or territorial prescription.

The telephone system operates in both East and West Germany, in both North and South Korea. The international corporate body is indifferent to national limitations. Its personnel think, plan, and operate on an international basis: the telephone line is broken in Ghana; there is an oil shortage in Paraguay; the Catholic priest in a church near Pittsburgh has stepped beyond permissible doctrine and Rome has suspended him; a scientific congress has refused to seat a delegate from Rumania or Switzerland because it considers his work incompetent. The international corporate body "governs" functionally across all borders wherever it has found a natural role, a service that it alone can perform.

We thus really have two systems of "sovereignty" in the world: the state, large and small, and the international corporate body. The first is on the defensive and is probably on the decline; it is anxious over its security and is living by permission of those who could annihilate it on any day. Even the great powers stand in fear that the "balance of terror" will break down or that some fallible human being will miscalculate and blunder to produce a cataclysm that may see the end of all life on the face of the earth. This nation-state has tried to build an international political system for its own salvation but has always failed. Its commitment to national security has made it impossible for it to contrive an extranational body within which it could be submerged. If we live by the experience of the past the modern national state cannot build an extranational body to its own undoing as a national state.

The second "sovereignty" is the international corporate body. It is growing and it cannot be stopped. Except for the very great powers, the smaller nations are increasingly dependent upon the international corporate body for the means of economic development if not for survival. These corporate bodies perform their essential services for a fee— such as interest on a bank loan or a profit on oil distribution. They are apolitical but possess great political influence if not political power. Their international character makes them indifferent to local political squabbles. Their supranational structure places them beyond the need for security so essential to the state. In fact, they by-pass the security problem.

Clearly, if the state manages to blunder into a holocaust and consume the races of men that people the earth, then the international corporate bodies will go down the stream and be washed away as if they had never existed. But if we assume that life is carried by some creative impulse that will not die, that man has always contrived a new structure when the old one was worn out, when it could no longer provide for and protect those whom it was meant to serve, then one would expect what has happened in the past to be repeated in the present impasse. The international corporate body, like the itinerant merchant who settled outside the castle wall with the consent of the baron and ultimately displaced him by developing a new political order, would seem the logical basis for the contrivance of a noncompetitive international order. This is perhaps a strange destiny for the corporation. But examples of it have been seen in the past: the Knights Templars and the Hanseatic League, for instance. The international corporate body seems destined for this role. It is international in structure and function. It knows not the tribulations of the state. The reduction of the earth to the size of a large ancient parish with many autonomous governments makes the international corporate body the logical bond between them. The speed of communication, the increased mobility and proliferation of the sciences, make corporate organization increasingly evident, necessary, and inevitable. Our industrialized world is held together by the increasing number of corporate bodies and by their widening role.

The international corporate body involves the citizen in a different loyalty—a functional identity with a stateless order that knows no borders. The day may well come when the majority of people in all nations will have their deepest political loyalties to one or more international corporate

64   bodies. They may well become absorbed in identities, values,
and interests unrelated to the state or the nation. This is
probably inevitable if industrialization works its way as it
seems bound to do. The international corporate bodies may
have differences with other similar organizations. But the differences would have little to do with nationalism or security.
What seems implicit in this development is a new international order based not upon the state obsessed by fear of
subversion or conquest but upon the natural extranational
bodies that are visibly by-passing the security problem of the
national state and are enveloping all men and all states.

Time is the essence of change and transition. How long
will it take for the corporate body to be so evidently the
international structure as to make the formal legal organ
contrived by the nation-state—the United Nations—visibly
irrelevant because the state itself will become irrelevant to
international dealings? One cannot assume that so profound
a structural change as here envisioned can go on without
political implications, and without a shift in political power.
What is not clear is the way this shift of political power will
occur; but that it will take place there can be little doubt.
Will the national state hold on long enough to permit this to
occur or will it destroy itself and mankind as well? What
about Russia and China? The answer here seems clear. If
Russia and China are going to become industrialized in the
sense that the United States is, then they will go the same
way—the international corporate body will reach over the
closed state, as in some measure it already does. The international corporate body is a natural functional institution
and it can only be kept from its role if there is no extensive
industrial development. In either case the question is the
same. Will the Communist and the non-Communist states per-
severe without annihilating each other long enough to allow
the unforeseen growth of the international corporate body to
take on the requisite political role in the international field,
while leaving to the state the police powers for internal civil

needs? This seems to be the major issue confronting mankind. It is a question of time, and no one can say whether man will allow himself the mercy of surviving long enough to find a way of transferring international powers to the corporate bodies that have come into being for other purposes but unwittingly foreshadow an international order resting on a natural international base untroubled by the burdens of national security.

the American tradition
4 in foreign relations

A GREAT PEOPLE WEATHERS a period of stress like that through which Americans are now living if its institutions are sound and express its deepest convictions. The American institutions, molded by time and experience, contain values that give meaning to the things we do. Time, place, and fortune have wrought their own special imprint upon the American conscience and endowed our folk with an ethical bias peculiarly their own. The indefinable something we call the American outlook adds up to a philosophy of life and a political morality. But Americans are inclined to take their ethical notions for granted and busy themselves with immediate issues. They do not worry about their ideology and would not recognize the meaning of the word if used to describe their beliefs. If in the present crisis they are troubled and confused by the contradictory policies urged upon them, it is because some of their counselors speak a language alien to American experience and indifferent to the inspiration of

 Reprinted, with permission, from *Foreign Affairs*, October 1951, pp. 31–50. This essay became the base for *The American Tradition in Foreign Policy* (Norman, Okla.: University of Oklahoma Press, 1967).

American polity. We seem to have lost sight of the recognizable drift of our own history and of the sweep of its great energy.

This exuberant and restless power, so recognizably descriptive of the United States, has been disciplined by an equally strong moral bias which has not only canalized and contained it within bounds, but humanized it as well. How else explain this crude and boundless might, which fought two great wars 3,000 and 6,000 miles distant from its own shores, and then, at the height of its military glory—with the enemy defeated and the world helpless to resist the strength of its armies—dismantled its gathered force and returned to the pursuit of peaceful ways, asking only that the other nations of the world do the same? It has placed no other people under duress and has exacted neither homage nor obeisance from the weak and the powerless, as well it might have done. Nay, more than that. It has not only denied itself any compensation for the burden and cost laid upon it by two wars, but at the end of the fighting it has offered its resources and its skill to help bind the wounds and assuage the pain that the wars had imposed upon other peoples—including the enemies it had just defeated. The Hoover Commission, in the First World War, UNRRA, and the Marshall Plan at the end of the second, are but parts of the effort by the American people to make life livable again for those who had suffered in the conflict. But the story does not end there. After the First World War, Wilson became the architect of a League of Nations that would protect the weak against the strong—against ourselves in fact; and, after the Second World War, Roosevelt and Hull became the chief movers to do over again through the United Nations what had been attempted after the First World War by Wilson. To say that a people that on two such occasions behaved in this way has no philosophy of politics, no sense of direction, and no international policy is to speak the sheerest nonsense. What may be said is that the United States has never elaborated its implicit values

68   into a conscious doctrine. This, however, is an evidence of strength and vitality. A formal ideology is an unconscious apology, a claim for validity that needs to be defended. A vigorous, spontaneous life calls for no explanation and overflows any doctrine.

The tenor of American polity, both internal and external, is clear enough if we will only look at it. If we have not looked at it in recent times, this is in part due to the distorted doctrines in which our generation and the one before it have been caught up. Many of those doctrines are not descriptive of our behavior and do not stem from American experience. We have—and here our intellectuals and teachers are perhaps more guilty than others—permitted ourselves to be beguiled by theories of economic determinism and "power politics." We have attempted to explain American foreign policy on grounds in which we really do not believe—the proof of which is that we do not act upon them. Our behavior is a standing contradiction of the theories taught us in books based upon the beliefs and practices of other peoples. And when—as happened on occasion—our government through the executive departments has behaved as if the theories of "power politics" and economic determinism were true, the American people repeatedly repudiated the policy, and forced a return to the traditional though inadequately formulated American belief that the little nations of the world have the same right to live their own life as the strong and powerful. In fact, our sympathy for the weak has always been greater than our admiration for the strong. The "big stick" formula of Theodore Roosevelt is an anomaly in our experience, was condemned by large numbers of Americans from the beginning, and formally repudiated within a few years after his death. The Reuben Clark memorandum on the Monroe Doctrine, written inside the State Department in 1928, represents the official demise of the big stick theme in American foreign policy. But even Theodore Roosevelt explained many times that he meant to strengthen the weaker states in the Caribbean rather than permanently to control them.

In short, the American people have always had a principle of foreign policy. They have had it from the very beginning. The basic motivation that has governed American relations with other states became evident during the earliest dissidence that led up to the War of Independence, was the chief cause of the Revolution itself and (to use William H. Seward's phrase) "is in reality the chief element of foreign intercourse in our history."

The controlling proposition in American foreign policy was clearly enunciated by James Madison when he said "The fundamental principle of the Revolution was, that the colonies were coordinate members with each other and with Great Britain, of an empire united by a common executive sovereign, but not united by a common legislative sovereign. The legislative power was maintained to be as complete in each American Parliament, as in the British Parliament. . . . A denial of these principles by Great Brtain, and the assertion of them by America, produced the Revolution." The "fundamental principle . . . that the colonies were coordinate members with each other and that . . . the legislative power was . . . as complete in each American Parliament, as in the British Parliament" has remained the unbroken popular theme in American foreign relations. It was this inspiration that ultimately made Rhode Island and Texas equal within the American federal union. The Pan American system of equal states rests upon the same fundamental principle, and to this basic motivation we must ascribe the gradual evolution of the Monroe Doctrine from unilateral to multilateral policy. It explains the "hands off" injunction imposed upon European Powers in regard to the Western Hemisphere and is the reason for the non-aggressive attitude in the Monroe Doctrine. This fundamental principle was the keystone for our advocacy of the Open Door in China, as it was the justification for a continuing opposition to Japan. We accepted the challenge of a war in the Far East rather than yield the governing principle in our foreign policy.

The American commitment to the ideal of the juridical equality and moral integrity of states explains our participation in two world wars. It explains our effort to develop a League of Nations so as, in Woodrow Wilson's words, to expand "the doctrine of President Monroe as the doctrine of the world . . . that every people should be left free to determine its own polity, its own way of development, unhindered, unthreatened, unafraid, the little along with the great and the powerful." In such words President Wilson was simply restating the version of the "fundamental principle" which Madison knew was the chief cause of the War of Independence. But the same motivation was also one of the chief reasons for the defeat of the League of Nations. One need but turn back to the debate in the Senate to recognize that what defeated the League of Nations was in no small degree the conviction that America's belief in the "coordinate" membership of all peoples had been repudiated. There is a peculiar consistency in this belief of ours that the little nation has the same rights as the big one. Our quarrel with Russia is upon this ground. The Truman Doctrine is a modern version of the basic propositions of President Monroe; and our defense of Korea is explainable only on the grounds that the only kind of a world the American people can comfortably live in is one in which Korea has no more right to attack and dismember Russia than Russia has to attack and dismember Korea—or Finland. We really believe that Ecuador and Haiti are coordinate with the United States, just as we believe that Poland and Bulgaria are coordinate with Russia.

To some these American notions seem impractical and foolish. Influential scholars and counselors would have us abandon them. They suggest that we cease being childish and idealistic and recognize that the national interest requires us to become disciples of Machiavelli, take our lessons from Richelieu, Bismarck, or Clemenceau. The fact that

Germany and Japan have committed national suicide by consistent adhesion to these doctrines seems not to dampen the eloquence of those who would persuade us to abandon the beliefs and practices by which we have lived and prospered from the beginning.

THE United States is the oldest international society (excepting Switzerland) in existence. It is also the largest. It is composed of [50] "indestructible," "sovereign" states, greatly differing in wealth and population. How great the difference between them is can be seen by comparing Rhode Island to Texas in area, and Nevada with about 160,000 population to New York with more than 14,000,000. And yet there is no invidious distinction between them, and a Senator like Borah from a small state could be a dominant voice in the foreign policy of the United States for some 20 years. In the United States, the representative of the smallest member of the Federation can speak for the entire system without anyone being aware that he represents the least of the states. This is a profound political miracle and was made possible by our acceptance of the principle of equality. Without it, no nation based upon a federal system could have been built to span an entire continent and grow to be not merely the most powerful but perhaps the stablest political entity on the face of the earth.

The issue of juridical equality had to be settled first in the history of the United States, or this nation might never have been born. The Constitutional Convention which advised a "more perfect union" found, as had already been shown in the Continental Congress, that the little states would not yield their juridical equality, their equal sovereignty, or their territorial integrity. This was the stumbling block to union. The warm debates revealed the danger of a permanent dismemberment of the newly born nation. Oliver Elsworth from Connecticut said on June 29, 1787: "If all the states are to exist, they must of necessity have an equal vote in the general government. Small communities when associating with greater can only be supported by an equality of votes." And Luther Martin from Maryland laid it down that "you must give each state an equal suffrage, or our business is at an end." The course of the debates need not be reviewed here, but the compromise—reluctantly agreed to by the large states—adopted the older practice of Connecticut, that of an equal vote for the political units and a popular vote for the governor. Each state was to have two members in the Senate; representation in the House was to be determined on the basis of population in the states. In effect, this means that the smaller states can outvote the larger ones in the Senate, and that in any crucial legislative issue the states are equal, because a bill has to be passed by both houses. It also means that in foreign relations the smaller states could play the decisive role if they voted as a bloc. But they do not vote that way. Equality has eliminated jealousy.

The extension of this principle of equality to the new states to be carved out of the Western Territories is, next to the formation of the union, the most important political decision in our entire history. Without it there would have been no federal union that spans a continent. It was recognized that in time the new states would outnumber the original 13, it was argued that the East would be surrendering itself into the hands of the new states, and among other limitations it was proposed that the representatives of the new states should never be allowed to outnumber those of the original 13. But the principle of equality prevailed. Madison insisted that "the Western States never would nor ought to submit to a union which degraded them from an equal rank with other states." The resolution adopted by the Continental Congress to govern the admission of the new states said that new districts "should become and ever after be and constitute a separate, free, and sovereign state, and be admitted into the union as such, with all the privileges and immunities of those states which now compose the Union." This is what coordinate membership means. This same principle was applied to the lands that came with the Floridas, the Transcontinental Treaty, the Louisiana Purchase, and those ceded to the United States as a result of the war with Mexico. The principle was further evidenced by the agreement that no large state could be divided and no small state united with another without its own consent.

The juridical and political equality of the "indestructible" states has made possible sharp difference of opinion over questions of interest and policy without undermining the union. What we have not quarreled about is the right of each state to its full share in a common judgment and in the formation of a common policy. And herein lies the basic issue in international relations. We forget that the United States is an international society because we do not quarrel over the right to partake in common decisions.

The principle of equal membership within the federal union ultimately eventuated in Calhoun's doctrine of a dissoluble compact between the states, and in the Civil War. The South still speaks of the War Between the States. But it also explains the even more remarkable political event of the readmission of the defeated states on a par with the victors. If the union was to survive, no other course was possible. A federal union built upon the principle of equal sovereignty is not a proper instrument for military government nor for the arbitrary denial to others of the rights and immunities which the individual states claim for themselves. The American ideal of coordinate states is in its essence anti-imperialist.

THIS is well illustrated in our relations with Latin America. The Monroe Doctrine is woven of many contradictory strands and influences, but the firm hand of John Quincy Adams, more than that of any other, shaped its final form. Two years before it was given to the world, Adams had declared that

74 "colonial establishments cannot fulfill the great cbjects of governments in the just purpose of civil society." They were, he said, "incompatible with the essential character of our institutions"; they were "engines of wrong," and in time it would be "the duty of the human family to abolish them, as they are now endeavoring to abolish the slave trade." The Monroe Doctrine, therefore, has in its background the broad proposition, again in Adams' own words that: "The whole system of modern colonization is an abuse of government and it is time that it should come to an end."

Our government chose to act separately when announcing the new policy rather than with Great Britain, as originally proposed by Canning. But it is worth recalling that John Quincy Adams urged the British to follow our example and recognize the independence of the Latin American nations because "upon this ground . . . a firm and determined stand could now be jointly taken by Great Britain and the United States in behalf of the *Independence of Nations.*"

President Monroe before issuing the declaration consulted Jefferson and Madison, who had preceded him in office. Jefferson thought that it was a good occasion "of declaring our protest against the atrocious violations of the rights of nations" begun by Bonaparte and "now continued" by the Holy Alliance. Madison suggested that it might encompass not merely the Western Hemisphere but Spain and Greece as well. The full significance of the Monroe Doctrine must be read against the anti-imperialism of its chief American sponsors. And William H. Seward, writing to the French Government, declared that: "The practice of this Government, from its beginning, is a guarantee to all nations of the respect of the American people for the free sovereignty of the people in every other State."

This same theme comes, surprisingly perhaps, from Richard Olney, famous for his boast in the Venezuelan dispute that a fiat of the United States "is law upon the subjects to which it confines its interposition" in this continent. He added, however, that the Monroe Doctrine "does not contemplate any interference in the internal affairs of any American state." And in what seems like a reminder of the great debate in the Constitutional Convention here transferred to a debate between nations, he said that "the United States would cherish the territorial rights of the feeblest of those states, regarding them . . . as equal to even the greatest nationalities."

It was left to Theodore Roosevelt temporarily to twist the Monroe Doctrine beyond its historical intent. He argued that, "however reluctantly," the United States might be compelled "to the exercise of an international police power" in the Caribbean area. But even Roosevelt's exuberance was modulated by the basic American tradition, and he declared that the Doctrine did not imply or carry "an assumption of superiority, and of a right to exercise some kind of protectorate" over the Latin American countries. It was during Theodore Roosevelt's administration that Elihu Root, speaking as Secretary of State, made the ever-memorable statement: "We wish for no territory except our own. . . . We deem the independence and equal rights of the smallest and weakest member of the family of nations entitled to as much respect as those of the greatest empire." And it was during Root's administration of the Department of State that the United States' delegates to the Second International Peace Conference at The Hague sought "a limitation upon the use of force" in the collection of public debts, because such a practice was inconsistent "with that respect for the independent sovereignty of other nations which is . . . the chief protection of the weak nations against the oppression of the strong." In 1915 Wilson proposed the formalization of the idea of co-ordinate membership in the hemisphere by a treaty which would guarantee the territorial integrity and political independence of the American nations, "so that," to use Colonel House's words, "the Monroe Doctrine may be upheld by all the American Republics instead of by the United States alone as now." Hughes, when Secretary of State, said that "our interest does not lie in controlling foreign peoples; that would be a policy of mischief and disaster," and quoted Jefferson on "the advantages of a cordial fraternalization among all American nations." While Reuben Clark in 1928 declared that "the so-called 'Roosevelt corollary' [is not] justified by the terms of the Monroe Doctrine."

The Good Neighbor policy is the logical sequence to a tradition as old as our government. Bolívar's effort of 1826 to form a federation of American nations was resuscitated by Blaine when he called together a Pan American Congress in Washington in 1889. These nations, to use Blaine's words, "shall meet together on terms of absolute equality." Secretary Hull's definition of the coordinate position of the American states as consisting of "the absolute independence, the unimpaired sovereignty, the perfect equality and the political integrity of each nation large and small" has a classic finality about it. The Non-Intervention Doctrine enunciated by Franklin D. Roosevelt in Montevideo in 1933, and the series of resolutions beginning with the Havana Conference in 1940 and culminating in the Rio de Janeiro Treaty of 1947, converted the Monroe Doctrine from a unilateral to a multilateral policy. Wilson's hope, embodied in the proposed treaty of 1915, had been fulfilled. The growth of the Organization of American States extends to the Western Hemisphere the ideal of a federation of "indestructible states" upon which the United States itself is founded.

THE more than a century-old history of our relations with the independent countries of this hemisphere illustrates the slow and sometimes painful working out of this doctrine. When, during the Grant Administration, an attempt was made to annex Santo Domingo, Senator Sumner of Massachusetts vigorously opposed the project because: "Santo Domingo is the earliest of that independent group . . . towards which our duty is as plain as the Ten Commandments. Kindness, beneficence, assistance, aid, help, protection, all that is implied in good neighborhood—these we must give . . . their independence is as precious to them as is ours to us, and it is placed under the safeguard of natural laws which we can not violate with impunity." After the War with Spain, when the question of Cuba came up for consideration, President McKinley wrote: "I speak not of annexation, for that cannot be thought of. That by our code of morality would be criminal aggression." And he instructed the military commander to administer the island for the benefit of the Cubans.

The controversy with Mexico, which began in 1912, when Taft was President, and continued almost unabated for 30 years through periods of great tension, ended in a peaceful settlement because the people of the United States would not destroy a nation in defense of material interests. Wilson said: "It is none of my business and none of your business how long they [the Mexicans] take in determining their form of government. It is none of my business and none of yours how they go about the business. The country is theirs, the government is theirs, the liberty, if they can get it—God speed them in getting it—is theirs, and whilst I am President nobody shall interfere with them." His statement prevailed in the end in spite of Coolidge's assertion in 1927 that, "The person and property of a citizen are a part of the general domain of the nation, even when abroad."

Theodore Roosevelt's boast, "I took the Canal," is less impressive than the fact that Panama was encouraged to set up as an equal member within the American family of nations. And after the Second World War it exercised its equality by requiring the United States to surrender, much against its will, the use of air bases which it had constructed for the defense of the Canal. In some ways the Panamanian rebellion is comparable to the secession of West Virginia during the Civil War. It is not a good instance of imperial conquest. And to appease our bad conscience we paid $25,000,000 to Colombia.

The series of interventions in the Caribbean and Central America that followed the Roosevelt Corollary are fruitful demonstrations of the workings of the American fundamental principle. The significant point to remember is that intervention is taken to be a temporary intrusion. No one believed—neither the Americans, nor the Haitians, Dominicans, or Nicaraguans—that the United States was there to stay. In each case the President was placed on the defensive. The Senate appointed investigating committees, individual senators attempted to attach riders to the naval appropriation bills denying the use of public funds for the payment of the Marines in the occupied countries. The different administrations were compelled repeatedly to justify their activities before the country, and for half of the time were busy explaining that we were trying to withdraw the Marines from foreign soil. The Clark memorandum officially denied the legitimacy of the government's policy of intervention, and Hoover said in 1928 that "dominion of other people is repugnant to our ideal of human freedom," and in 1929, that "in the large sense we do not wish to be represented abroad [by Marines]." The liquidation of the policy of intervention was begun under Coolidge and Hoover and was completed by Roosevelt. The Platt Amendment, supported and opposed with so much heat, was also repudiated. The American adventure in imperialism in this hemisphere evaporated in one generation.

The one real deviation in the application of the fundamental principle in our foreign relations in this hemisphere is to be found in the annexation of Texas and the war with Mexico. Both of these events are so closely tied to the struggle for position between the slave-holding and free states that they do not really make a clear case of repudiation of the principle. The opposition to both was bitter. John Quincy Adams, "the architect of American foreign policy," signed a public manifesto opposing the annexation of Texas; Lincoln, Webster, and Clay, among many others, condemned the Mexican War and the acquisition of Mexican territory. Clay said: "This is no war of defense, but one of unnecessary and of offensive aggression. It is Mexico that is defending her firesides, her castles, and her altars, not we." He then compared the war with Mexico to the partition of Poland. American historians have generally criticized the war with Mexico. H. H. Bancroft calls the war "a deliberately calculated scheme of robbery on the part of a superior power" and contemporary historians repeat Lincoln's accusation that President Polk simulated an attack by Mexico. One unhappy historian attempts a defense of the war because "every American father ought to be able to say to his boy: 'Your country never fought an unjust nor an inglorious war.'" The question has continued to trouble our conscience, and Henry L. Stimson, speaking in New York before the Council on Foreign Relations in 1931, while Secretary of State, referred back to this period as an aberration "directly attributable to the influence of slavery in this country, then at the height of its political power."

THIS same doctrine has worked its way into the Far East. After the Spanish-American War, President McKinley was sorely troubled by what we ought to do about the Philippines. He explained his decision to a delegation of the General Missionary Committee of the Methodist Episcopal Church: "I went down on my knees and prayed Almighty God for light and guidance. And one night it came to me . . . to take them all, and to educate the Filipinos, and uplift and civilize and Christianize them, and by God's grace do the very best we could by them, as our fellow-men for whom Christ also died." But this explanation failed to convince the American people. The Anti-Imperialist League declared that "the subjugation of any people is criminal aggression and open disloyalty to the distinctive principles of our government. . . .

80   A self-governing state cannot accept sovereignty over an unwilling people." And while the President was explaining the inspiration that led him to disregard the fundamental principle of our foreign relations, one of his chief supporters in the Senate was saying that, "I do not know of anybody, from the President to his humblest follower, who is proposing by force and violence to take and hold these islands for all time to come." The bill for the annexation of the Philippines passed by a majority of one vote and that slim victory was due to the news of the rebellion of the Filipinos against the United States; it arrived the day before the vote was taken. Still the act was on our conscience. [William Howard] Taft, who became Governor General of the Philippines, spoke of "our little brown brothers," and implied an attitude that expressed itself by gradually including in increasing proportion Filipinos in the local administration. The Jones Act of 1916 promised the full autonomy that was given the Filipinos in 1936.

The Filipinos were saved their self-respect, the leaders of the rebellion against the United States became our chief supporters, and when the American flag was lowered and the Filipino flag raised the people of the islands spoke of *Ang Ulalin Watawat*—the orphan flag. When the crisis was upon us in 1941, instead of joining our enemies, they fought on our side. In spite of conquest, annexation, and foreign administration, the basic American belief in coordinate membership had made itself felt in the relationship that had grown out of the original conquest. In some ways this is the most eloquent testimony to our inability to treat any nation as a "subjugated" people. The episode came to an end with complete independence in 1946.

THE much older story of the Open Door in China led to the tragedy of a great war and to the contemporary heartburning of a lost cause. But what we have done in China through

more than a century is so typically American that we probably 81
could not have acted differently.

Our fundamental attitude toward China antedates the
Open Door Policy of Hay by nearly 70 years. In 1832, when
Edward Livingston wrote out the instructions to Edmund
Roberts, our first diplomatic agent to the Far East, he told
him to inform the rulers of those strange countries that "it is
against the principles of our nation to build forts, or make
expensive establishments in foreign countries," and "that we
never make conquests, or ask any nation to let us establish
ourselves in their countries." This statement of American
policy toward China reappears over and over again in the
instructions from the Secretary of State to our representatives
in China. Caleb Cushing asked our Minister to make it clear
to the Chinese that they need stand in no apprehension of
territorial ambition on our part. W. L. Macy informed Robert
M. McLean, who had urged our joining Great Britain and
France in a more aggressive policy, that there was "no hope
that such authority could be obtained from Congress." Lewis
Cass told our Minister that "this country, you will constantly
bear in mind, is not at war with China, nor does it seek to
enter that empire for any other purpose than those of lawful
commerce. . . . You will, therefore, not fail to let it be known
to the Chinese authorities that we are not a party to the . . .
hostilities and have no intention to interfere in their political
concerns." Hay's well-known statement of 1900 that our policy
is one "which may bring about permanent safety and peace
to China, preserve Chinese territorial and administrative
entity," is but a logical sequence to what had originally been
stated in 1832.

The only major deviation in a century-long policy toward
China is to be found under the administration of Theodore
Roosevelt, who made so many others as well in American
relations to the world. In the Taft-Katsura memorandum of
July 1905, Japan was given a free hand in Korea, and the
Root-Takahira Agreement of November 1908 "suggests," to

82   use Professor S. F. Bemis' words, "that Roosevelt was preparing to give to Japan a free hand in Manchuria as he had done already in Korea." It is worth noting that both of these were executive agreements and were not submitted to the Senate for confirmation. But Taft, when he became President, sought to safeguard China against further depredations. He suggested a loan to China for the purchase of the Manchuria Railroad, as "perhaps the most effective way to preserve the undisturbed enjoyment by China of all political rights in Manchuria."

President Wilson opposed the International Consortium. Within two weeks after he took office—on March 18, 1913—he made the far-reaching public statement which reasserted the traditional position of the American people toward China: "The conditions of the loan seem to us to touch very nearly the administrative independence of China itself. . . . Our interests are those of the Open Door—a door of friendship and mutual advantage. This is the only door we care to enter." And Bryan in 1915 told the Japanese that "the United States cannot recognize any agreement or undertaking between the Governments of Japan and China, impairing the political or territorial integrity of the Republic of China, or the . . . Open Door policy."

The Nine-Power Treaty of 1922 brought the principles so long maintained by the United States into a formal international agreement of the signatory Powers, including Japan, Great Britain, and France. Those Powers agreed: "To respect the sovereignty, the independence, and the territorial and administrative integrity of China; to provide the fullest and most unembarrassed opportunity to China to develop and maintain for herself an effective and stable government."

To Japan, however, the Nine-Power Treaty, the Pact of Paris, and the Kellogg-Briand Pact were in the nature of plausible sentiments uttered to satisfy the mood of the moment. As others have done and still do, she made the profound mistake of assuming that we could not really mean what we said. And when she saw the opportunity—when the

Western World was distraught by the economic and political difficulties of the Great Depression, when the League of Nations was a council divided, when the United States and Great Britain had both permitted their navies to fall below even the permitted strength under the Washington Naval Treaties—she attacked Manchuria.

China was weak, the United States was pacifist and isolationist, and Great Britain could not and would not fight alone against Japan in defense of China. The United States protested, Secretary Stimson reminded Japan of her signatures to the Nine-Power Treaty and the Kellogg-Briand Pact, but the Japanese pursued their fateful adventures, regardless of the judgment of the world.

On January 7, 1932, the American Secretary of State announced the now famous Stimson Doctrine that the United States does not "intend to recognize any treaty or agreement . . . which may impair . . . the sovereignty, the independence, or the territorial and administrative integrity of the Republic of China . . . or the Open Door policy." America gave her adherence to the Lytton Commission's report which condemned Japanese actions in China. Japan walked out of the League. In 1940–41 the old story was drawing to a dramatic close. We had frozen Japanese assets and had placed an embargo against oil shipments. Japan had occupied most of China and had invaded French Indo-China. On November 20, 1941, the Japanese Ambassador handed a note to Secretary Hull containing the conditions of peace for the Pacific. Japan promised to withdraw from French Indo-China in return for the lifting of the embargo, removal of the order freezing Japanese assets, and restoration of normal commercial relations. Those were the things Japan asked from the United States as a condition of peace. They seemed very simple and realistic. Surely they would serve the national interest of Japan and would not injure that of the United States. But Secretary Hull and the American people thought otherwise. The American Secretary of State replied on November 26, 1941. The reply was as follows: "The Government of the

84   United States and the Government of Japan, both being solicitous for the peace of the Pacific, affirm that their national
policies are directed toward lasting and extensive peace
throughout the Pacific area, that they have no territorial designs in that area, that they have no intention of threatening
other countries or of using military force aggressively against
any neighboring nation, and that . . . they will actively support the following fundamental principles: [1] The principle
of inviolability of territorial integrity and sovereignty of each
and all nations. [2] The principle of non-interference in the
internal affairs of other countries. [3] The principle of equality, including equality of commercial opportunity and treatment. [4] The principle of reliance upon international cooperation . . . and pacific settlement of controversies . . . and
that the Government of Japan will withdraw all military,
naval, air, and police forces from China and from Indo-
China."

Japan's answer was Pearl Harbor, December 7. And so
the climax had come. The statement made by Hull in November 1941 is not unlike the first one made by Livingston in
January 1832. Roosevelt and Hull fulfilled an original American commitment: the pledge that we would not be a party
to the destruction of another nation.

Why were we so idealistic as to insist upon an affirmation
of national integrity at a moment when the "wave of the
future" seemed so overwhelming? Our acceptance of the
Japanese challenge involved us in mortal danger and the
staggering military expenditure that no possible benefits from
an Open Door policy would have justified. Our investments
in China in 1914 were smaller than those of England, Japan,
Russia, France, or Germany, and in 1931 they were only
about equal to those of France, representing only 2.8 percent
of our investments abroad; our exports and imports to and
from China hovered between one and two percent of our
international trade. To argue that we accepted so dangerous
a challenge in order to defend so small a material interest is
a conclusion which could only be drawn in an age when

economic determinism is the great obsession. When the Japanese offered us peace in the Far East, after they had already occupied most of China and a large part of French Indo-China, we refused. They even agreed to evacuate Indo-China if we would but recognize their conquest in China and Manchuria. We declined. Because of economic interests? No. Because Roosevelt and Hull, speaking for the American people, recognized that no settlement which compromised Chinese political independence and territorial integrity would be acceptable to our sense of justice or consistent with our basic tradition. No American President could have satisfied the Japanese demands without risking repudiation, not merely by the opposition, but by his own party as well.

The fundamental principle of the coordinate state ruled this decision as it has most others in our foreign policy from the beginning.

THIS attitude does not imply any special virtue on our part. It has not saved us from serious errors in dealing with other nations, and it has not endowed us with any special grace in cultivating the good will and friendship of foreign people. On the contrary, our record for irritating our friends by saying the wrong things in the worst way is well above the average. Our good intentions are a small excuse for the unwelcomed preachments we like to indulge in, and the "holier than thou" tone which we often adopt does not add to our persuasiveness in the world of diplomacy. Nor is our record for cooperation, even by our own standards, by any means above reproach. But our failings are within a consistent historical tradition that leads back directly 150 years—and indirectly much further. The policy derives from the assumption that security rests upon cooperation, that cooperation is possible only among equals, that equality eliminates the basic reason for political disruption because those equal politically are coordinate in dignity and in rank.

The doctrines of "power politics" now being preached by

such persuasive scholars as Professor Hans J. Morgenthau of the University of Chicago are a denial of this tradition and a repudiation of the lessons of American experience. The advice offered is exactly that which has ruined half of the nations of the world. Historically these doctrines have always led to war, and often to national suicide. The new school of *Realpolitik* advances its arguments for a settlement with the Soviets on the basis of "spheres of influence," and in terms of the "national interest." The "national interest" is a beguiling phrase: everyone desires to advance the interests of his country. But what country, concretely, is to be sacrificed in the power deal which would determine the *quid pro quo?* Which national interests do not count? Intellectuals abroad who urge upon us this "return to diplomacy" (as the fashionable slogan goes) should be sure of one thing—that we will not bargain away the independence of any other nation.

Fortunately, with all our errors and misjudgments, Americans have never successfully been persuaded that in foreign policy might makes right, or that Machiavelli was a great moral teacher or even a good guide for an understanding of human motives. Our repudiation of "power politics" in this sense of the term does not mean that we do not believe that policy must not be backed by strength, or that we do not possess strength. Germany and Japan can testify to that. When Dean Acheson speaks of a "position of strength" he means strength to resist aggression. To assume that this position is mere sentimentalism and utopianism is to miss the basic point of American history. We are a strong nation because we are an "indestructible union" of weak states. The very essence of American international relations rests upon the idea of a cooperative relationship.

The United States entered the First World War because we were convinced that we could not abide a world dominated by such brutal disregard of the rights of other nations as imperial Germany displayed. The German attack upon Belgium was seen by the American people with absolute horror. Here was a little peaceful nation bound by treaty to remain neutral, cultivating its fields and following in quiet its own affairs, suddenly destroyed without a declaration of war, without cause and in complete repudiation of a solemn treaty. The declaration that the treaty was a scrap of paper merely confirmed the callousness of the German Government. The burning of the library of Louvain, the unrestricted submarine warfare, the braggadocio, and the contempt for the small and the weak all confirmed the American people in the belief that the German régime was a present danger to all nations. And we went to war not to increase our power, not to expand our territory, not for aggrandizement, but to end such practices. That was the meaning of the Fourteen Points; that too was the purpose of the League of Nations. And paradoxically that too was one of the major reasons why the League was defeated. One needs but read the debates in the Senate to recognize that the bitter feeling that turned on Wilson stemmed in part from disillusionment at a peace which repudiated the moral purpose that had taken us into the war.

Our entrance into the Second World War was no less an expression of the great tradition. The surrender at Munich had made it seem that there was no moral principle left in Europe that was worth defending. The spheres of influence settlement at Munich was a yielding of the basic principle of national integrity and political equality for which we had gone into the First World War and crossed the ocean a million strong to maintain. It would have been infinitely easier for the American people to have joined Great Britain in war if she had in 1938 thrown herself against Hitler on the grounds that she would not be a party to the destruction of an independent nation. When Britain became the small bastion that resisted destruction by the evil reborn in Hitler, the attitude of the American people changed. In 1939 when Roosevelt, who clearly saw the meaning of the Nazi threat, had addressed himself to Hitler and Mussolini to exact from them the terms of a possible peace, he spelled out the old American tradition in favor of the security of the independent nation by listing separately all of the nations within the

88   possible reach of the European dictators. Again when in 1940 Russia occupied the Baltic countries, Sumner Welles reasserted the old tradition on the grounds that the very basis of our civilization rested upon the respect for the little nations. This same doctrine of the equality, freedom, and independence of the small nation along with the great reappeared in the Atlantic Charter and gave the Second World War the meaning that the First World War had had. Those ideals reappear in the Moscow Declaration, in the statements issued after the Teheran Conference, and are embodied in the Charter of the United Nations: "The organization is based upon the principle of the sovereign equality of all its members." These same principles reappear in President Truman's speech on the fundamentals of American foreign policy delivered in October 1947, "We shall not recognize any government imposed upon any nation by the force of any foreign power." And in the Truman Doctrine the same old proposition is reasserted. It is implied in the North Atlantic Treaty and in the national defense assistance policy. The fundamental principle of the coordinate state with which our history as a nation began has remained a continuing philosophy of international relations to the present.

No swing away from it lasts long. The deviation in some of the Yalta agreements has, characteristically, met bitter and continuous opposition. The announcement that the United States had asked for three votes in the General Assembly to offset Russia's demand for three votes was made on March 29, 1945, and repudiated April 3: a major policy reversal in five days. The Great Power veto has been widely criticized in America from the beginning. It since has lost much of its effect by the transfer to the Assembly of issues that could be blocked by the Russian veto. The fact that that transfer of jurisdiction was made in an effort to protect the sovereignty of an independent nation—Korea—is eloquent testimony to the soundness of the American tradition. The provisions for permanent membership of certain Powers in the Security Council seem to Americans just as unreasonable as it would have been for the Constitutional Convention to have named the states of New York, Pennsylvania, Massachusetts, and Virginia as the great states of the Union with special power and privileges—a proposition which was indeed made and rejected. One may predict that if the United Nations is to survive it will in time adopt, perhaps in stages, the proposition of "coordinate" membership in the fullest sense. On this point the lesson of American experience is plain, for, as we have noted, the American Federal Union and the Pan American system have grown stronger with the years: the principle of equality, by providing an equal opportunity to participate in a decision which affects all members, removes the fundamental obstacle to international cooperation. International security can stem only from the loyal cooperation of people associated in the enterprise of peaceful existence in a recalcitrant universe. Power derived from conquest, exploitation, and abuse is insecure precisely because it is unjust. There is neither an alternative nor a substitute for the strength that comes with union. But a true union depends upon voluntary adhesion, only possible among those possessed of equal dignity.

It would be good for the world, and for ourselves, to be clear about the concrete significance of this tradition at the present moment. Americans want peace with Russia, but will not buy it at the expense of other nations. The American tradition has no room for a settlement which would divide the world into spheres of influence. It has no room for the sacrifice to Russia of any nation, small or large, for the sake of securing an abatement of the "cold" war or for the sake of avoiding a hot one. The only kind of peace acceptable to it is one based on collective security—again, the principle of the coordinate membership of all states in the family of nations. Much misunderstanding would be avoided if, in their reasoning about us, our friends began with that simple fact.

The enormous energy of the United States has been disciplined by the ethical conception of political equality, and harnessed to the ideal of collective security resting upon a

90   federation of coordinate states. These are the grounds of our difference with Russia. We are not quarreling over economic interests, political doctrines or her internal policies, even if we do not like them. We cannot accept Russia's denial of the coordinate character of other states. We do not believe in the Big Five, the Big Three or the Big Two. The day the Soviet Union learns, if it can, to accept its neighbors as of equal rank with itself, the world will be united again and the Iron Curtain will melt into thin air. Our quarrel is not about Russia, but about her contempt for the independent sovereignty of other nations.

the balance of power
versus *5*
the coordinate state

A GREAT DEBATE on the character and purpose of American foreign policy has been precipitated by those who would persuade our people to abandon their humanitarian and pacific traditions and frankly adopt the doctrine of power politics and of the balance of power as the basis of their foreign policy. This doctrine is confessedly, nay gleefully, amoral. It prides itself upon being realistic and takes Machiavelli as its great teacher. It is contemptuous of the simple beliefs of honest men, jeers at the sentimentalism of those who believe that men may strive for peace among nations, and looks upon democracy as a hindrance to skilled diplomacy. It looks with a certain derisive superiority upon the great leaders of this nation from Jefferson and John Quincy Adams to Woodrow Wilson and Franklin Delano Roosevelt and describes them as moralistic and sentimental, and suggests that our models ought to be Richelieu, Clemenceau, and Bismarck. Its adherents believe that international wars instead of being made by men and supported by institutions humanly contrived have their origin in the nature of man himself and are inevitable. The best they foresee is an armed

91

Reprinted, with permission, from *Political Science Quarterly*, LXVII (June 1952), pp. 173–197.

balance of power—until the next war—and after that, more skilled diplomacy toward the achievement of the same inevitable end, a new balance of power ending in a new war.

This dreadful doctrine has now won wide acceptance by teachers and scholars in the field of international relations and has, in fact, become the leading theme in such circles in many of our largest universities. It has become the *science* of international relations—and who would quarrel with science, especially when it comes packaged in good clear English and from high sources? But it is not science. It is make-believe. Its scientific basis is false and spurious. It is, in fact, only poor logic based upon false premises, and its claim to be a science is only a bit of unholy conceit. For what we are dealing with is not a tentative hypothesis put forth by humble men as a possible clue for other students to analyze, criticize, modify, and reject—or partially accept. No, we are offered a doctrine for national behavior which runs counter to the very essence of the American tradition and are told to accept it in the name of the national interest because this science has discovered what that interest is.

This debate is of greater import to the future of the United States than the long running argument between the "interventionists" and the "isolationists." Both of these accepted the basic American belief in international good will, in the doctrine of friendship among nations, in the right of the little nation to abide in security and without fear, in the possibility of finding a way to peace among nations, in the sanctity of international treaties, in the authority of international law, and in the hope that the democratic way, by enhancing human dignity and widening human freedom, would ease the burden of conflict among men and nations. The "interventionists" and "isolationists" differed about how best to translate these ideas into formal policy, but they did not, with strikingly few exceptions, repudiate the doctrine by which this nation has lived from its very inception.

Now the advocates of *Realpolitik* would sweep away all

of our old beliefs as foolish, sentimental, and moralistic. They would have us build our future upon the concept of the balance of power in international realations, throw all morality and law out of the window as a hindrance and nuisance to skilled diplomacy, divide the world between Russia and ourselves, repudiating our past beliefs, as well as our promises, obligations and treaties that bind us to our many allies, and girdle ourselves by a permanent and huge military establishment—for what?—to carry the happy game of skilled diplomacy from one war to the next. Most of this is explicitly stated in the argument. Some of it, though not stated, is implicit, and constitutes a challenge to the democratic process itself. These doctrines, if adopted and implemented, would convert the United States into a centralized military empire, and in due time destroy the basic democratic institutions by which this government has prospered these many years.

This debate is just beginning. A good deal more will be heard of it in the coming years. The fact that so erudite a scholar as Professor Hans J. Morgenthau, of the University of Chicago, and so subtle a mind as George F. Kennan are the chief proponents of this dreadful doctrine in the United States will add zest to the debate. The appointment of Mr. Kennan as Ambassador to Russia gives his views immediate significance in American foreign policy. But the American people will not take this advice, for they cannot act upon it without ceasing to be both a Christian and a democratic people.

This essay is an attempt to state what has always been the American philosophy of international relations. It brings to the surface the beliefs and the ideals upon which this nation was built as a great federal system, and shows how these same commitments have shaped our foreign policy from the beginning.

We want to be clear on what the debate is about. One side believes that it is necessary, even inevitable, that the relations between nations be built upon the principle of the

balance of power. The other believes that it is possible and
desirable, if man wishes to save himself from destruction, to
organize international relations on the basis of the coordinate
state. The first derives its conclusions and its law from the
modern national state system of Europe, the other from the
experience of the federal system of the United States, from
the development of the Organization of American States,
from the recent adoption of the principle of the coordinate
state on which to frame the Commonwealth of Nations and
from the federal history of Switzerland. These two different
conceptions of the basis of international organization carry
with them underlying assumptions of the nature of man, of
the possible role of human institutions as well as implicit
attitudes toward the democratic process. The international
relations of the United States have unconsciously been dominated by the belief that the relations between states can be
made to rest only upon the ideal mutuality, the equal right to
abide in freedom and the dignity of all nations—great and
small.

An international society, built upon the coordinate state,
must of necessity behave differently from one resting upon
the concept of centralized power. The first makes cooperation
both the means and the ends of its policy. It can, in fact, have
no other objectives. Its ends are determined by its means. Its
objectives in international as in internal affairs can only be
cooperation for the resolution of common difficulties, and its
means can again only be cooperation. It accepts the doctrine
of live and let live as a matter of course, for its own life is
conceived of as a process of continuing accommodation
within a world of nonviolent friction.

Friction and differences are taken for granted. They are
recognized as a persistent phenomenon. There is no effort at
an absolute or perfect solution. The meaning of peace is unwittingly redefined to mean, not the absence of serious difficulties or the disappearance of differences of interest, but the
daily haggling over issues toward a workable compromise.
An international society composed of "equal" members en-

dowed with unequal resources requires the surrender of the
simplistic notion of a "solution" of "problems." The very idea
of "solution," and the concept of "problem" for which a permanent "solution" is to be had, are both felt to be delusive.
There are no "problems" and no "solutions" in the complex
of political society or in international relations. There are, in
fact, no "social sciences" from which these final ends can be
derived. And the beginning of wisdom in these matters is the
recognition that man abides in a recalcitrant and imperfect
universe.

The world is not fully malleable to the hand of man. All
of life, all of society, all of international relations is a developing and changing series of forces upon which no stable form
can be imposed by any method. The best that man may contrive are means toward a workable compromise so that change
may take place without violence. Friction will go on, differences old and new will continually emerge, and no formula
the "scientists," politicians, and statesmen can devise will
freeze the fleeting moment and permanently balk the hidden
and contradictory flux that always moves through the world,
and must do so as long as man survives on the face of the
earth. These contradictory processes are life itself. If they
ceased to be, life—personal, social, or international—would
also cease. The feasible is not a permanent "solution," but a
channel for continuing adjustments among contradictory
drives.

A substantial amount of balance between the forces of
nature is essential to survival, but the balance is never absolute and is always changing. A stable world is best described
as one of relative instability. It is in that sense that there are
no solutions and no problems, either within the nation or between the nations. But these compromises can be made only
between recognized and existing entities. These entities must
not only exist, but be recognized as existing, whether they be
men, institutions, societies, corporations, or nations. The recognition of their existence implies an acknowledgment of a
claim upon all other similar beings because they can only sur-

vive mutually, and cannot live in absolute isolation. The condition of mutuality is an equal opportunity to survival, which in turn requires the acceptance of the equal dignity of the existing entities mutually interdependent.

This is the meaning of the "coordinate state" in international relations. It implies a position of equal dignity. It has nothing to do with wealth, power, size, population, or culture. It has everything to do with the recognition that compromise is a continuing means of nonviolent friction (peace). It has everything to do with the acknowledgment of the unique sense of "historic personality" which each state has of itself as the only basis of a friendly relationship. It is only if all the states continue to have equal dignity among themselves that changes in power and wealth can be absorbed without undue violence. That is the essence of federalism in international relations. The coordinate state relationship makes it possible to accept the inevitable growth of some and the decline of other states without war and without the loss of "face," because the changes are gradual and absorbed through a process of accommodation by all the members who are equal to each other. Federalism embodies these traits and has been illustrated in many ways by the history of the United States.

The essential character of the American system derives from a federal relationship of coordinate states. Our expectancies and demands upon the world are conditioned by that fact. This does not mean that we have not in our relations to the outside world committed grave errors, and on many occasions denied our own beliefs. The traditional twisting of the "British Lion's tail" is but one example of a species of irresponsibility in international relations. Theodore Roosevelt's interference in the arbitration of the Alaska boundary dispute; his, "I took the Panama Canal"; Wilson's intervention in Haiti and Santo Domingo; the Platt Amendment; the arbitrary senatorial action on Japanese migration; the century-long bullying of Mexico; the numerous landings of American marines in Central America; the indifference to the feelings of foreign nations often expressed in Congressional debates; our constant preachments and moralizations; the subordination of our foreign policies to domestic politics; the support of "big business" and American investors in foreign countries, sometimes without due regard to the legitimacy of their claims; the lack of sensitivity to foreign culture and foreign values and, since the Second World War, the conscious but faltering support of colonialism—these are all part of the story of our failure to abide by our own commitments.

However, these variations from our own professed ideas are the side currents at the edge of the broad stream of our foreign policy. The major drift of our relations with the rest of the world have with more or less consistency responded to the basic tradition of the coordinate state. We have, with the exception of the short but more than memorable episode of the Freedmen's Bureau and Reconstruction, never for long deviated from the idea of equal dignity of the state inside our own federal system, and have therefore never long permitted ourselves to act overtly toward other nations as if we were a centralized state, concerned primarily with the security that rests upon military force and military alliances. We have always sought our security either in isolation or in cooperation with other nations of equal dignity.

This conception of the equal dignity of the state is therefore fundamental to our own thinking about the world. Just what do we mean by the equal dignity of the state? This is a crucial question, for it defines the character of our own federal system. More than that, this concept of the equal dignity of the cooperating state not only represents a basis for our own federal system, but lies at the root of the Organization of American States. What is more, it is a similar concept, not uninfluenced by the American experience, which has come to govern the British Commonwealth of Nations. This same basic definition of the equal dignity of the related members has shaped the long-successful Swiss Confederation. We are therefore dealing with a general principle of organization, of which the American federal system is but a type. And this system of international organization stands in the world as a contrast to the alternative idea of the balance of power between states, and to the doctrines of power politics advanced by the schools of *Realpolitik,* of which Professor Hans Morgenthau and Mr. George Kennan are, at the moment, the most widely recognized proponents in the United States.

Under the American Constitution the states are, in fact, equal in their political authority; and this equality is the condition of the survival of the federal system. It is true, of course, that the powers of the central government have greatly expanded in recent years, due largely to the interpretations of the commerce and welfare clauses of the Constitution. But this increase of the powers of the federal government was by consent of the Congress, and affects all of the states equally. It has set no discrimination between one state and another. Furthermore, the states could by a constitutional amendment, were they so minded, recover whatever part of the powers of the federal government has accrued to it in recent years.

In the American federal system, therefore, there can be no member of lesser dignity or lower status. Legally, they are all endowed with the same kind of independence, possessed of like privileges and subject to similar limitations and duties. The differences between the states are measured by size, population, resources, and wealth and not by status and privilege. There are within our federal system no high and no low, no great and no lesser, states.

This description of the place of each separate state in the United States can be applied to the position of each nation within the Pan American system. The differences between the United States and the Pan American system are very great. The first is a nation with a central government, the other is a loose organization resting upon the consent of its members. But each separate entity of either structure in relation to the other members is very much the same.

In the Pan American system (the Organization of American States as it is now called) each nation is legally equal to any other. Every member nation has one vote. There is no veto. There are no privileged nations grouped in a council possessed of powers denied to the other members. The charter of the organization guarantees each nation its territorial integrity, its sovereignty and independence. No nation or group of nations may intervene in any way in the internal or external affairs of any nation in this hemisphere. All international issues that arise between the member states "shall be settled by peaceful procedures," and attack upon one member is an attack upon all the others. No nations may use economic or political pressure to "force the sovereign will" of any other state for the purpose of gaining some advantage to itself. The territory of each member nation is inviolable, and no territorial acquisitions or other privileges gained by force or other coercion are recognized. All members have an equal place on all of the important committees of the organization, and decisions are, in most instances, made by an absolute majority, in a few by a two-thirds vote.

In commenting on the relationship which exists between the nations in this hemisphere, Dr. Alberto Lleras, formerly president of Colombia and now Secretary General of the Organization of American States had this to say:

> Those nations have enjoyed, and will continue to enjoy, the inestimable advantage of being neighbors to one of the greatest empires in all history without suffering the fear of imperialism or the threat of violence, basking in an international order based on law which preserves their independence and guarantees their security and sovereignty more fully with each passing day.[1]

After pointing out that equality of voting power, democratic procedure, and majority decisions characterize the working

[1] *The Results of Bogatá.* Lecture series on the Bogatá Conference, May 24, 25 and 26, 1948, Washington, D.C., p. 4.

100   methods of the Organization of American States, Dr. Lleras added, "The same fundamental principle that guides the political life of this country [the United States] prevails in the basic rule of the Organization of American States." Clearly enough, the sixty-year-old organization that includes all of the twenty-one nations of this hemisphere has gradually acquired increasing power and prestige and has developed greater unity and identity. The charter itself speaks of the "spiritual unity" of the continent. This achievement was a matter of slow growth. But that it has grown to its present role and future promise is due to the acceptance of the principle that nations may differ in size, population, resources, and power, but that they are alike in dignity and status, possessed of equal privileges and bound by equal duties. The Foreign Minister of Guatemala, Dr. Manuel Salich, expressed the basis upon which the Pan American system has survived—the older ideal of the coordinate state: "here . . . geographic, economic, and other differences do not count [and] our voice, which is that of a small country . . . has, thanks to the generosity of the other twenty Republics, the same moral rank as the rest." [2]

If the ideals of the coordinate state lie at the base of our own federal system and of the Organization of American States as well, they have also come to play the chief role in the development of the British Commonwealth of Nations. It is interesting to note that, at about the period of the American Revolution when James Wilson, Benjamin Franklin, Thomas Jefferson and James Madison were asserting the doctrine that each colony was coordinate within the Crown and legislatively independent of Parliament, some English publicists were advocating similar ideas as a basis for the reconstruction of the British Empire.[3]

[2] Fourth Meeting of Consultation of Ministers of Foreign Affairs, Washington, D.C., *Proceedings,* Conference and Organization Series Number 12, p. 193.

[3] Robert Livingston Schuyler, *The Fall of the Old Colonial System* (New York, 1945), pp. 55–63.

Major John Cartwright, in a series of letters addressed to Parliament in 1774, pleaded for a reform of the British imperial system on substantially the same grounds as those urged by the leaders of the American colonists. He believed that the Empire consisted of a group of states "equal in constitutional status," with coordinate legislatures and a common king.[4] The relations between the American colonies and the mother country he said were similar to those between Hanover and Great Britain or between Scotland and England before 1707. He argued that "I would consider the American governments, like that of Ireland, as sister kingdoms, and I would cement a lasting union with them as between the separate branches of one great family." [5] He wanted the colonies "to be free and independent states" with the King to remain sovereign "in like manner" as he is of Great Britain. He wanted them to be individually and collectively protected against every foreign Power and each guaranteed in its independence with respect to the other colonies. He also urged a treaty to establish a perpetual League of Friendship for mutual security against all other states. This change would be of great advantage to the Empire for then the King would "receive fifteen independent kingdoms in exchange for as many dependent, and *hardly dependent* provinces, and become the father of three million of free and happy subjects, instead of reigning joint tyrant over so many discontented slaves, or losing by revolt so many of his people." [6]

Similar ideas were advanced by Granville Sharp, the famous abolitionist who in 1774 urged in a pamphlet that the permanent recognition of separate legislative power for each colony ought to be adopted because they would then with the mother country "form *one vast Empire,* which will never be divided" because the maintenance of the British Constitution inviolate in all the colonies would provide "a sufficient

---

[4] *Ibid.,* p. 50.
[5] *Ibid.,* quoted, p. 58.
[6] *Ibid.,* quoted, pp. 59–60.

band of union" between the imperial Crown of Great Britain and the overseas colonies.[7]

Another proponent of similar views was the widely known radical, Dr. Richard Price, who propounded his ideas in the *Observations of the Nature of Civil Liberty, the Principles of Government, and the Justice and Policy of the War with America* published in 1776. Professor Schuyler summarizes Dr. Price's views in the following words: "His ideal was a voluntary, co-operative alliance of self-governing states, co-ordinate with each other but united through the crown." [8]

The ideas advocated by Cartwright, Sharp and Price are strikingly similar to those that now provide the theoretical groundwork upon which the Commonwealth is made to rest. Winston Churchill gave eloquent expression to this basis of Commonwealth unity while paying tribute to late King George VI.

> There is no doubt that of all the institutions which have grown up among us over the centuries or sprung into being in our lifetime, the constitutional monarchy is the most deeply founded and dearly cherished by the whole association of our peoples. In the present generation, it has acquired a meaning incomparably more powerful than anyone had dreamed possible in former times. The Crown has become the mysterious link, indeed I may say the magic link, which united our loosely bound but strongly interwoven Commonwealth of nations, states and races. Peoples who would never tolerate the assertions of a written constitution which implied any diminution of their independence are the foremost to be proud of their loyalty to the Crown. We have been greatly blessed amid our many anxieties and in the mighty world that has grown up all around our small island, we have been greatly blessed that this new, intangible, inexpressible, but, for practical purposes, apparently all-powerful element of union, should have leapt into being among us.[9]

It required the American independence, the difficulties in Canada that led up to the Durham Report in 1839, the

---

[7] *Ibid.*, pp. 60–61.
[8] *Ibid.*, p. 62.
[9] *New York Times,* February 8, 1952.

slow growth of constitutional federalism in Canada, Australia, and New Zealand, the tragedies of the First World War, the bloody strife in Ireland, and the stubborn, nonresistance movement in India before these ideas could come into their own. The change that has taken place is reflected in the new name for the old British Empire. It came to be called the British Commonwealth of Nations and more recently just the Commonwealth. The Commonwealth is, therefore, composed of formerly subject peoples. These have now become completely independent nations joined in a voluntary association, each enjoying the fullest sovereignty and complete equality of right. Great Britain is, in fact, only the older member of the Commonwealth and having the greater prestige and moral authority that has come to it from age, experience and a great historical role. It can make no law for, nor veto one made by, its former dominions; the members of the Commonwealth have no compulsory allegiance to Britain. A member of the Commonwealth can, as Eire did during the Second World War, remain neutral, deny the use of its ports to the Allied navy, continue diplomatic relations with the enemy and still be considered a member of the Commonwealth. The members of the Commonwealth pay neither tribute nor taxes to Britain. They control their own foreign affairs, have their own diplomatic representatives, their own armed forces, and make their own immigration policies. A member nation can secede and break its ties with the Commonwealth, as Burma has done, or remain within the Commonwealth and become a republic as Pakistan and India have done. The connection between the members does not rest upon a written constitution or a formal body of law. It would even be difficult to discover a fully documented theory that would describe the association. It is neither a nation nor a formal federation.

It is not, however, a mere collection of independent units. It is a flexible association of nations, capable of showing great strength and loyalty in a crisis.

Similarly, Switzerland is a federation composed of mem-

104 bers possessed of identical legal status. The twenty-five cantons of the Swiss Confederation differ greatly in size. Grisons,
for instance, has an area of 2,773 square miles and Zug of 92,
while Bern has an estimated population of 790,000 and Uri
only 29,000. These twenty-five cantons have varying forms
of government, and the 3,107 communes of which they are
comprised retain large degrees of home rule. The federal
government, based on the Constitution of 1848, which was
strongly influenced by that of the United States, has only limited powers, and, by more recent constitutional changes,
federal legislation is subject to rejection and modification by
popular referendum and initiative. The Swiss cantons have
reserved for themselves more of their powers of government
than the states of the United States. Federalism in Switzerland dates back to the Alliance between the three forest
districts, Uri, Schwyz, and Unterwalden in 1291. Other districts gradually adhered to the original three and, in spite of a
turbulent and warlike history, the principle of federalism
survived all vicissitudes. For centuries, general affairs were
determined by a Diet composed of ambassadors acting under
instructions. For nearly 600 years, the original members of
the federation abided by the rule that all disputes between
them should be settled by arbitration. Other members gradually joined the original league; Lucerne in 1332, Zurich in
1351, Glarus and Zug in 1352, Bern in 1353. As early as 1481
at the Diet of Stans, the principle of collective security was
adopted in the resolution that they would come to the aid of
a member attacked by another member. In 1815, the principle
of absolute political equality of the cantons was embodied
in allotting one vote to each canton, and [the] territorial
integrity of each [was] secured by prohibiting the attack of
one member by another. Switzerland stands as the oldest
and, in some ways, the most successful federation in the
Western World.

The history of the four widely different federations we
have just discussed merits careful scrutiny by the student of
international organization, for they each, in their own way,

illustrate the principle of the coordinate state. They also make it clear that the acceptance of that principle is necessary to the growth and survival of a federal system. In the case of the United States, the debate ending in the Missouri Compromise reaffirmed the original proposition that all states stand in relation to each other as equals; that the older states could not sell "a provincial status" to a new state without undermining the foundations of the Union itself. This decision reaffirmed the earlier agreements on an equal vote in the Senate regardless of size of population, on nonintervention by one state in the affairs of another, through the provision for judicial settlement of disputes between states, on territorial integrity established in the rule that no state could be divided or united with another against its own will, and that the states reserve all of their powers not deposited in the federal government by the Constitution. The federal government is thus an indestructible union of indestructible states.

Similarly, in the case of the Organization of American States, it was necessary to reaffirm the coordinate position of each nation before the Pan American system could move forward to become a cohesive international body. That reaffirmation required the surrender of the right to intervention in the internal or external affairs for any reason whatsoever, the guaranteeing of the territorial integrity and the political independence of each member nation, the assertion of the principle of collective security, and the affirmation of political and juridical equality which could be fulfilled only by the outlawing of intervention. And, as in the case of the United States, it required that all disputes between members "shall be settled by peaceful means."

These same conditions have come to define the relations between the members of the Commonwealth of Nations. It is an association of equally independent and sovereign states. There are no great and no lesser members.[10] The Imperial

[10] Richard Frost, ed., *The British Commonwealth and World Society* (London, 1947), p. 149.

106   Conference of 1926 agreed that the dominions were "equal
in status, in no way subordinate to one another in any aspect
of their domestic or external affairs. . . . Equality of status
so far as Great Britain and the Dominions are concerned is
thus the root principle governing our inter-imperial relations." [11] In February 1948, Ceylon's Independence Act declared that she was "a fully responsible member of the
British Commonwealth of Nations, in no way subordinate in
any aspect of domestic or external affairs, freely associated
and united by a common allegiance to the Crown." [12] But in
South Africa "the King for the purpose of reigning in and
over the Union is created by our statutes. . . . The King is,
therefore, the King of South Africa and not of the Commonwealth. But the Crown has not a 'vestige' of functional reality." [13] In Ireland the symbolic character of the Crown proved
unacceptable and the oath was repudiated because it was,
according to Mr. de Valera, "an intolerable burden." [14] The
Irish preferred to be "externally associated." Mr. de Valera
declared that "we are associated with the States of the British
Commonwealth of Nations. We are not members of it." [15] To
the Burmese, however, the idea of remaining even as an associate of a British Commonwealth proved unacceptable because they considered that the word British implied ownership
or subjugation. In 1947, Mr. Thankin Nu, the Burmese Prime
Minister, said that they were, however, prepared to consider
association with a United Commonwealth. The change of
name was made in 1948 in the Amendment of the British
Nationality Act, but it was then too late.[16]

The demand for independent sovereignty of the members
of the Commonwealth which was first fully manifested by

[11] Quoted in *The Commonwealth and the Nations,* by Nicholas
Mansergh (London, 1948), p. 33.
    [12] *Ibid.,* p. 22.
    [13] "The Changing Commonwealth," F. H. Soward, ed., *Proceedings
of the Fourth Unofficial Commonwealth Relations Conference, September 8–18, 1949* (Toronto, 1950), pp. 3–4.
    [14] Mansergh, *op. cit.,* p. 201.
    [15] *Ibid.,* p. 202.
    [16] *Ibid.,* p. 11.

the Irish in 1921 who wanted "external association" has been completely fulfilled. The concepts of dominion status, of a "British" Commonwealth, of the Crown as an essential symbol of unity for all members, have been rejected. The Commonwealth is a free association among completely sovereign states held together by tradition, common historical experience, interest, convenience and a belief that their common history is a bond much stronger than that which rests upon force or upon a symbol which, for reasons of past resentment, is unacceptable to some of the members. Unity here lies in freedom and identity.

It has been a slow process to convert a world-wide Empire into a free association. But the fact that such a change was possible reflects the resiliency of English constitutional traditions. The milieu of the twentieth century made the symbols of dominion over other peoples incompatible with the passionate nationalism that has dominated our time. The insistent claim by every people across the face of the earth of a "historical personality" which must not be denied or impugned has made imperialism, or even the mere trimmings of foreign rule, unacceptable. If the association of many nations, races, and cultures which the British Empire represented was not to break up in hatred and strife, then the constitutional design that would hold them together had to be accommodated both to the political realities of the times and to the emotional overtones which they reflect. But once the reconciliation between the older ideas of empire and the more recent belief in the free "historical personality" has been achieved, then the association finds a sounder and more flexible basis of cooperation than it had before. For now all the associates are equal members of the same family. They are all inside the same house. They are strong with a strength that comes from moral identity and voluntary adhesion. In comparison, a military alliance resting on a balance of power is a rope of sand. On a much smaller scale and differently, the Swiss Confederation has found a similar unity based upon a recognition of diversity of race and language, differences of constitutional forms, and varying historical traditions.

It will be objected that the use of the United States and Switzerland as examples of international organization distorts the meaning of the word "international." It ought, however, to be clear by now that what saved the American federation, and made it the kind of organization it is, is precisely the acceptance of the principle of identical sovereignty of the several states among themselves. If the Missouri Compromise had gone differently, our federal system would have gone with it, and the Union, if one had survived, would have been a centralized government plagued with the very difficulties of empire we have just been considering. The same is, of course, also true of Switzerland. The long federal history of that remarkable nation illustrates, in a hundred crucial points, the vitality of the principle of equal status. And it was not until that was finally and fully accepted for all cantons that the country settled down to a peaceful political history. It is, therefore, the same principle which operates in all of these four instances of successful international organization based upon the idea of the coordinate states. In the American point of view, the concept of the coordinate state is a general principle of universal applicability. Otherwise how explain our ceaseless penchant for international organization?

The Continental Congress, the United States, the Organization of American States, the League of Nations, the United Nations, the North Atlantic Pact, and the effort to stimulate a European Union are all parts of the same story. In each of these instances, there is visible the common ideal of cooperation among equal states. How congenial that concept is to the American experience is illustrated at the very beginning of our history not only by the doctrine of equal legislative sovereignty for the colonies advanced by the early leaders as a proper basis for the organization of the British Empire, but in Benjamin Franklin's suggestion after the for-

mation of the American Constitution that Europe follow our
example and establish for itself a federal system. Benjamin
Franklin was sagacious and experienced beyond most men
and he not only knew the United States but had deep knowledge of England and the Continent. In the ripeness of his
years, after helping frame the American Constitution, he felt
that it represented a political system that Europe might well
adopt for itself. In the year 1787, Franklin wrote to a European friend:

> I send you enclosed the proposed new Federal Constitution
> for these States. I was engaged four months of the last sum-
> mer in the Convention that formed it. . . . If it succeeds, I
> do not see why you might not in Europe carry the project of
> Good Henry the 4th into execution, by forming a Federal
> Union and One Grand Republic of all its different States and
> Kingdoms; by means of a like Convention; for we had many
> interests to reconcile.[17]

The concept of federalism is, with the American people,
bred in the bone as part of the idea of political freedom. We
believe that security rests upon cooperation, that cooperation
is possible only among equals, that equality eliminates the
basic reason for political disruption because equals politically are "coordinate" in dignity and in rank, that this common identity is essential for different states to achieve that
unity which makes them members of the same political family. International cooperation from our point of view requires
that all participating members be insiders, and that such a
fellowship is in the end an "indestructible union." That is why
the concept of a "balance of power" is alien and repugnant
to the American people. We have condemned in others the
policies derived from that concept and have rejected them
for ourselves. Illustrative of this attitude is President Wilson's
statement: "the centre . . . of the old order was that un-

---

[17] Oct. 22, 1787, to Mr. Grand. *Documentary History of the Constitution of the United States of America*, Department of State, IV (1905),
pp. 341–342.

stable thing which we used to call 'balance of power' . . . a thing determined by the sword . . . thrown in on one side or the other." [18] And "If the future had nothing for us but a new attempt to keep the world at a right poise by a balance of power, the United States would take no interest, because she will join no combination of power that is not the combination of all of us." [19]

To the advocates of power politics and the balance of power, however, these American convictions and beliefs derived from their own experience are "intoxication with moral abstractions [which] has become the prevailing substitute for political thought." [20] And Wilson, because he advocated a League of Nations, was driven to "substituting for the concrete national interest of the United States the general postulate of a brave new world where the national interest of the United States, as that of all other nations, would disappear in a community of interest comprising mankind." [21] These same errors were committed by the leaders of the Second World War, Roosevelt and Hull. The reason for their failure is simple and obvious.

> How could statesmen who boasted that they were not "believers in the idea of balance of power"—like a scientist not believing in the law of gravity—and who were out "to kill power politics," understand the very idea of the national interest which demanded, above all, protection from the power of others? [22]

The American mind, according to Dr. Hans Morgenthau, has been "weakened in its understanding of foreign policy by half a century of ever more complete intoxication with moral

[18] Albert Shaw, *Messages and Papers of Woodrow Wilson* (New York, 1924), p. 584.
[19] *Ibid.*, p. 591.
[20] Hans J. Morgenthau, *In Defense of the National Interest* (New York, 1951), p. 4.
[21] *Ibid.*, p. 26.
[22] *Ibid.*, pp. 32–33.

abstractions."[23] The difficulty with American foreign policy is that it is burdened with "utopianism, legalism, sentimental- ism [and] neo-isolationism."[24] It does not understand that

> Foreign policy, like all politics, is in its essence a struggle for power, waged by sovereign nations for national advantage. . . . By its very nature this struggle is never ended, for the lust for power, and the fear of it, is never stilled. . . . In the life of nations peace is only respite from trouble—or the per- manent peace of extinction.[25]

Our great mistake was to assume that the United Nations could be a substitute for the balance of power. We defined it in "Utopian terms of permanent peace and non-competitive, trustful cooperation among the great powers." American pol- icy is wrong because it is interested in the "well-being of all mankind."[26] A nation is under no obligation to keep a treaty. It is, in fact, an "iron law of international politics that legal obligations must yield to the national interest." There is ap- parently no difference between nations that "have a flair for throwing burdensome obligations overboard in an elegant, unobtrusive fashion, or of chiseling them away with the fine tools of legal misinterpretation" like France has done, and Russia and Germany who "have the disconcerting habit [of] announcing . . . that a treaty has become a 'scrap of paper.'" These matters are, after all, only "the lawyers' con- cern" which the statesman can take in his stride in pursuit of the "national interest." Nor need the great Powers be con- cerned about the interests of third parties; "great powers . . . have by tradition and logic . . . settled their disputes . . . over the regions where their interest, power and responsibili- ties were paramount." The business of statesmanship could not be carried on any other way.[27]

[23] *Ibid.*, p. 39.
[24] *Ibid.*, p. 92.
[25] *Ibid.*, p. 92.
[26] *Ibid.*, p. 114.
[27] *Ibid.*, pp. 142–146.

112   It is a legalistic illusion to believe that the United Nations is a substitute for power politics because it is obvious "from the political history of the human race that the balance of power and concomitant spheres of influence are of the very essence of international politics. They may be disregarded at the peril of those who choose to do so but they cannot be abolished." [28]

American policy, therefore, operates with "defective intellectual equipment." [29] Our difficulties derive from our failure to recognize that the "balance of power" is as much a law of politics as gravity is a law of physics and is illustrated by all of human history. This law which apparently is basic to the "science" of international relations has been understood by all the great statesmen, who, each in turn, have successfully ruined their nations and made a shambles out of all those parts of the world where they have been free to work out the "law" and practice the science. Now we too, who have prospered by refusing to apply the science or believe in its basic law, are urged, on grounds of the "national interest," to join the historical procession to national suicide by dividing the world between Russia and ourselves. The fact that it runs counter to every political instinct of the American people merely proves that we are possessed of a "defective intellectual equipment" and, if we consider it immoral and contrary to our experience to trade away the independence and freedom of other nations as part of the bargain, it shows that we are sentimental, moralistic, Utopian, and neo-isolationist and we can refuse to take this advice only at our own peril because the balance of power like the law of gravity will work its way regardless of what foolish men may do.

Now we submit that all this has nothing to do with science, and little to do with the infinitely complex influences that have shaped the history of man through time. We suspect that it is a very subjective and private view of the nature of

[28] *Ibid.*, pp. 154–155.
[29] *Ibid.*, p. 159.

man and of his role on earth. And that view seems to be that man is now and has always been in a sad estate from which he cannot extricate himself. He has no one to help him. He has no law to live by, no morality to support him; he has nothing except the "balance of power"—and if he will not believe in that, then God help him—but in this view of the world even that comfort is denied to man, for it could not abide any concept of a teleological universe. The interesting thing about this point of view is that it should either remain oblivious to or scorn the vast record of cooperative experience among men and nations, and that it should treat the relatively short and exceptional history of the European state system as equivalent to the history of the race across the face of time, and that it should deny the possibility and presumably the desirability of institutional development in the relations between nations. Institutions are presumably, by some undivulged "law," confined to grow only inside of the "sovereign" state. There must be no extra-national institutions; they would deny the "national interest" and make for "a brave new world" which is the greatest of political sins.

There is another statement of this theme of *Realpolitik* and the balance of power that comes from the influential and highly skilled pen of Mr. George F. Kennan.[30] In this exposition of the case, there is a kind of urbanity, a kind of sensitivity for the values and shortcomings of the American milieu and a kind of compassion for human frailty that robs it of much of its sting. It is so gently, so persuasively stated, that the reader finds himself carried along almost to the point of agreement until he realizes that this modest and restrained presentation is, in fact, a repudiation of every value we hold:

> I see the most serious fault of our past policy formulation to lie in something that I might call the legalistic-moralistic approach to international problems. This approach runs like a

[30] George F. Kennan, *American Diplomacy, 1900–1950* (Chicago, 1951).

red skein through our foreign policy of the last fifty years. It has in it something of the old emphasis on arbitration treaties, something of the Hague Conferences and schemes for universal disarmament, something of the more ambitious American concepts of the role of international law, something of the League of Nations and the United Nations, something of the Kellogg Pact, something of the idea of a universal "Article 51" pact, something of the belief in World Law and World Government.[31]

This is more than a challenge to our international policies of the last fifty years. It is a denial of the American beliefs that have sustained American political life from the beginning; for our ideas of foreign policy are part and parcel of our belief in human freedom, in the equality of men, and in the dignity and independence of nations. The extenuating feature of Mr. Kennan's presentation is its lack of consistency. There is internal evidence that the author has not really made up his mind about these important matters. He is still ambivalent and groping for the truth, and the "balance of power" has not achieved the status of a "law" like the law of gravity. This is, in our view, a saving grace—but the damage has been done, for an influential voice has been added to the attempt to persuade the American people that their traditional policy based upon the coordinate state is wrong and has proved a failure.

The proof often presented by those who would force us off our beaten path is the failure of the League of Nations. A particular instance is made to serve the ends of a universal law. The League having failed, then all international organizations must fail. But the reasons for the failure were numerous. That the League was not based upon the idea of the coordinate state was, in our view, one of its major weaknesses. If all the members of that body had had an equal voice, Italy's attack upon Ethiopia would have been defeated, and sanctions both economic and military would have been effec-

[31] *Ibid.*, p. 95.

tively applied. It will be said in reply that the small Powers would have committed the large ones to a possible war in which they would have borne a minor part. That may or may not be true. But the way to have avoided the greater tragedy which ultimately destroyed or weakened both the great and the small states was to have acted as the small states would have acted—to enforce the principle that in the modern world there are no separate interests for the small or the large state, that their destinies are collectively involved in each other, and that the violation, by war and oppression, of the independence of even the smallest Power is, in the end, the denial of the possible survival without war even of the largest Power. For such violation, whatever the grounds on which it is justified, is in effect the building of aggressive power against other nations until they, too, are placed in jeopardy. In this view of the matter, the structuring of international organization on the coordinate state is the alternative to the balance of power, and to security without permanent militarization. Nor must we permit ourselves to be confused by the argument that the United Nations has failed and that the Atlantic Security Pact is the true substitute in the form of a military alliance. The Atlantic Security Pact is conceived of as a temporary and instrumental association of a defensive character organized for the purpose of implementing the ideal of the United Nations. It has nothing to do with the balance of power idea and less to do with dividing the world into spheres of interest between Russia and ourselves. Its objectives are aimed precisely at an attempt to prevent the permanent militarization which dividing the world into spheres of influence would require, and to escape the destruction of the democratic process which would follow in its wake.

The American people will not accept the program. They will not consent to the destruction of all that a hundred and fifty years of democratic life has brought them for the sake of being the masters of that part of the world which they

116   could lay hold of. They will not do it because it runs against
their grain, and because they have an alternative which seems
more difficult to those hypnotized by the ideal of force and
craft but is, in fact, easier and more consistent with our own
traditional way with other people, and one we know how to
live with because we have always done so. And that is the
organization of as much of the world as we can upon the
basis of the coordinate state, not for the sake of achieving
a balance of power, but for the sake of building a basis of
common defense upon a system of collective security open
to all the nations of the world who wish to join it, without
losing their independence or their dignity. It may prove impossible under present conditions to build such a system
without having to fight a war with Russia, but then at least
we will be fighting, as we did before, for the thing we consider worth defending with our lives and treasure. Equally
important, our allies and partners will be fighting for things
as dear to them as ours are to us. They will find their own
values secured in a common defense and a common victory.
And our enemy, Russia, will find the peoples of its own satellites striving to enter our common security system just because it is made to rest on the ideal of the coordinate state.

A balance of power settlement would lead our many allies
and associates to conclude that they are mere pawns in a
game of international politics played at their expense. They
would cease to be partners in a great cause; for the division
of the world into spheres of influence would automatically
destroy the basis of the partnership in the West. That partnership rests upon the assumption that all the members are
equal, that their rights cannot be bargained away, that they
have to be consulted, that they have to consent freely to
changes that affect them. It also rests upon the assumption
that there are *no* spheres of influence—that the United States
has no rights greater than the least of its members, and that
the defense is a joined defense of a common interest, but that
the common interest rests upon the particular and unique

political personality of each member. It assumes a coordinate relationship, not the position of a great Power with many satellite Powers. The mere acceptance of the idea of a balance of power would undermine the basis of the relationship among free partners formed together and would convert it into an empire with satellites to be ordered about. It would convert the United States from a federal republic to an empire and ultimately destroy the republic. That is what the proposal really means, and that is why it will be resisted by the American people.

Such an arrangement would lead our friends to fall away from us feeling that they had been betrayed, as, in fact, they would have been. They, too, would seek the best bargain—temporarily—and play for higher stakes when the occasion offered. We would find ourselves weaker in the international field, not stronger. We would have voluntarily accepted a great moral defeat, and the power derived from a common cause among nations, all of whom felt identified through interest, belief, and outlook, would have been irretrievably lost. The only remaining hope that an association of coordinate states could be gathered together to resist the attempt by Russia to dominate the world would evaporate. It is difficult to foresee a day more dark and hopeless than the one on which the American people could be persuaded to seek a temporary peace through deliberately sacrificing the principle of voluntary association among nations, and agree to divide the world between Russia and the United States.

No. With all of our shortcomings and failings, we will not accept the new science and follow the "will-o'-the-wisp" of *Realpolitik*. We will not abandon the faith we have lived by, nor deny the other nations the right to live in freedom and without fear. Our commitments are to a world of free men working together in free nations. The democratic faith that lies at the base of everything we cherish is the overriding law of American policy both at home and abroad. We cannot surrender our belief in the equal dignity of little nations without,

118   in the end, abandoning our belief in the equal dignity of men. We will, if we have to, resist to the death the effort to subvert the world to a totalitarian despotism, but we will not bargain with it at the expense of other people and to the destruction of that sense of human integrity and national morality which is part of the substance of our very being. This may not be "science," but that is the way it is. We can do no other. Therein lies our strength.

the destiny of the negro
in the western hemisphere *6*

THE SETTLING OF THE WESTERN HEMISPHERE by peoples coming from Europe and Africa was an adventure on a grand scale, involving diverse peoples, varying cultures, millions of human beings, and hundreds of years. The common element was the New World. Its physical features and cultural types were strangely dissimilar, but the student discerns many an analogous design, patterned by the newcomers as they established themselves in the strange and unexplored regions. It is natural, therefore, for Gilberto Freyre to draw revealing similarities between the history of Brazil and the United States.[1] Like everything that he writes, this volume has a freshness and a lucidity that endow the reader with insight and understanding of the complex instrumentalities for life and labor contrived by man in his new world. Freyre finds in the development of Brazil, for example, the impact of the frontier and the dominion of the plantation so typical of our own South. The disparity, implied rather than expressed in the study, is

Reprinted, with permission, from *Political Science Quarterly,* LXI (March 1946), pp. 1–41. This essay was later expanded into book form as *Slave and Citizen* (New York: Alfred A. Knopf, 1946).

[1] Gilberto Freyre, *Brazil: An Interpretation* (New York: Alfred A. Knopf, 1945), pp. vii, ix, 179.

120   the divergent position of the Negro within the two areas. For
the Negro—and especially the Mulatto—had an access to the
culture in Brazil, and a role in social life, unknown in the
United States. In politics, in the arts, and in society, the
Mulatto found the door ajar even if not fully open, and a
markedly different social milieu has come into being. Even
under the Empire, the Negro and the Mulatto—and, socially,
the attractive Mulatto women—found an acceptance unthink-
able in the North American scene. Freyre quotes from Ewbank this revealing picture:

> I have passed black ladies in silks and jewelry, with male
> slaves in livery behind them. Today one rode past in her car-
> riage, accompanied by a liveried footman and a coachman.
> Several have white husbands. The first doctor of the city is a
> colored man; so is the President of the Province.

In another place, Ewbank points out that gentlemen of dark
color achieved the dignity of president of the cabinet under
the Emperor.[2]

A social atmosphere so dissimilar in two nations built in
the New World by immigrants from the Old challenges
analysis. It cannot be a mere accident. The way these two societies have gone must have an explainable etiology, and an
examination of the source of the difference may illumine the
present.

We are really concerned with one of the major race and
population problems of the western hemisphere. The Negro
is found everywhere in this hemisphere except Greenland,
and there are regions where he is so numerous that long ago
Humboldt spoke of a possible colored empire in the Caribbean. From Rio de Janeiro northwards, the coastal stretches
of Brazil, French, Dutch, and British Guiana, Venezuela,
Colombia on both the Atlantic and Pacific, Ecuador, and Peru

[2] Thomas Ewbank, *Life in Brazil; or Journal of a Visit to the Land
of the Cocoa and the Palm* (New York, 1856), pp. 266; [quoted in]
Freyre, *op. cit.*, p. 101.

have significant and, in certain districts, preponderant numbers of people of African origin. This holds true, likewise, for both coasts in Central America. In Mexico, the Negro on the coastal plains has largely merged with the Indian population, but even here traces of African influence are still visible, while our southern states, bordering on the Gulf of Mexico, the Mississippi and the Atlantic, have a colored population of many millions that in some rural sections outnumbers the whites. Even Canada and Alaska have a fraction of Negroes in their population. It is, however, on the islands in the Caribbean, rather than on the mainland of North or South America, that the Negro has acquired a dominating place. If Humboldt's reference is taken in a demographic rather than a political sense, the colonization of the western hemisphere has involved the settlement of many thousands of square miles by peoples who came from Africa rather than from Europe; and, if we draw an arc from Rio de Janeiro to Washington, D.C., and include the West Indian islands within it, we will have in outline the empire Humboldt talked about.

. . .

The settlement of America was not a purely European enterprise. It is more accurately described as a common undertaking by the folk coming from both Europe and Africa. For the slave trade is better viewed as a migratory movement —forced migration, if you will—but still one of the greatest population movements of all time. This movement stretched over more than four centuries (1442–1880) and was integrally related to the colonization of large parts of the western hemisphere.

Negro migration to Europe from Africa began in 1442, half a century before the discovery of America. In 1443, there was a shipment of 235 slaves to Portugal.[3] In 1448, the first

---

[3] Fray Bartolome de las Casas, *Historia de las Indias* (Madrid, Edition of M. Aguilar, 1927), I, p. 129. Bryan Edwards, *History of the Island of St. Domingo* (Edinburgh, 1802), p. iii. J. P. Oliveira Martins, *O Brazil e as colonias portuguezas* (Lisbon, n. d.). J. Lúcio de Azevedo, *Epocas de Portugal económico* (Lisbon, 1929), p. 71.

122   "factory" was established in the island of Arguim for the
purpose of the new commerce. By 1461, the trade had been
regularized and was carried on peacefully in Senegambia,
and the island of Arguim alone supplied, during the latter
half of the fifteenth century, an average of seven to eight
hundred slaves per year.[4] What had hitherto been an internal
migration in Africa had now become water-borne, first to
Europe across the Mediterranean, and, later, with the discovery of America, across the Atlantic to the New World. African
participation in the New World adventure began early, and
in 1501 Nicholas Ovando, the new governor of Española, was
advised to import Negroes born in Christian lands.[5] The first
fifty Negroes from Africa were brought to the Antilles in
1511, and by 1517 the trade had been so well established that
a regular *asiento* was given to the governor of Bressa to intro-
duce 4,000 Negroes to America. The migration to America
did not interrupt the flow to Portugal itself, and in 1552, in
a population of 100,000, Lisbon had some ten thousand
slaves with from sixty to seventy slave markets. There were,
among them, 1,550 washerwomen, 1,000 street cleaners, and
400 who peddled crabs or cooked rice and other delicacies.[6]

From this time on, the movement was in full swing, and
all of the European nations facing the Atlantic were drawn
into it to a greater or less extent, and for longer or shorter
periods. Portugal, France, the Netherlands, England, Den-
mark, Sweden, Spain, and even Brandenburg participated in
it, while, on the American side of the Atlantic, the English
colonies, Brazil, and Cuba at one time or another imported
Negroes on their own account. The number of Negroes trans-
ported will never be known. The subjection of the trade to
fiscal ends by various governments led to extensive contra-
band, and the more officers set to watch the lawbreakers, the

---

[4] Oliveira Martins, *op. cit.*, p. 71.
[5] *Colección de documentos ineditos, Relativos al descubrimiento,
conquista y organizacion . . . de Indias* (Madrid, 1842–95), XXXI,
p. 23.
[6] Azevedo, *op. cit.*, pp. 75–76.

more participants in the illegal traffic there came to be. Nor did the abolition of the slave trade by Great Britain and the United States, in 1808, end the traffic. If anything, it may have increased it; for it is clear from the records that both Cuba and Brazil imported greater numbers annually after that date than before it. In fact, the transfer of Negroes did not cease until the abolition of slavery itself, not only in the United States but in Cuba in 1880, and in Brazil in 1888, and even then it continued out of Africa to Sãn Thome.[7] Portugal, which had been the first to enter the trade, was the last to leave it. There is no way of giving even seeming accuracy to the numbers imported, but a rough estimate may be obtained from the records for individual countries and periods.

Between 1511 and 1513, 1,265 Negroes of both sexes passed through the "Casa do Escravos" in Lisbon for the account of the king; and the Jesuit Father Garcia Simoëns describes the active commerce out of Angola in 1576, esti- mating the annual export from there alone at 12,000.[8] Between that year and 1591, 52,000 were shipped to Brazil; while the British West Indies, between 1680 and 1786, imported 2,130,000; and Cuba, between 1790 and 1820, imported 225,574, and from 1821 to 1847, an average annual number of some 6,000 to 7,000, not counting the numbers smuggled in.[9] The total number up to 1853, for Cuba alone, has been stated to be over 644,000, and we know that the importations continued after that.[10]

For Brazil, the importations all through this period were large and increasing. Between the years 1759 and 1803, the

---

[7] Johnston, *op. cit.*, p. 84.

[8] Dieudonné Rinchon, *La traité et l'esclavage des Congolais par les Européens* (Bruxelles, 1929), p. 59.

[9] *Ibid.*, p. 63; Bryan Edwards, quoted by Amos K. Fiske, *The West Indies* (New York, 1899), p. 105; Alexander Humboldt, *The Island of Cuba*, tr. J. S. Thrasher (London, 1856), p. 218; Oliveira Martins, *op. cit.*, p. 62.

[10] Humboldt, *op. cit.*, p. 219, footnote by translator. William R. Manning (ed.), *Diplomatic Correspondence of the United States, Inter-American Affairs, 1831–1860*, XI: *Spain*, 1854 (Washington, 1939), p. 765. *United States Foreign Relations, 1865*, p. 665.

124   exports to Brazil from Angola are said to have amounted to 642,000, or an annual average of 14,000 to 15,000. Some Brazilian writers have put the numbers imported at an annual rate of 44,000 for the seventeenth century and 55,000 for the eighteenth. The imports into Brazil continued heavy until about 1850 and have been placed as high as 50,000 per year for the ten years between 1842 and 1852.[11]

All general figures are guesses, but the estimates are significant. One author [12] estimates the general migration from the Congo to America to have been 7,000 annually during the sixteenth century, 15,000 during the seventeenth, 30,000 during the eighteenth. And, for the first half of the nineteenth century, he places the number at the incredible sum of 150,000 annually to 1850, and as high as 50,000 between 1850 and 1860, and 2,000 between that date and 1885—a total of over 13,000,000 from the Congo from the beginning of the commerce. Exaggeration, it seems—but, how much? Another author estimates the total exported from all Africa for the entire period at 20,000,000.[13] Again an exaggeration? But by how much? Even a conservative estimate would hardly cut this figure in half. It really makes little difference how much it is cut, for the enterprise lasted over four centuries and engaged the energies of many commercially minded people in many parts of Africa, Europe, and the western hemisphere.

Some check on these generalizations is provided by scattered records of the number of ships engaged in the traffic. Toward the last third of the eighteenth century, there were forty "factories" on the African coast belonging to the leading nations in Europe engaged in the African trade. Of those, ten belonged to the English, three to the French, fifteen to

[11] Oliveira Martins, *op. cit.*, p. 62. Pandiá Calogeras, *Formação historica do Brasil* (Rio de Janeiro, 1930), p. 53. Percy Alvin Martin, "Slavery and Abolition in Brazil," *The Hispanic American Historical Review*, XIII (May 1933), p. 159.

[12] Rinchon, *op. cit.*, p. 133.

[13] Oliveira Martins, *op. cit.*, p. 64.

the Dutch, four to the Portuguese, and four to the Danes.[14]
Each of these nations had ships of their own plying the
Atlantic, carrying Negroes across the ocean. In 1600 and
later, more than a hundred Spanish and Portuguese ships
entered Loanda every year, while 192 British ships were used
in the year 1771 to bring 47,146 Negroes to the West Indies.[15]
In 1788, the French engaged 98 ships to carry over 29,000
slaves to Santo Domingo.[16] Long after the active campaign
to abolish the slave trade got under way, anywhere from
33 to 50 ships a year, between 1833 and 1840, entered the
ports of Cuba, loaded with Negroes from Africa.[17] American-
built vessels to the number of 64 were sold in Rio de Janeiro
alone in the year 1845, and most of these were put to the
slave trade; and, as late as 1848, 93 vessels sailed in the slave
trade from Bahia.[18]

It can be seen from even these fragmentary illustrations—
and they could be very greatly increased—that the ships were
numerous and the trade continuous. How many ships, on an
average, sailed annually during the four centuries? The ships
were not large and most of them, perhaps, carried less than
three hundred Negroes at a time. There were, it is true,
toward the later part of the eighteenth century, ships that
carried five hundred or more Negroes on a single voyage. But
on the whole these were exceptions. If we put the number at
three hundred Negroes per voyage—and that is probably an

---

[14] Bryan Edwards, *The History, Civil and Commercial, of the British Colonies in the West Indies* (Philadelphia, 1806), II, p. 255.

[15] Rinchon, *op. cit.*, p. 68. Edwards, *History . . . of the British
Colonies in the West Indies*, II, p. 258. "Dicky Sam," in *Liverpool and
Slavery*, by a genuine "Dicky Sam" (Liverpool, 1884), cites thirteen
years between 1771 and 1806 when more than 100 ships sailed in the
slave trade every year, out of Liverpool alone.

[16] Henry Brougham, *An Inquiry into the Colonial Policy of the
European Powers* (Edinburgh, 1803), I, pp. 530–531.

[17] James Bandinel, *Some Account of the Trade in Slaves from
Africa* (London, 1842), p. 232.

[18] Lawrence F. Hill, *Diplomatic Relations between the United
States and Brazil* (Durham, 1932), p. 129; William Hadfield, *Brazil,
the River Plate, and the Falkland Islands* (London, 1854), p. 147,
footnote.

exaggeration—it took many hundreds of ships in the trade to carry that number of men across the Atlantic. Hundreds of ships, thousands of sailors, and hundreds, perhaps thousands, of individuals, partnerships and companies were engaged in bringing to the New World, south of the United States, more Africans than Europeans for the entire colonial period.

The Negro, much against his will, was to become a participant in the building of the New World. The migration continued for so long a time because of the heavy mortality ("almost half of the new imported Negroes die in the seasoning, nor does the poligamy which they use add much to the stocking of a plantation"); [19] because, in parts of the New World, the Negro did not reproduce, and because men were more readily welcomed for the heavy labor than women. On the average, only one woman was imported for every three men. There were plantations in Cuba in the nineteenth century, for instance, that had as many as seventeen males to one female —and these women became common wives, prostitutes, incapable [of] or unwilling to bear children. The life of the Negro plantation laborer in the West Indies is said to have lasted an average of seven years, and the replenishment went on; but if the migration had been by families, it would have been smaller in numbers and of perhaps shorter duration.

Despite the cost in life, sorrow, and broken bodies, the Negro became the effective means for the colonization of vast American regions. Cotton and tobacco in the United States, sugar in the West Indies, cocoa in Venezuela, sugar, coffee, and mining in Brazil, and a thousand other industries everywhere else were dependent upon the Negro. In Brazil, the Negro was so much the laborer that no one else seemed to labor at all, and until very recently it was something unseemly even to carry a small parcel in the city of Rio. As Mawe puts it, in Brazil the Negro seemed to be the most intelligent person he met, because every occupation, skilled

[19] Charles Leslie, *A New and Exact Account of Jamaica* (Edinburgh, 1739), p. 328.

and unskilled, was in the hands of Negroes. Even in Buenos
Aires, theirs were the hands that built the best churches. They
were the field hands; and in many places they were the
miners. They were the cooks, the laundresses, the mammies,
the concubines of the whites, the nurses about the houses,
the coachmen, and the laborers on the wharves. But, they
were also the skilled artisans who built the houses, carved the
saints in the churches, constructed the carriages, forged the
beautiful iron work one sees in Brazil, and played in the
orchestras. The Negro, slave and free, was the living hand
that embellished the setting and provided the art and the
spice for the cultured, easy, and carefree life in which some
of the New World plantation centers luxuriated for so long
a time. The very pattern so characteristic of a large section
of colonial and post-colonial life in this hemisphere derived
from their skills, their loyalty, and their participation in the
world about them, even as slaves.

Without the Negro, the texture of American life would
have been different—different in lore, family, social organization, and politics, and, equally important, different in economy. Conceivably, even the crops that the Negro cultivated
in gangs, and sometimes under the lash, would not have been
grown at all; and large parts of tropical and semitropical
American land would have remained untilled and unnur-
tured. Viewed from any angle—biologically, in terms of physical labor, socially, and in the molding of the culture so
typical of the Western world—the Negro was for those areas
where he labored and lived in large numbers just as important as his master; and his contribution to the population
and settlement of this hemisphere is part of a common adventure of the folk from across the sea who have molded a
new and a different social milieu for themselves. American
colonization is, therefore, a joint Afro-European enterprise.

. . . In spite of the slave trade, in spite of the horrors of
the middle passage, in spite of the centuries of slavery, the
Negro has accommodated himself to the New World in a

128   manner not merely creditable but surprising. The Indian, on
the other hand, has either withered away and disappeared, as
he did in the West Indies, or been killed and driven off, as in
the plains of the United States and Argentina. Where he has
not been extirpated from the earth, he has remained mostly
a pariah in his native habitat. For example, compare the
Negro in Cuba and Brazil to the Indian in Peru. The Negro
in Cuba and in Brazil is an active member of the body politic;
in Peru, the Indians form an isolated body, apart from the
rest. Whereas the Negro has learned the language of the
European, the Indian, by the million, has remained stubborn,
uncommunicative, and isolated in his own linguistic universe.
The same has happened with many other elements of European culture—dress, food, social customs, song, art, and matters of faith. The Negro is a magistrate on the city bench of
New York, a member of Congress; he is a senator and a
member of the cabinet in other places. He is part of the nation. He is active, vocal, self-assertive, and a living force. He
has become culturally a European, or, if you will, an American. The Indian, where he has survived in large numbers, as
in Guatemala for instance, has not identified in this way—it
might almost be said in any way—with the European; for
those things which he has taken over he has so amalgamated
with his own native customs that their European origin is
hard to recognize.

This adventure of the Negro in the New World has been
different in the United States than in the other parts of this
hemisphere. In spite of his adaptability, his willingness, and
his competence, in spite of his complete identification with
the mores of the United States, he is excluded and denied.
A barrier has been drawn against the Negro. This barrier has
never been completely effective, but it has served to deny
to him the very things that are of the greatest value among
us—equality of opportunity for growth, and development as
a man among men. With us, the shadow of slavery is still cast
ahead; and we behave toward the Negro as if the imputation

of slavery had something of a slave by nature in it. The emancipation may have legally freed the Negro, but it failed morally to free the white man, and by that fact denied to the Negro the moral status requisite for effective legal freedom.

This did not occur, however, in the other parts of this world which we call new and free. It did not occur because the very nature of the slave institution was developed in a different moral and legal setting, and in turn shaped the political and ethical biases that have manifestly separated the United States from the other parts of the New World in this respect. The separation is a moral one. We have denied ourselves the acceptance of the Negro as a man because we have denied him the moral competence to become one, and in that we have challenged the religious, the political, and the scientific basis upon which our civilization and our scheme of values rest. This separation has a historical basis, and, in turn, it has molded the variable historical outcome.

The Negro slave arriving in the Iberian Peninsula in the middle of the fifteenth century found a propitious environment.[20] The setting, legal as well as moral, that made an easy transition possible developed out of the fact that the people of the Iberian Peninsula were not strangers to slavery. The institution of slavery, which had long since died out in the

[20] Elizabeth Donnan, *Documents Illustrative of the History of the Slave Trade to America*, Vol. I: *1441–1700* (Washington, D.C., 1930), p. 29: "For as our people did not find them hardened in the belief of the other Moors, and saw how they came in unto the law of Christ with a good will, they made no difference between them and their free servants, born in our own country. But those whom they saw fitted for managing property, they set free and married to women who were natives of the land, making with them a division of their property, as if they had been bestowed on those who married them by the will of their own fathers, and for the merits of their service they were bound to act in a like manner. Yea, and some widows of good family who bought some of these female slaves, either adopted them or left them a portion of their estate by will, so that in the future they married right well, treating them as entirely free. Suffice it that I never saw one of these slaves put in irons like other captives, and scarcely any one who did not turn Christian and was not very gently treated." Quoted from *The Chronicle of the Discovery and Conquest of Guinea* by Gomes Eannes de Azurara.

rest of western Europe, had here survived for a number of reasons, especially because of the continuing wars with the Moors which lasted until the very year of the discovery of America. At the end of the fifteenth century, there were numerous slaves in Portugal and Spain, and especially in Andalusia. Among them were not only Negroes, but Moors, Jews, and apparently Spaniards as well.[21] Indeed, we have records of white slaves sent to America by special permission of the Crown. We know that Rodrigo Contreras, the governor of Nicaragua, was allowed by a special *cedula* of July 15, 1534, to import two white slaves; and Fernando Pizarro in 1535 was permitted four white slaves. There are a number of similar records.[22] But the mere survival of slavery in itself is perhaps less important than the persistence of a long tradition of slave law that had come down through the Justinian Code. The great codification of Spanish traditional law, which in itself summarizes the Mediterranean legal mores of many centuries, was elaborated by Alfonso the Wise between the years 1263 and 1265. In this code, there is inherent a belief in the natural equality of men; and slavery, therefore, is something against both nature and reason.[23]

This belief that equality among men is natural and reasonable is both pagan and Christian. It stems from the Stoics as well as from the Christian fathers. The conception that men are free and equal, especially equal in the sight of God, made slavery, as such, a mundane and somewhat immaterial matter. The master had, in fact, no higher moral status than the slave; and spiritually the slave might be a better man

[21] Rinchon, *op. cit.*, p. 44.

[22] Georges Scelle, *La traité négrière* (Paris, 1906), I, pp. 219–220.

[23] "Servidumbre es postura et establescimiento qui ficieron antiguamente las gentes, por la qual los homes, que eran naturalmente libres, se facian sivervos et se sometian a señorio de otri contra razon de natura." *Las Siete Partidas del Rey Don Alfonso el Sabio, Cortejadas con Varios Codices Antiguos por la Real Academia de la Historia, y Glosadas por el Lic. Gregorio López del Consejo Real de Indias de S. M.* (Nueva Edicion, precedida del Elogio del Rey Don Alfonso por D. J. de Vargas y Ponce, y Enriquecida con su Testamento Politico; Paris, 1847), Ley I, título XXI, partida IV.

than his master. *Las Siete Partidas* were framed within this Christian doctrine, and the slave had a body of law, protective of him as a human being, which was already there when the Negro arrived, and which had been elaborated long before he came upon the scene. When he did come, the Spaniard may not have known him as a Negro, but the Spanish law and mores knew him as a slave and made him the beneficiary of the ancient legal heritage. This law provided, among other matters, for the following.

The slave might marry a free person, if the slave status was known to the other party. Slaves could marry against the will of their master, if they continued serving him as before. Once married, they could not be sold apart, except under conditions permitting them to live as man and wife. If the slave married a free person with the knowledge of his master, and the master did not announce the fact of the existing slave status, then the slave by that mere fact became free. If married slaves owned by separate masters could not live together because of distance, the church should persuade one or the other master to sell his slave. If neither of the masters could be persuaded, the church was to buy one of the slaves, so that the married slaves could live together. The children followed the status of their mother, and the child of a free mother remained free even if the mother later became a slave. In spite of his full powers over his slave, the master was forbidden either to kill or to injure him, unless authorized by the judge. If the master abused the slave or attempted to starve him, the slave could complain to the judge, and upon verification of the complaint the judge was to sell the slave, giving the price to the owner. The slave was never to be returned to the original master. Any Jewish or Moorish slave became free upon turning Christian; and, even if the master himself later became a Christian, he recovered no rights over his former slave.[24]

[24] *Las Siete Partidas,* Ley I, tit. V, part. 4; Ley II; Ley II. tit. XXI, part. 4; Ley III; Ley VIII.

132   *Las Siete Partidas* go into considerable detail in defining
the conditions under which manumission may occur. A master may manumit his slave in the church, or outside of it,
before a judge or other person, by testament, or by letter;
but he must do this in person. If one of the owners of a slave
wishes to free him, then the other must accept a just price
fixed by the local judge. A slave becomes free against his
master's will by denouncing a forced rape upon a virgin, by
denouncing a maker of false money, by discovering disloyalty
against the king, by denouncing the murderer of his master.
The slave could become free if he became a cleric with the
consent of his master or, in certain cases, without his consent,
by providing another slave in his place. And if the former
slave became a bishop, he would have had to put up two
slaves, each valued at the price that he himself had been
worth while still a slave. A Christian slave living among the
Moors might return to live among the Christians as a free
man.[25]

The slave could appeal to the courts [1] if he had been
freed by will and testament, and the document maliciously
hidden (under these circumstances he could appeal against
anyone holding him); [2] if he had money from another and
entrusted it to someone for the purpose of being bought from
his master and given his liberty, and if then this person refused to carry out the trust, by either refusing to buy him
or to free him if he had bought him; and [3] if he had been
bought with the understanding that he would be freed on
the receipt of the purchase price from the slave and there
had been refusal either to accept the money or to release him
after accepting it. He could appeal to the courts for defense
of the property of his master in his master's absence, and the
king's slaves could appeal to the courts in defense of the
king's property, or of his own (the slave's) person—a special
privilege permitted the king's slaves in honor of their master.[26]

---

[25] *Ibid.*, Ley VI, tit. XXII, part. 4, Ley II, Ley IV, Ley VII.
[26] *Ibid.*, Ley VII, tit. II, part. 3; Ley IX, tit. II, part. 3.

A man considering himself free, but demanded as a slave, might have a representative to defend him; a man held as a slave, but claiming to be free, might argue his own case, but could not have a representative; the slave's relatives might plead for him, even a stranger could do so, for "all the laws of the world aid towards freedom." [27] Slaves could be witnesses, even against their masters, in accusations for treason against the king; in cases of murder of either master or mistress by either spouse; or in cases of adultery against the mistress; when one of the two owners of a slave is accused of killing the other; or in case of suspicion that the prospective heirs had killed the master of another slave. A slave who became the heir of his master, in part or in totality, automatically became free. If a father appointed a slave as the guardian of his children, the slave by that fact became free; and if the slave of more than one person became an heir of one of his masters, the other must accept a price in reason for that part of the slave which belonged to him. He who killed his slave intentionally suffered the penalty for homicide; and, if a slave died as a result of punishment without intention to kill, then the master must endure five years' exile.[28]

This body of law, containing the legal tradition of the Spanish people and influenced by the Catholic doctrine of the equality of all men in the sight of God, was biased in favor of freedom and opened the gates toward manumission as soon as slavery was transferred to the New World.[29] The law in Spanish and Portuguese America facilitated manumission, the tax gatherer did not oppose it,[30] and the church

[27] *Ibid.*, Ley IV, tit. V, part. 3.
[28] *Ibid.*, Ley XIII, tit. XVI, part. 3; Ley XXI, tit. V, part. 6; Ley VII, tit. XVI, part. 6; Ley XXIII, tit. III, part. 6; Ley IX, tit. VIII, part. 7.
[29] The *Real Cedula* of 1789 on the treatment and education of Negro slaves is a formal summary of older rules and practices long part of both the legal and social environment in the Spanish colonies.
[30] "In the Cuban market freedom was the only commodity which could be bought untaxed; every negro against whom no one had proved

134   ranked it among the works singularly agreeable to God. A hundred social devices narrowed the gap between bondage and liberty and encouraged the master to release his slave, and the bondsman to achieve freedom on his own account. From the sixteenth to the nineteenth century, slaves in Brazil could, by offering the original purchase price, compel their masters to free them.[31] In Cuba and in Mexico, the price might be fixed at the request of the Negro, and the slave was freed even if he cost "triple of the sum." The right to have his price declared aided the Negro in seeking a new master, and the owner was required to transfer him to another.[32]

The law further permitted the slave to free himself by installments, and this became a widely accepted custom, especially in Cuba.[33] A slave worth 600 dollars could buy himself out in twenty-four installments of 25 dollars each, and with every payment acquired one twenty-fourth of his own freedom. Thus, when he had paid 50 dollars, he owned one-twelfth of himself.[34] On delivering his first installment, he could move from his master's house, and thereafter pay interest on the remaining sum, thus acquiring a position not materially different in effect from a man in debt who had a specific monetary obligation. There seem to have been many instances of slaves paying out all of the installments due on their purchase price except the last 50 or 100 dollars, and on these paying one-half a *real* per day for every 50 pesos. The advantage in this arrangement apparently lay in the fact that a Negro, thus partially a slave, could escape the payment of taxes on his property and be free from military service.[35]

---

a claim of servitude was deemed free. . . ." Quoted from *British Slavery and Its Abolition, 1823–1838* by William Law Mathieson (London, New York, 1926), pp. 37–38.

[31] Johnston, *op. cit.*, p. 89. D. P. Kidder and J. C. Fletcher, *Brazil and the Brazilians* (New York, 1857), p. 133.

[32] Alexander Humboldt, *Political Essay on the Kingdom of New Spain,* translated by John Black (New York, 1811), I, p. 181. Richard Henry Dana, Jr., *To Cuba and Back* (Boston, 1859), p. 249.

[33] Fernando Ortiz, *Los negros esclavos* (Havana, 1916), p. 313.

[34] Humboldt, *The Island of Cuba*, p. 211.

[35] Ortiz, *op. cit.*, pp. 315, 317.

In effect, slavery under both law and custom had, for all practical purposes, become a contractual arrangement between the master and his bondsman. There may have been no written contract between the two parties, but the state behaved, in effect, as if such a contract did exist, and used its powers to enforce it. This presumed contract was of a strictly limited liability on the part of the slave; and the state, by using the officially provided protector of slaves, could and did define the financial obligation of the slave to his master in each specific instance as it arose. Slavery had thus from a very early date, at least in so far as the practice was concerned, moved from a "status," "caste," "by law of nature," or because of "innate inferiority," or because of the "just judgment and provision of holy script" to become a mere matter of an available sum of money for redemption. Slavery had become a matter of financial competence on the part of the slave, and by that fact lost a great part of the degrading imputation that attached to it where it was looked upon as evidence of moral or biological inferiority. Slavery could be wiped out by a fixed purchase price, and, therefore, the taint of slavery was neither very deep nor indelible.

In addition to making freedom something obtainable for money, which the slave had the right to acquire and possess, the state made manumission possible for a number of other reasons. A Negro could be freed if unduly punished by his master.[36] He was at liberty to marry a free nonslave (and the master could not legally interfere); and, as under the law the children followed the mother, a slave's children born of a free mother were also free.[37] Slaves in Brazil who joined the army to fight in the Paraguayan war were freed by decree on November 6, 1866, and some twenty thousand Negroes were thus liberated.[38]

In the wars of independence, many thousands of slaves in

[36] Humboldt, *Political Essay,* p. 181.
[37] Henry Koster, *Travels in Brazil* (Philadelphia, 1817), II, p. 202; Ortiz, *op. cit.,* p. 337.
[38] Martin, *op. cit.,* p. 174.

Venezuela and Colombia were freed by Bolivar and enlisted in the army of liberation. In Argentina, perhaps as much as a third of San Martin's host that crossed the Andes was composed of freed Negroes. Finally, as early as 1733, by a special *cedula* repeated twice later, slaves escaping to Cuba from other West Indian islands, because they wished to embrace the Catholic religion, could be neither returned to their masters, nor sold, nor given in slavery to any other person.[39]

Significant and varied as were these provisions of the law in the Spanish and Portuguese colonies, they were less important in the long run than the social arrangements and expectancies that prevailed. It was permissible for a slave child in Brazil to be freed at the baptismal font by an offer of 20 milreis, and in Cuba for 25 dollars. A female slave could seek a godfather for her baby in some respectable person, hoping that the moral obligation imposed upon the godfather would lead to freedom for the child. It was both a meritorious and a pious deed to accept such a responsibility and to fulfill its implicit commitments, and it bestowed distinction upon him who accepted them.[40] In the mining regions of Minas Garaes, a slave who found a seventeen and a half carat diamond was crowned with a floral wreath, dressed in a white suit, carried on the shoulders of fellow slaves to the presence of his master, and freed and allowed to work for himself.[41] Any parent, male or female, having ten children could claim freedom.

The freeing of one's slaves was an honorific tradition, and men fulfilled it on numerous occasions. Favorite wet nurses were often freed; slaves were manumitted on happy occasions in the family—a birth of a first son, or on the occasion of the marriage of one of the master's children. In fact, the

[39] Ortiz, *op. cit.*, p. 351.
[40] Robert Southey, *History of Brazil* (London, 1819), p. 784; Mathieson, *op. cit.*, p. 37; Koster, *op. cit.*, p. 195.
[41] John Mawe, *Travels in the Interior of Brazil* (London, 1812), p. 318.

excuses and the occasions were numerous—the passing of an examination in school by the young master, on a family festival, on a national holiday, and, of course, by will upon the death of the master.[42] A cataloguing of the occasions for manumission in such a country as Brazil might almost lead one to question the persistence of slavery; but, as we have pointed out above, the importations were large and continuous in Brazil all through the colonial period and late into the nineteenth century.

Opportunities for release from slavery were further facilitated by the system of labor that prevailed in many places, particularly in cities. Slaves were often encouraged to hire themselves out and bring their masters a fixed part of their wages, keeping the rest. Skilled artisans, masons, carpenters, blacksmiths, wheelwrights, tailors, and musicians were special gainers from the arrangement.[43] Even ordinary laborers were allowed to organize themselves in gangs, *gente de Ganho*, as they were called. Preceded by a leader who guided them in a rhythmic chant, they would offer their services as carriers on the wharves of the city, or for any heavy work that came to hand. The description of these chanting gangs of Negro slaves in the city of Rio, carrying bags of coffee on their heads, their sweating bodies stripped to the waist, marching in rhythm to their song, is like nothing else in social history. Their wages were their own after they paid their master his share. Individual persons in Rio, otherwise poor, would make their living from the owning of one or more of these male or female slaves who were permitted to hire themselves out.[44] Women often hired themselves out as wet nurses, or peddled through the streets the colorful cloth of their own weaving or embellishing. With all of its cruelty, abuse, hardship, and inhumanity, the atmosphere in Brazil and the Spanish American countries made for manumission. Even in

[42] Martin, *op. cit.*, p. 170.
[43] Ortiz, *op. cit.*, p. 318.
[44] R. Walsh, *Notices of Brazil in 1828 and 1829* (Boston, 1831), II, p. 20.

138   the rural regions, some slaves were allowed to sell the products from their own plots given them to work for themselves, and to save their money toward the day of freedom. In Cuba, one writer notes that the raising of pigs by slaves provided a ready source of the accumulation of sums for such a purpose.[45] It should be further noticed that, in addition to their Sundays, the Negroes in Brazil had many holidays, amounting all together to 84 days a year, which they could use for their own purposes, and for the garnering of such funds as their immediate skill and opportunities made possible. The purchase of one's freedom was a tradition so firmly established that many a Negro bought the freedom of his wife and children while he himself continued laboring as a slave; and among the freed Negroes, societies were organized for the pooling of resources and the collecting of funds for the freeing of their brethren still in bondage.[46]

These provisions favoring manumission were strongly influenced by the church. Without interfering with the institution of slavery where the domestic law accepted it, the church early condemned the slave trade and prohibited Catholics from taking part in it. The prohibition was not effective, though in some measure it may have restricted the Spaniards to a rather limited participation. The slave trade had been condemned by Pius II, on October 7, 1462, by Paul III on May 29, 1537, by Urban VIII on April 2, 1639, by Benedict XIV on December 20, 1741, and, finally, by Gregory XVI on the third of December 1839. The grounds of the condemnation were that innocent and free persons were illegally and by force captured and sold into slavery, that rapine, cruelty, and war were stimulated in the search for human beings to be sold at a profit.[47] The Franciscan father, Thomas Mercado,

[45] Abiel Abbot, *Letters Written in the Interior of Cuba* (Boston, 1829), p. 97.

[46] Arthur Ramos, *The Negro in Brazil,* translated from the Portuguese by Richard Pattee (Washington, 1939), p. 70.

[47] José Antonio Saco, *Historia de la esclavitud de la raza Africana en el Nuevo Mundo y en especial en los Paises Americo-Hispano* (Havana, 1938), III, pp. 64–66.

had condemned the slave trade in the strongest terms in the year 1587, on the grounds that it fostered two thousand false-hoods, a thousand robberies, and a thousand deceptions. The church, however, did not interfere with the customary insti-tution derived from known practices in a given community; such as the status of persons born into slavery, persons en-slaved in a just war, or who had sold themselves, or who had been condemned by a legitimate court.

The presumption against the slave trade was that it forced people into slavery outside the law and against their will. More important in the long run than the condemnation of the slave trade was the church's insistence that slave and master were equal in the sight of God. Whatever the formal relations between the slave and master, they must both rec-ognize their relationship to each other as moral human beings and as brothers in Christ. The master had an obligation to protect the spiritual integrity of the slave, to teach him the Christian religion, to help him achieve the privileges of the sacraments and to guide him into living a good life, and to protect him from mortal sin. The slave had a right to become a Christian, to be baptized, and to be considered a member of the Christian community. Baptism was the sign of his entrance into the community, and, until he was sufficiently instructed to be able to receive it, he was looked upon as out of the community and as something less than human.[48]

From the very beginning, the Catholic churches in Amer-ica insisted that the masters bring their slaves to church for the learning of the doctrine and participation in the com-munion. The assembled bishops in Mexico, in the year 1555, urged all Spaniards to send the Indians, and especially the Negroes, to church. It was the same in Cuba, in 1680.[49]

In fact, Negroes were baptized in Angola before leaving for their Atlantic adventure on the journey to Brazil. Upon

[48] Koster, *op. cit.*, p. 199.
[49] *Concilios Provinciales, Primero y Segundo, Mexico, En los Años de 1555 y 1565* (Mexico, 1769), Concilio primero, Cap. III, p. 44. Saco, *op. cit.*, T. I, pp. 165–167.

140   arrival, they were instructed in the doctrine, and, as evidence of their baptism, carried about their necks a mark of the royal crown. As a Catholic, the slave was married in the church and the bans were regularly published.[50] It gave the slave's family a moral and religious character unknown in other American slave systems. It became part of the ordinary routine on the slave plantations for the master and slaves to attend church on Sundays, and, regularly before retiring at night, the slaves gathered before the master's house to receive his blessings.[51] If married by the church, they could not be separated by the master. Religious fraternities sprang up among the slaves. These were often influential and honorific institutions, with regularly elected officers, and with funds for the celebration of religious holidays subscribed to by the slaves out of their own meager savings. In Brazil, the slaves adopted the "Lady of the Rosary" as their own special patroness, sometimes painting her in black. In a measure, these religious fraternities emulated those of the whites, if they did not compete with them, and the slaves found a source of pride in becoming members, and honor in serving one of these religious fraternities as an official.[52]

If the Latin American environment was favorable, the British and American was hostile to freedom.[53] Obstacles

[50] Koster, *op. cit.*, pp. 198, 202.
[51] Alfred R. Wallace, *A Narrative of Travels on the Amazon and Rio Negro* (London, 1853), p. 92.
[52] Southey, *op. cit.*, p. 784.
[53] There were, briefly speaking, three slave systems in the western hemisphere. The British, American, Dutch, and Danish were at one extreme, and the Spanish and Portuguese at the other. In between these two fell the French. The first of these groups is characterized by the fact that it had no effective slave tradition, no slave law, and that the religious institutions were little concerned about the Negro; and, at the other extreme, there [was] both a slave law and a belief that the spiritual personality of the slave transcended his slave status. In between them, the French suffered from the lack of a slave tradition and slave law, but did have the same religious principles as the Spaniards and Portuguese. If one were forced to arrange a scale of slavery in terms of the severity of the system, the Dutch would seem to stand as the hardest, the Portuguese as the mildest, and the French, in between, as having elements of both.

were placed in the way of manumission legally, and it was discouraged in every other manner. The presumption was in favor of slavery. A Negro who could not prove that he was free was presumed to be a runaway slave, advertised as such, and, if no claimant appeared, was sold at public auction for the public benefit.[54] In Demerara, no slave could be manumitted without the consent of the Governor and Council. In many of the British colonies, heavy taxes had been imposed on manumission, and, as late as 1802, a law was passed in the Northern Leeward Islands requiring the owner who would register his slave for manumission to pay £500 into the public treasure,[55] and this sum had to be provided in the will if it made provision for the liberation of the slave. The slave could not be freed without the master's consent, even if the full price of the slave were offered. In the fear of an increase of freedmen, Barbados, in 1801, passed a law taxing the manumission of a female slave much more heavily than a male. St. Christopher, which taxed manumission for the first time in 1802, declared it to be a "great inconvenience . . . that [the number of] free negroes and . . . free persons of color was augmented" by releasing slaves from bondage, and provided that a slave who had been released by his master, but not formally enfranchised, should be "publicly sold at vendue." [56]

In Virginia, in 1691, it was provided that a Negro could not be set free unless "pay for the transportation of such negro" out of the "country" within six months be provided. In 1723, an act provided that a Negro could be set free only by the action of the Governor and Council, and only for some "meritorious service." In 1805, Virginia prohibited emancipation unless the Negro left the state. In 1824, the Virginia courts ruled that the freeing of a mother by will after she reached a certain age did not apply to her children born

---

[54] Mathieson, *op. cit.*, pp. 38–40.
[55] Johnston, *op. cit.*, p. 231.
[56] Mathieson, *op. cit.*, pp. 38–40.

142   after the date of the will.[57] Many similar statutes were passed in other states.

The slave had no protector to appeal to, and the master had, in some instances, complete power over him. An early Jamaican statute provided: "If any slave by punishment from his owner for running away, or other offence, suffer in life or limb, none shall be liable to the law for the same; but whoever shall kill a slave out of wilfulness, wantonness, or bloody-mindedness, shall suffer three months imprisonment and pay £50 to the owner of the slave." Thus, willful murder had been reduced to a misdemeanor if committed against a slave; but even more surprising is the fact that, if the murder was committed by an indentured servant, he too could expiate the crime by 39 lashes and 4 years' service.[58] Tennessee provided that the law defining the killing of a slave as murder shall not apply "to any person killing a slave . . . in the act of resistance . . . or dying under moderate correction." The Georgia Constitution again safeguards against the charge of murder, if the "death should happen by accident in giving such slave moderate correction." In South Carolina, the act of 1740 provided that willful murder of a slave should cost the perpetrator "seven hundred pounds current money," and this law remained on the statute books till 1821, and further provided that if the murder occurred "on sudden heat and passion" it shall cost him only £350. But for such minor punishments as willfully cutting out the tongue, putting out the eye, castrating, scalding, and similar offenses, it would, according to the above law, involve the culprit in a cost of merely "one hundred pounds of current money." [59]

[57] *Judicial Cases Concerning American Slavery and the Negro*, by Helen Tunnicliff Catterall (Washington, 1937), I, pp. 72, 73, 74.

[58] Leslie, *op. cit.*, p. 234. *The Laws of Jamaica Passed by the Assembly and Confirmed by His Majesty in Council April 17, 1684* (London, 1684). In 1696 willful killing of a slave was, on the second offense, to be considered as murder and punishable as such without benefit of clergy. *Acts of Jamaica, 1681–1737* (London, 1738), p. 8. In 1717 anyone ordering a slave dismembered was to pay £100. *Ibid.*, p. 160.

[59] George M. Stroud, *A Sketch of the Laws Relating to Slavery in the Several States of the United States of America* (Philadelphia, 1856), pp. 60–61, 64, 66.

The slave had no protector to appeal to and he could not
have his price specified for purposes of redemption and was
not allowed to accumulate property to buy himself out. Thus
the law of South Carolina, cited above, prohibited the slave
from raising any horses, mares, cattle, sheep, or hogs; and
Georgia prohibited the master from allowing a Negro slave
to hire himself out for his own benefit. This was true also in
the case of Virginia. In 1779, North Carolina prohibited the
ownership of animals by slaves. Mississippi prohibited a
master from allowing his slave to trade like a free man; and
in Maryland the slave was forbidden to keep "stock of any
description" and could not acquire money, beyond his wages,
for the purchase of the freedom of his children.[60]

There was no custom of freeing the children at the baptismal font for a nominal price, there was nothing known of
the moral role of the godfather for the slave child, and his
family had no status either in law or in public recognition.

The law recognized no marriage relation in law between
slaves. There followed no inheritance of blood even after
manumission,[61] and they were permitted to bear witness
against one another. It was part of the record that "A slave
never has maintained an action against the violator of his
bed. A slave is not admonished for incontinence, or punished
for fornication or adultery; never prosecuted for bigamy, or
petty treason, for killing a husband being a slave, any more
than admitted to an appeal for murder." [62] Under the law,
generally a slave could not acquire property by earning it,
by gift, or by inheritance. Not having any property, he could
make no will, and could not take by descent, "there being in
him no inheritable blood." [63]

The right of redemption seems to have been nonexistent,
and the right to change masters for cruel and unusual pun-

[60] *Ibid.*, pp. 76–77, 81.
[61] *Ibid.*, pp. 243, 245.
[62] "Opinion of Daniel Dulany, Esq., Attorney-General of Maryland,"
Maryland Reports, 561, 563, quoted in Stroud, *op. cit.*, p. 99.
[63] Thomas R. R. Cobb, *An Inquiry into a Law of Negro Slavery in
the United States of America* (New York and Savannah, 1858), p. 238.

144   ishments was possible only in Louisiana and Kentucky, and in these states only under great difficulties, made harder because no slave could testify against his master.[64]

This contrast between the Spanish and Portuguese slave law on one side, and the English and American on the other, was further heightened by the different role of the church in the life of the Negro. The slaves in the British West Indies were almost completely denied the privileges of Christianity. The plantation owners opposed the preaching of the gospel on the grounds that it would interfere with the management of the slaves, make them recalcitrant, and put notions of rebellion and freedom in their minds. The argument that the Christian doctrine would make the slaves more obedient, and therefore, more docile, aroused little response that was favorable among the planters. More surprising than the attitude of the slaveowners is that of the church itself. It was but slight exaggeration to say, as does one writer on the West Indies, that "The English Church did not recognize them as baptisable human beings." [65] Although the Society for the Propagation of the Gospel, organized in 1701, declared through the mouth of Bishop Fleetwood, in 1710, that the three hundred Negroes which it had inherited in Barbados, had to be brought into the church, "that if all the slaves in America and every island in those seas were to continue infidels forever, yet ours alone must yet be Christian," [66] the church remained indifferent to its responsibility.

The official church did little indeed for the hundreds and thousands of West Indian Negro slaves. The Episcopalians confined their activities to the whites and left the Negroes to the dissident denominations. Even these came late upon the scene, and found little opportunity to preach the gospel. As a general rule, the missionary preachers were opposed, ridi-

[64] Stroud, *op. cit.*, p. 93.
[65] Fiske, *The West Indies*, p. 108.
[66] Quoted in H. A. Wyndham, *The Atlantic and Slavery* (London, 1935), p. 235.

culed, and, in some instances, driven out. The Quakers seem to have come first to the island of Barbados, but their efforts proved unfruitful, and it was not till the Moravians established their first settlements in Jamaica, in 1732, that the Protestant gospel found a voice among the slaves. By 1787, there were missionary stations, in addition to Jamaica, in Antigua, St. Christopher, and Barbados. But the opposition to the preaching of the gospel continued into the nineteenth century and beyond the passage of the act abolishing the slave trade in 1808.

This persistent refusal of baptism "touched the English conscience to the raw," [67] but custom, tradition, hostility, and fear on the part of the planters proved stronger than missionary zeal. As one writer puts it, "I sincerely believe and am well assured that the slaves being instructed would be less attentive to labor, less inclined to obey their overseers and other deputies, and would be more anxious and more easily enabled to throw off the yoke of slavery altogether." [68] The law had, in contrast to Spanish provisions, set up no requirements for the religious training of the Negroes,[69] and it was not till 1816 that the Assembly of Jamaica ordered the vestries to provide chapels, and the curates to attend on Sunday afternoons for the instruction of the Negroes, and to visit on two days a week the neighboring plantations for the same purpose. Action, however, was slow and indifferent, and as late as 1820 no chapel had been built in spite of the fact that some ten or twelve curates had by then been appointed, although some chapels were built after that.

We see, therefore, that it was only after the abolition of the slave trade, and when the very institution of slavery

---

[67] Charles Booth, *Zachary Macauly* (London, 1934), p. 32.
[68] R. Bicknell, *The West Indies as They Are* (London, 1825), p. 120.
[69] In 1696 the Assembly of Jamaica had suggested that owners and overseers "shall as much as in them lies endeavour the instruction of their slaves in the principle of the Christian Religion" and shall do their best "to fit them for baptism." *Acts of Jamaica*, p. 80.

146   itself was on the verge of extinction in the British West Indies, that legal action favoring Christian teaching to the Negroes was adopted. The effect of all this upon the fortunes of the Negro was very serious. [As he was not] a Christian, marriage in his case was not considered a sacrament and was not encouraged. The wife had no legal status, and the family, as such, was not a unit. Legally, the British slaves could not be married and the religious unions could be dissolved at any time. In the years of 1821–1825, one devoted missionary had married, in his own parish, 1,085 couples, and, in some of the others, the marriages in this period ranged from one to five.[70] This was in a slave population of over 300,000, while in most of the other British West Indies no marriages had ever taken place. Under an act of the British Parliament, slaves could be sold by the sheriff in the satisfaction of all debts.[71] It was not uncommon to break up the families of the slaves in the payment of debts as well as taxes.

The contrasts, therefore, between the Spanish and Portuguese slave system on the one hand, and that of the British and the American on the other, were very marked and worked themselves out in their effect not merely upon the slave but, even more significantly, upon the social position and moral status of the freedman. Under the influence of the law and religion, the social milieu in the Spanish and Portuguese colonies made easy room for the Negroes passing from slavery to freedom. The older Mediterranean tradition of the defense of the slave, combined with the effect of Latin American experience, had prepared an environment into which the Negro freed from slavery could fit without visible handicap. Slavery itself carried no taint. It was a misfortune that had befallen a human being, and was in itself sufficiently oppressive. The law and religion both frowned upon any attempts to convert this into a means of further oppression. A *Real Cedula,* dated

[70] Mathieson, *op. cit.,* p. 41.
[71] Edwards, *History . . . of the British Colonies in the West Indies,* II, p. 366.

the 14th of November 1693, and directed to the Captain
General of Cuba, expresses, in the name of the King, the
following very revealing sentiments:

> That after privately calling the masters of these slaves, you
> say to them in my name that they must not, for whatever mo-
> tive, rigorously tighten the wage they receive from their slaves,
> for having been tried in other places, it has proven incon-
> venient harming the souls of these people, which is a matter
> for grave scruples that for their own conscience' sake, the mas-
> ters must avoid. . . . And at the same time, I command you
> that if at any time [these masters] mistreat [the slaves] you
> will apply the necessary remedy. It is not just to consent to,
> or permit any excess in this matter, for their slavery is a suffi-
> cient sorrow without at the same time suffering the distem-
> pered rigour of their masters.[72]

If the law was solicitous to protect the Negro slave against
abuse and defended him as a human being, the church
opened its doors to him as a Christian, and, as early as the
eighteenth century, in Brazil there were not only Negro
priests, but even black bishops. And in Brazil, anyway, the
Negro clergy seem to "have been more reverent, better living,
more earnest than the Portuguese clergy." [73] Many things
had conspired to give the Negro in Latin America a special
place in the community. The fact that he had come with the
conqueror, that in a measure he was part of the conquering
host, that he was used by the whites as bosses and foremen

---

[72] Quoted in Saco, *op. cit.*, II, pp. 169–170. We may contrast this
with the following: "No man who knows anything of his own nature
can suppose it to be possible that two races of men, distinguished by
external and ineffaceable marks obvious to every eye, who had held towards each other from time immemorial the relation of master and slave,
could ever live together as equals, in the same country and under the
same Government. If, therefore, slavery be abolished, the one or the
other of the races must leave the country or be exterminated. This choice
would be for the slaves, because they are the weaker party." Abel P.
Upshur, Secretary of State of the United States, to Edward Everett,
United States Minister to Great Britain, Washington, Sept. 28, 1843, in
Manning, *op. cit.*, VII, p. 12.
[73] Johnston, *op. cit.*, p. 90.

148 over Indians in Mexico, Venezuela, and other places, the fact that he, unlike the Indian, had learned the language of his masters and had taken many of his habits and customs, all combined to identify him with and make him part of the European community. In every instance, the Negro participated on equal terms with the whites in their wars, and, in some of them, he achieved the prestige of a national hero. Thus, in Brazil, one of the two national heroes, dating from early colonial wars against the Dutch, is Henrique Dias, a Negro. In Brazil, too, the Negroes had established their reputation for physical courage and military prowess in their mighty defense of the Negro Republic of Palmares (1650–1696), which required an army of six thousand men and many years to destroy. In the wars for independence, the Negro was an important element, and in Cuba the Negroes provided a majority of the army in the long struggle against Spain.

It is not surprising, therefore, that the political and social environment in Latin America has proved different from that in North America. Not only was the Negro encouraged to secure his freedom, but, once free, no obstacles were placed in the way of his incorporation into the community, insofar as his skills and abilities made that possible. In Brazil, the Negroes had done all of the work during the colonial period. It was in their ranks that all of the skills, crafts, and arts were to be found, and it was from the ranks of the Negroes and Mulattoes that some of the great artists, musicians, and sculptors were drawn. Rich planters in Brazil often educated their bright Mulatto children and even sent them to Lisbon in pursuit of learning. Negro slaves were often specially educated in specific arts, and Koster notes an instance of a planter who had trained up a private band of musicians by sending some of them to Rio and others to Lisbon.[74] The ranks of the regular army were open to free Negroes and Mulattoes, and special Negro regiments were common, some-

[74] Koster, *op. cit.*, p. 174.

times with their own Negro officers, not merely in Brazil but in Cuba, and during the revolution in Venezuela.

A peculiar feature of the slave system in Brazil and in other areas was the large plantation belonging to different religious orders—the Franciscans, the Dominicans, and the Order of Jesus. On these plantations, the Negroes, who were seldom sold, were especially well treated and protected, and their moral and religious training was carefully supervised. In fact, the Negroes on these plantations considered themselves as belonging to the Saint rather than to the friars who looked after them.[75]

Upon gaining their freedom, the Negroes and their children found openings in private and public employment, and even in public office. If the question of color was raised, it became evident that the office took precedence over color, so that a Mulatto captain was declared to be white. This happened even in cases of the nobility in Brazil. Where a Negro probably could not have found a place, a Mulatto could. How could a member of the nobility be anything but white?[76] Free Negroes had the same rights before the law, were allowed to hold property, and, from the beginning, took part in public life. The Negro had, in fact, acquired a moral personality while slavery still flourished; for all of these rights were enjoyed by the Negro when hundreds of thousands, and, in some instances, millions, of his fellow blacks were still suffering the evils of slavery.

Nothing said above must induce the reader to believe that slavery was anything but cruel. It was often brutal. The difference lies in the fact that the cruelties and brutalities were against the law, that they were punishable, and that they were perhaps not so frequent as in the British West Indies or in the American colonies. But these abuses had a remedy at law, and the Negro had a means of escape legally, by compulsory sale if the price were offered, and by many other

[75] *Ibid.,* pp. 217–218.
[76] Wyndham, *op. cit.,* p. 250.

150   means. More important was the fact that the road was open to freedom, and, once free, the Negro enjoyed a legal status equal to that of any other subject of the king, or to that of any other citizen of the state.

If we now contrast the position of the freed Negro and people of color in the British possessions with those we have just described, it will become evident that, whereas freedom in one place meant moral status, in the other it meant almost the opposite. In the British West Indies, the achievement of manumission merely involved a release from the obligation to serve a special master. It did not carry with it any new rights. As Edwards puts it:

> . . . the courts of law interpreted the act of manumission by the owner, as nothing more than an abandonment, or release of his own proper authority over the person of the slave, which did not, and could not, convey to the object of his bounty, the civil and political rights of a natural-born subject; and the same principle was applied to the issue of freed mothers, until after the third generation from the negro ancestor.[77]

In most of the islands, freed Negroes or Mulattoes could not give evidence in court against white persons, or even against people of color. They were thus less protected than slaves who had their master to defend them against abuse or maltreatment. They were not permitted to serve even as petty officers of public trust, such as in parochial vestries or as constables. They could not hold office in the black militia, they could not vote. By a law of 1762 in Jamaica, they were deprived of the right to inherit more than £2,000, unless born of lawful marriage; and in Antigua a Negro could not own more than eight acres of land.[78] It was not till 1796 that people of color were allowed to give evidence in court against

[77] Edwards, *History . . . of the British Colonies in the West Indies*, II, p. 217.
[78] "Laws of Jamaica," from John Henry Howard, *The Laws of the British Colonies in the West Indies and Other Parts of America* (London, 1827), II, p. 58; "Laws of Antigua," *ibid.*, p. 452.

whites. Freed Negroes could not be tried by jury and were subject to the same procedure as slaves, and freed persons could not even testify against slaves till after 1748. It was not until 1824 that free Negroes were permitted to give evidence in the courts under oath. One of the difficulties in the situation was the fact that the Negroes, not being, as a general rule, members of the Christian church, were considered incapable of taking an oath, and, being deprived of that privilege, were automatically eliminated from all responsibilities and opportunities wherein the taking of an oath was a prerequisite.

The position of the manumitted Negro, or even of the Mulatto born of a free mother, was not propitious. The legal and social environment was discriminatory and hostile. The English community opposed manumission, feared the growth of the free colored population, and reduced those few who had found a route to freedom to as nearly a servile state as possible. In the United States, a very similar policy toward the freedmen developed. An act of manumission was merely a withdrawal of the rights of the master. It did not confer citizenship upon the freedmen. That power rested with the state.[79] They were not privileged to bear arms, they had to have a guardian to stand in the relation of a patron to them, and they were, in some instances, denied the right to purchase slaves as property. They tended to be placed on the same footing as slaves in their contacts with whites. These restrictions placed the freedmen but little above the slaves with respect to civil privileges. The penal slave code usually applied to freedmen. South Carolina, in 1740, applied a penalty of $100 to anyone who used a Negro as a scribe, or taught him how to write, and this law was further strengthened in 1834 to punish a free person of color by fifty lashes for the same offense.[80] Similar laws were adopted in a number of states. The law, the church, and social policy all con-

[79] Cobb, *op. cit.*, p. 313.
[80] Stroud, *op. cit.*, pp. 189, 240.

spired to prevent the identification of the liberated Negro with the community. He was to be kept as a separate, a lesser, being. In spite of being manumitted, he was not considered a free moral agent.

The different slave systems, originating under varying auspices, had achieved sharply contrasting results. If we may use such a term, the milieu in Latin America was expansive and the attitude pliable. The Negro may have been racially a new element, but slavery was a known and recognized institution—known especially to the law. The law had long since struggled with the subtleties of freedom and servitude, and had, over a period of centuries, created an elaborate code for the slave; and the new Negro slave was automatically endowed with the immunities contained in the ancient prescription. He was no stranger to the law. His obligation and freedoms within the code were both known. In fact, *the element of human personality was not lost in the transition of slavery from Africa to the Spanish or Portuguese dominions.* The Negro remained a person even while he was a slave. He lost his freedom, but he retained his right to become free again, and, with that privilege, the essential elements in moral worth that make freedom a possibility. He was never considered a mere chattel, never defined as unanimated property, and never under the law treated as such. His master never enjoyed the powers of life and death over his body, even though there were abuses and cruelties. Even if justice proved to be blind, the blindness was not incurable. The Negro slave had, under this system, both a juridical and a moral personality, even while he was in bondage.

This legal tradition and juridical framework were strengthened by and were part of the doctrine and practice of the Catholic religion. The church made him a member of the Christian community, it imposed upon both the slave and the master equal obligations of respecting and protecting the moral personality of the other, and for practical purposes it admitted the slave to the privileges of the sacraments. In the mundane world, it meant that marriage was a sacred union that could not be broken by mere caprice, that the slave had a right to his wife, and that the slave's family was, like other families, a recognized union in a moral universe, not different from that of his master's family. Here again, the religious prescriptions were perhaps as often violated as obeyed. But both the state and the church combined to maintain the principle of the rule by the exercise of civil and canon law. The church could and did thunder its opposition to the sins committed against the family—against all Christian families—regardless of color, and regardless of status. The church, further, in its emphasis upon the moral equality between master and slave, came to favor manumission and to make it a deed laudable in the sight of God.

The legal right to achieve freedom and the religious favoring of manumission, combined with a number of other features peculiarly Latin American, tended to make easy the path to freedom. That it was easy is seen by the large numbers of freedmen everywhere in Latin America during the colonial period and after independence.

It was the opinion of De Pons that in the Spanish colonies there were more freedmen and children of freedmen than slaves; and he cites for Venezuela that, out of a total population of 728,000, there were then 291,000 freedmen, or over 40 percent of the total.[81] In the 103 years between 1774 and 1877, for which we seem to have a fairly accurate record for Cuba, the number of freedmen never fell below 32 percent of the slave population, and in spite of the constant importation of new slaves, the freedmen were 41 percent in 1774, and over 55 percent in 1877.[82] In Brazil, it has been estimated that at the time of the emancipation there were three times as many free Negroes as slaves. In contrast, the free persons of color in the British West Indies were few. Cuba

[81] F. R. de Pons, *Travels in South America* (London, 1807), I, pp. 168–169.

[82] Ortiz, *op. cit.*, pp. 321–322.

154   alone, in 1827, had 20,000 more free Negroes than all of the British Caribbean islands.[83]

The endowing of the slave with a moral personality before emancipation, before he achieved a legal equality, made the transition from slavery to freedom easy, and his incorporation into the free community natural. As there were always large numbers of freedmen and children of freedmen, it never seemed especially dangerous to increase their number. There was never the question that so agitated people both in the West Indies and in the United States—the danger of emancipation, the lack of fitness for freedom. There was never the horrifying spectacle, so often evoked in the United States, of admitting a morally inferior, and, therefore, by implication, a biologically inferior, people into the body politic on equal terms.

The experience in this matter of slavery of the nations other than those of the Iberian Peninsula was very different. They had long since lost all vestiges of slavery and a slave code. In neither tradition, policy, nor law was there room for the slave. The law did not know him and could not make provision for him when he came upon the scene. This is equally true of public practice and policy. The fact that the slave was a Negro merely added to the confusion; it did not create it. What made the difficulty was that, when the Negro slave was first brought in contact with the English, they did not know what to do with him. There was no recognizable place for him in the law. He certainly was not a free man; and the law did not know a slave. It was, therefore, no accident that in the early days, both in the West Indies and in the American colonies, he was, in practice, assimilated with the indentured servant. But this effort was of short duration and broke down, among other reasons, because the slave was not an indentured servant. The master had a contractual relation with the indentured servant—there was no such contractual relation with the Negro slave. The indentured serv-

[83] Mathieson, *op. cit.*, p. 40.

ant's time was limited by contract to a specified number of years after which he was to be free. The master assumed with the indentured servant a certain number of future obligations. The indentured relationship was recognized by both sides as temporary and dischargeable with a specified emolument. The indentured servant was Christian, had his rights to his wife and children, over whom the master could exercise no legal compulsions. None of these terms fitted the slave. There was no contractual relationship with the slave. He had been bought from a third person. There was no time limit to the contract, there was no pecuniary obligation upon the master after the contract expired, and, finally, the Negro slave had no legal family. The master had bought the slave, the women and the children, paying separately for each. The slave had no rights in the law and acquired none by contract. The legal perplexity was real enough. It was made worse by the position of the Protestant churches. The slow, hesitant, and doubtful approach to the problem of conversion merely increased the legal isolation of the Negro within the community, because as a Christian he would have acquired certain immunities and privileges belonging to all members of the established church. But the established church was inordinately slow in moving to bring him into the fold, and the dissident churches were not very successful nor very much respected in their endeavors until nearly the end of slavery as an institution in the West Indies.

In the absence of either religious or legal provision for the slave, it was not illogical for the planters, both in the West Indies and in the American colonies, to settle the legal issue involved by legally defining the slave as chattel. If he was neither a free man nor an indentured servant, then declaring him to be chattel disposed of the puzzle legally. Once this decision was made, the definition of the Negro brought in its train a whole series of consequences, both for the Negro and for the white community, which are reflected even at the present time. As chattel, the Negro slave lost all claims

156   upon legal protection. The powers of the master were enormously increased, and, by definition, the Negro slave was reduced to a beast of the field. While the impact of the law did not and could not completely wipe out the fact that the Negro slave was human, it raised a sufficient barrier to make the humanity of the Negro difficult to recognize, and, legally, almost impossible to provide for. This legal definition carried its own moral consequences and made the ultimate redefinition of the Negro as a moral person most difficult.

The abolition of slavery found both the Negro and the white community unprepared for freedom. In the case of the Negro, there was almost a complete lack of preparation for the responsibilities characteristic of freedom. The number of freedmen was infinitesimal, their role in the free community greatly restricted, and they proved incompetent to absorb and direct the large body of slaves suddenly freed. The denial of a moral status to the slave as a human being was to prove the greatest handicap to the drawing of the Negro into the general community, because it kept the whites from that acceptance of the free Negro which would have facilitated the transition. Something of the same course, but much more disastrous in its consequence, worked itself out in the United States. Here, as in the West Indies, neither the law nor the church made adequate place for the slave as a moral person; here, as in the West Indies, the Negro family had no legal status; and here, as in the West Indies, the early attempts to identify the slave with the indentured servant broke down and the Negro was reduced to chattel. Here, too, the bias was in favor of slavery and against manumission, and the few Negroes who achieved the status of freedmen were frowned upon, isolated, discriminated against, and even expelled from many of the slave states. All of this does not deny the many thousands of instances of kindness, affection, and understanding between master and slave, but these were personal and with no standing in the law. Legally, there was no effective remedy against abuse, and no regular channel toward freedom. With us there were not, as in Brazil, Cuba, and Venezuela, large numbers of freedmen while slavery still existed, and, in our case, the slave had no moral status as a human being, and the Negro no experience in freedom.

It is, therefore, not entirely an accident that the abolition of slavery in the United States was achieved within the painful experience of a civil war, and followed by the almost equally painful and disintegrating process of a period of reconstruction. The Civil War gave the Negro legal equality with his former masters, but it could not and did not give him either the experience in the exercise of freedom, or the moral status in the sight of his white fellow citizens to make for them the freedom of the Negro an acceptable and workable relationship. The endowing of the Negro with a legal equality left a moral vacuum which remained to be filled. In Latin America, the Negro achieved complete legal equality slowly, through manumission, over centuries, and after he had acquired a moral personality. In our case, he was given his freedom suddenly, and before the white community credited him with moral status.

Herein lies the great contrast between the outcome of the two slave systems. The last eighty years in the United States may be characterized as a period within which the Negro has been struggling for moral status in the sight of the white community. It has been a painful, and for the Negro often a disillusioning, effort. But it cannot be denied that great progress has been made and that the moral position of the Negro within the United States is today much better than it was in 1865, after emancipation. The nature of our problem is conditioned by the time it will take for the Negro to have acquired a moral personality equal to his legal one. How long that will take is not predictable, but what is generally called the "solution" of the Negro problem is essentially a matter of establishing the Negro in the sight of the white community as a human being equal to itself. When that

158   finally occurs, then the problem will have solved itself. It
will have disappeared. But such an eventuality is a matter of
time, and here, too, the Spanish and Portuguese peoples have
a great advantage over the North Americans. They have
lived with the Negro much longer than we have. The first
Negroes were brought to Portugal in 1442, and in considerable numbers following that date, while the first Negro slaves
to reach Virginia came in 1619, a hundred and seventy-seven
years later. It will be the year 2113 before the people of the
United States will have had as long a contact with the Negro
as the Latin Americans now have. Taking the progress that
has been made in the eighty years since emancipation, there
is some hope that the Negro will, in time, have achieved in
the United States as good a relationship as he now enjoys in
Latin America. In fact, it may not be unreasonable to assume
that the Negro in the United States, because of the greater
opportunities available in our midst, will have forged morally
a position no less favorable, and economically a better one,
long before he has filled the time span of his sojourn among
the Iberian people.

an american dilemma 7

a book review

AN AMERICAN DILEMMA, by Gunnar Myrdal, is an important, perhaps a great, book.[1] It is predictable that in the future it will be classed with Tocqueville's *American Democracy* and Bryce's *American Commonwealth*. This is high praise, but the achievement is so clear and so broadly based that it has wider scope than the problem it is devoted to—the Negro. It is, in fact, a critical evaluation of contemporary American civilization. This achievement is the more remarkable because it stems from a deliberate undertaking, financed by a foundation. Instead of producing a dull, ponderous, and innocuous report on the Negro, we have a revealing study of the United States and the place of the Negro within it. To Frederick P. Keppel, so long and so fruitfully associated with Columbia College, belongs much of the credit for initiating and supporting the undertaking. It will long remain a monument to his breadth of interest and to his wisdom.

Mr. Myrdal brought to the study an active career in poli-

Reprinted, with permission, from *Political Science Quarterly*, LIX (September 1944), pp. 321–340.

[1] *An American Dilemma: The Negro Problem and Modern Democracy*, by Gunnar Myrdal, with the assistance of Richard Sterner and Arnold Rose. 2 Volumes (New York: Harper & Row, 1944). Carnegie Corporation of New York, "Negro in American Life Series."

tics, a wide training in the social sciences, and complete objectivity in regard to the special foilbles and shortcomings in American life. As an outsider, he achieved the kind of objectivity which would seem impossible for one reared within the American scene, but the study is neither impartial nor indifferent. The author is partial toward democracy and appreciative of the Negro. When viewed narrowly, this is a long, brilliant, and many-sided defense of the Negro against the charges of inferiority which buttress discrimination against him, and a justification of the Negro's claim to full acceptance as a member of the American community. The book is an extensive and oft-repeated demonstration of the failure of the American credo as it applies to the Negro. But the real theme is the credo, the American faith, the ethos of American life—freedom, equality, justice, opportunity, the right of man to claim his full share of the available chances for the good life. The American dilemma is the sense of inner defeat and frustration that comes from our failure to practice the faith we uphold.

The dilemma has its being in the American conscience. Its roots lie in the moralistic character of the American people and their restlessness in the face of a hypocritical situation. If the American people could only be indifferent to the contradictions in their own culture, then the dilemma would not exist—or, at least, not in this particular, unhappy form. (If they were less in earnest about their own values, then the hypocrisy would not matter—at least, not sufficiently to give rise to the surge of compassion and hatred which is so often evidenced in matters affecting the Negro, not only in the same person, but even at almost the same moment.) The nature of the dilemma is one that exists in each man and not just between men. It is not the North against the South; it is rather the believer in liberty, justice, equality, who also believes that the Negro ought to be kept in his place, against himself. It is he who feels like a good, even if not too lettered, child of the Enlightenment, of the American Revolution, of the Christian

Church, cherishing justice, equality, freedom, dignity, and self-respect, who often finds himself enmeshed in race prejudice, hatred, persecution, and even a lynching.

It is, however, not solely a white man's problem, as the author would have it (*p. xlvii*). If the Negro could be all things to all men, then the issues would have a different quality and the "problem" would be the white man's. But the Negro is not all things to all men—he is also a man with prejudices, attitudes, habits, wishes, and ambitions. More than that, he has become culturally a European, a white man with a black face. Had the Negro remained immune from the values of his American environment, then the problem would have had a different texture and might not have raised the moral issues that oppress our conscience. The difficulty is that the Negro believes the preachings of his white neighbors (*p. 4*); he believes in the doctrine of the equality of man in the sight of God, in the right to live, to work, to travel, to learn, to climb up and down the scale as other people. He believes in democracy—that is where he has learned to verbalize the values to which his community is attuned. In that sense, he helps create the problem of moral conflict, because he keeps prodding his white neighbors with the very words and ideas that express the ethos of American life. If the Negro were like a Gypsy, unconcerned, or like the American Indian who would rather be left alone in his community than disturbed by "progress," then the stress would not be so great. The trouble is that the Negro expects to be treated like any other American because he feels himself like any other American, and we expect him to feel that way, to think and to behave that way—except when the heavy burden of the past stands in our way, and we behave as if all that we believe, and have taught the Negro to believe, [were] not true. It is not true for the Negro, and, therefore, it is not true for anyone, not even for ourselves. Our doctrines have a universal reach and flavor; *all* men are created equal. All American citizens are equal before the law. We do not say that he of

162   the darker hue is not equal; we do not say that; we do not believe it; and yet we practice it. When our darker brother rises to taunt us with our hypocrisy, our weary conscience gives us no rest.

It is a white man's problem only in the sense that the American has made the Negro into a white man and refuses to recognize his handiwork. We have given the Negro our own set of values and refuse to acknowledge them. We either refuse to acknowledge that they are ours, or in despair insist that these are not the true values, that the Negro, because he is black, could not be as good as a white man. He simply could not! And we keep repeating it because we ourselves are not convinced by our own insistent protestations. Our conscience has got the best of us and will give us no rest—no rest at all until we forget about it. But we will not forget about it until we concentrate upon the ten thousand items of individual failings of our standards to carry over in universal terms, and talk about that—about poor housing, about insufficiency of education, about poor wages, about bad transportation, about the inequality of justice—talk about that, are burdened by and worried by that, rather than by the Negro problem. It is then, only then, that we will sleep in peace and stop protesting our good intentions, our lack of prejudice, our greater qualities and the poor Negro's "handicaps"—handicaps that God gave him so that we should not be blamed for the Negro's hurt, for his pain, for his failings, for his bitterness, for his crazy outbursts, for his escape into make-believe, for his "tomfoolery," for his "shiftlessness." It is not our fault. It is the nature of the Negro, his inner nature. Yes, but our conscience, our American conscience, with its gospel—Christian, democratic, equalitarian, so full of brotherly love and human kindness—keeps troubling us, and we have no peace. There will be no peace at home, because we have no peace in our hearts; these are torn and we will heal them only by accepting the inevitable: that all Americans are equal before the law, in the detail, specifically in each case where the problem arises; that the issues are the dignity and majesty of the law, not this man's darker hue, and action based on that belief. There is no other road to repose.

The Negro is part of the complex of American civilization (*p. xliv*), and not even segregation really isolates him or the issues his presence has precipitated. In that sense, at least, there is no Negro problem; there are only the stress and strains of American life. There is no way of abstracting the "Negro" and his problems from the rest of the community and looking at them in a kind of vacuum, as if the rest of the social structure did not exist. It is easier and truer to say that the structure exists rather than the Negro problem. There is no way of taking the Negro out of our American setting and looking at him as a separate item in our culture. Viewed from any angle—politics, political parties, labor, industry, agriculture, religion, art, music, dancing, speech and story, tradition and popular gossip—the whole flavor of American life is involved in any discussion of the Negro. The Negro as an isolated unit does not exist. What does exist is an entire culture—the American culture—which has been molded in a special way by the presence of a large segment of our population which comes from Africa instead of Europe. But "It," the Negro problem, does not exist. What we have instead is an American community that thinks, feels, plays, sings, writes, draws, and governs itself in a special way because of the penetration of the African immigrant into American life. We are a different people because of that. The problem is not a Negro problem; it is a problem of American culture we are talking about, and the specific issues are as wide and numerous as the culture contains. There are really as many problems as the culture presents, and as many "solutions" as the culture permits. It will be a glad day in American life when we begin talking about the issues in particular, rather than about a nonexistent problem in general.

In explaining the character of the issues raised by the Negro, the author argues (*p. liv*) that the moral latitude in

164   America between the "good" and the "bad" is so wide that
       there is no connection between them; that even in the large
       cities the good people have no more contact with political
       corruption, vice, and crime "than if they lived in another
       country" and that the race issue is, therefore, not typical of
       American culture. It "is only a corner—although a fairly big
       one—of American civilization." This seems to contradict what
       the reviewer believes to be a truer statement: "The Negro
       Problem is an integral part of . . . the whole complex. . . .
       It cannot be treated in isolation" (*p. xlix*). Not only can it
       not be treated in isolation, but it would be just as pertinent
       to say that it exists only as a part of the whole complex.

       There is no need for separating the virtuous from the evil
       in American life. American culture contains them both in full
       measure, and they are enough alike to recognize each other
       as Americans; it takes them both to give the American com-
       munity its special flavor. If we should not boast of our moral
       virtues, we need not unduly whimper our failings—the short-
       comings will change and the evils make room for other fail-
       ings than those complained of, as soon as the virtuous in our
       community become better than they are. If there is a gulf
       between the best of the culture and that part of it which is
       revealed by the Negro's place in the American community,
       that gulf may help explain the evils. Perhaps if there were
       no such gulf, the evils would be less conspicuous. It is just
       possible that the way out of the evils is to improve the char-
       acter of the "good" as much as it is to change the character
       of the "evil." The Negro problem belongs to the whole com-
       munity, not to a part of it. When the whole community be-
       comes immersed and slightly tarnished, if you will, then the
       Negro problem will become less of a strain upon our con-
       science. We would have more composure if we were less
       "pristine" white; we would improve the evils complained of,
       if in a measure we recognized that these shortcomings are
       ours—that we are our brothers' keepers, or, at least, that their
       grip upon us has something of a strangle hold in it.

Ours, as the author points out, is a self-conscious community. We are possessed, more than any other country, "large or small," of "the *most explicitly expressed* system of general ideas in reference to human interrelations" (*p. 3*); and these ideas are bent in the direction of freedom, of human dignity. Ours is the "land of the free," "the cradle of liberty," "the home of democracy." There is even something of a proselyting zeal about our sense of mission in the world. These self-evident truths have not merely an American, but a world-wide, import, and the four freedoms are but an extension of the American credo. The Negro and his ills, as well as his strivings, are within this frame of ideas and aspirations—their very poignancy is due to the failure to make the credo apply to him as fully as it is meant to apply to all members of the American community. Since the ideals that dominate American life are believed in by all groups—the conservatives as well as the liberals, the "old aristocrats" and the new immigrants, all worship at the same shrine—the American credo belongs to no special sect, caste, or class, and it is this "spiritual convergence" (*p. 13*) which makes "the nation great" and holds the promise of an even "greater future."

The author agrees, however, that the ideals of the American ethos are in conflict with the equally strong tradition of disregard for law and the readiness for personal violence. We have the ingrained habit of regulating every detail by a new law and the easy convenience of partial enforcement, no enforcement, or persistent violation. The story of Prohibition is but a conspicuous example of a wider pattern. The consequence is a certain defeatism that may well become "chronic" (*p. 20*). The task seems so great, the achievement so small, that a kind of negative natural law (*p. 19*) has affected even the Negroes, who feel that little can be expected from good intentions translated into law, that all efforts will be defeated, that the old evils will persist. Pessimism rather than optimism seems to have replaced the idealism implicit

166 in the ethos and this is particularly true among intellectuals (*p. 20*). For them, at least, it seems that "in principle the Negro problem was settled long ago, in practice the solution is not effectuated" (*p. 24*). The Negro problem appears as a lag, a century old. In outcome, however, the lag has very vivid consequences, especially for the people in the South. It has imposed upon them a kind of ambivalence in their attitude toward the Negro—he is good and bad, kindly and dangerous. They believe the good and evil report with half their minds. The Southerner has become incapable of facing the issues logically. A kind of addiction to half-truths has been devised, a readiness to indulge in gossip, an unconscious readiness to sacrifice truth to grace, a need to keep the surface unruffled—all of this just because it has become impossible to face the reality that the Negro is a man, just like other men, an American, endowed by the law with inalienable rights. Rather than face that, there is an escape into make-believe, because that is the only means to avoid a stark reality that ruffles tempers, rouses anger and opens the gateway to violence.

The Negro "is our problem," "let us deal with our own," "we know the Negro"—all of that and much more, because of a special insight and knowledge of the Negro which the Southerner claims as his special possession, but which is in a large part constructed and assumed insight. True or not, it serves to keep the surface polished, it helps to keep the "Negro low and the white high." This knowledge is in reality a kind of "high-strung" self-assertion; it serves to conceal a deep disturbance. What the white man has is an abstraction, untrue but satisfying. The conflict with the issues raised by the Negro in the South, at least, has tended spiritually to isolate the white man from the broad current of cultural and social development. He is so obsessed with the Negro that all issues are distorted and pulled out of joint. The obsession leaves him spiritually awry. The author quotes Weldon Johnson (*p. 43*) to the effect, "The race problem involves the saving of the white man's soul and the black man's body."

People in the South and many in the North would reverse the trend of American experience in so far as it affects the Negro. American experience works toward the dissolving of minority groups. The American ethos is all-embracing, and the minority, which in Europe strives to remain unique and isolated, here strives to become part of the majority, to be incorporated and lost within the great American folk. But, for the Negro, another doctrine is advanced (*p. 53*), that he is to develop a "race pride" of his own—a bit of advice offered by even the Negro's "best friends." There is an assumption that here the trend of American history will reverse itself; that instead of becoming part of the American folk, the Negroes will remain a nation within a nation, more and more isolated, more and more self-conscious, more and more pure. There are many indications in the volume under review that the author himself is inclined to accept, even if not approve of, this projected line of future development of the Negro in the United States. The reviewer disagrees with the advice, the assumptions, the policy, and the doctrine, not on the grounds that they are inadvisable—that would be presumptuous—but on the grounds that they are impossible, unrealistic and part of make-believe.

The Negro has been in other parts of this hemisphere for something more than a century longer than in what is now the United States (one need only look at Brazil, Venezuela, Cuba and other American nations), and, while other factors have played their part, a hundred additional years of common contact have also played their part. The problem, physically speaking, is of the essence of time and contact between the races, especially contact widely scattered over the face of the nation and amid all groups in the country. There are enough darker-hued folk in our population to make the distinction between Negro and non-Negro a line difficult to draw, and time will draw a veil over both. To assume otherwise is to assume that it is possible in a dynamic social structure, satu-

168   rated with a common ethos, to keep forever—and forever is a
long time—the peoples apart, when they go to the same
schools, work in the same shops, believe in the same gods,
wear the same clothes and die on the same battlefields. Those
who believe that, project their special description of the nature of man and the meaning of social differences into the
future. There is no single instance where a minority, placed
like that of the Negro in the United States, did not in time—
the long time—become a part of the majority. We say in time,
for, biologically speaking, there is no great hurry; there is
lots of time, and a thousand years are like unto a single day.

By widening the functions of the state, the New Deal has
increased the number of issues involving the Negro—social
security, housing, nutrition, child and woman labor, and now
the war, the army and the war industries. The Negro has a
"broader" and more varied field to defend. There is, however, the growing notion that there is no longer a Negro
problem, but only a class problem, and that is "escapism" in
a new form.

> The reason, of course, is that there is really a common tie
> and, therefore, a unity in all the special angles of the Negro
> problem. All these specific problems are only outcroppings of
> one fundamental complex of human valuations—that of Amer-
> ican caste. This fundamental complex derives its emotional
> charge from the equally common race prejudice, from its mani-
> festations in a general tendency toward discrimination, and
> from its political potentialities through its very inconsistency
> with the American Creed (*p. 75*).
>
> If, for example, we assume that for some reason white
> prejudice could be decreased and discrimination mitigated,
> this is likely to cause a rise in Negro standards, which may de-
> crease white prejudice still a little more, which would again
> allow Negro standards to rise, and so on through mutual inter-
> action. If, instead, discrimination should become intensified,
> we should see the vicious circle spiraling downward. The
> original change can as easily be a change of *Negro standards*
> upward or downward. The effects would, in a similar manner,
> run back and forth in the interlocking system of interdepend-

ent causation. In any case, the initial change would be supported by consecutive waves of back-effects from the reactions
of the other factor (*p. 76*).

There is an apparent assumption of something static in
this description of the relations between the races. But the
opposite seems to be true. The Negro is not outside the general milieu of white society. It is impossible to isolate the
Negro for special treatment, for separate standards, for
greater or poorer opportunities. If the social structure is
modified at any point, it is modified at all points, and the
Negro's position is modified by it. It is not possible, for instance, to evolve new standards of health for the community
without improving the health standards of the Negro community. What is required is a changed attitude, belief, practice, ideal, habit, system, involving public and private health.
That automatically affects the health position of the whole
community, the Negro included, and the author recognizes
this fact (*p. 169*). The same is true of education; the same is
true of public welfare. It is very dubious to this reviewer to
assume, as seems implicit in the above quotation, that "prejudice" against the Negro would keep health standards for the
Negro stationary, low, or even permit them to become lower,
while the health standards of the rest of the community were
improving. It may be true that these health standards for the
Negro would progress at a slower rate, but it is still true that
if the standards of health were improving, they would also
improve for the Negro. Standards of health are a matter of
knowledge and habit, attitude and belief. By their very nature, these things transcend barriers of race; they are of a
universal quality and pervasive in effect. What is true of
health is true of education, of public welfare, economic well-
being, employment, income, and so on. If the resources of the
community increase and are multiplied, their consequence
spreads throughout the community; if they diminish and
become more restricted, then that too spreads throughout the
community. Prejudice might affect the rate of change in either

direction, but even this is something that may not be true, for the change is impersonal and makes itself evident unevenly and at different places in the structure. If the community were becoming poorer, then all groups in the community would be affected by the change, and, more specifically, in those employments, opportunities, income, and standards that were first affected; and in that case all the people in that area, white or black, would be first affected. We might have, and we have had, "normal standards" for Negroes and whites at their respective levels, while in other areas—in mining, for example, during the early nineteen-thirties—all groups, both colored and white, might feel the effect of a depression long before it reached the rest of the community. Perhaps in each specific case the Negroes, because of their historical position, might be the first to suffer, but it is not true that "prejudice" would, in our kind of a dynamic society, complex and impersonal, make possible the decline in the standards of any group—not even the Negro—while the standards in the community as a whole were improving.

The author, however, has a full sense of the dynamic character (*pp. 75-78*) of American society and recognizes that change, when it occurs at one point, will, according to the "principle of cumulation," spread its influences in many directions. He recognizes that "panacea" at any point is impossible, but he still seems to feel that the Negro complex is a unit in the social structure in some way independent of the whole, but affected by it; that standards and opportunities for the Negro are something separate from these same influences within the white community. That seems to the reviewer to be unrealistic. The Negro began with lower standards when he left the status of slavery; he also began in a society very much poorer and less complex than the present. The changes in the position of the Negro represent total changes in the whole society. He has gained a great deal, probably in the total more than any other single group in the community, just because the level from which he began was so much lower.

But to assume that there is some way of improving the position of the Negro in any field, even in that of voting, without in effect changing the situation of the whole community is to believe in "panacea." The poll tax, for example, disenfranchises many Negroes, but it also disenfranchises many, perhaps more, whites. If the poll tax is abolished, the vote will probably increase in the South, but not in proportion to the total number of voters who will be empowered to vote by the change. If the Southern voters increase in number it will be because a multitude of influences will have stimulated a greater interest in voting, and that will affect both the Negroes and the whites. It may be true that such a change will increase efforts to keep the Negro from exercising his franchise, but that will be evidence that the change in direction of greater participation in politics has already occurred. It will be discrimination after the fact and not before it, and it is bound to fail, just as any effort to keep the Negro from benefiting from changed attitudes toward public health or public education have failed. Only in a static caste system, where the separation is complete at all points, can the social groups live in comparative isolation. *To keep the Negro from sharing all of the benefits of the changes in social policy and attitude it would be necessary to keep him from sharing in any of the changes—a perfectly impossible position in an industrial society.*

The only issue is one of the rate of speed at which the changes become inclusive. The quality of the changes, or improvements, is involved in the rate and in the available surplus of energy and income which is diverted in that particular direction. If public housing takes a great spurt after the war, then the Negro will benefit most from that as will the rest of the community; if education, then he will benefit from education. Prejudice may affect, let us repeat, the rate at which he will benefit, but not the results of the spreading policy. In that sense there is no Negro problem. The problem is a moral one and not a material one. It lies in the conflict within the conscience of the white man and is made acute by the very fact that he cannot effectuate his prejudice fully in either direction. He cannot keep the Negro "down" and he cannot "uplift" him, as a separate entity. The Negro suffers from the fact that he is poor and that he lives in the poorest section of the country. Neither of these facts can be changed by itself. His income can increase only if the income of the community increases and he can share in the greater wealth of the South only when the South achieves greater wealth. He is not an isolated something, living in a vacuum, which can be depressed or inflated at will or by prejudice.

There is an implicit contradiction in Myrdal's study. He recognizes that the American creed—and, he ought to add, industrialism—makes inevitable uniform application of social policy to all groups, and, at the same time, argues that there is a homogeneous—increasingly homogeneous—isolated, segregated, self-conscious group called the Negro, which lives, and will continue to live, outside the rest of the social structure. But such an outcome would deny the force of the American creed and could, perhaps, be effectuated only in an agricultural society. It is not feasible, even if desired, in an industrial society, where the population is unstable, where population movement is fluid, and where skills are always changing in number and complexity. The author repeatedly, when describing specific policies, points out that we "will be compelled to extend to the Negroes the population measures taken primarily to build up the white population . . . a unity of purpose becomes established on the basis of the American creed" (*p. 170*). It simply remains true that at whatever level, whether in population policy, education, unemployment, social justice, the difference between the Negro and the white man is measured by a lag. The Negro falls in behind in the line, but he goes the same way. The difference is not a difference in kind, but in amount. He is not denied higher education. His difficulties in securing it are greater. He is not denied better housing. He gets it in lesser amounts and, perhaps, somewhat later than other elements in the population, and that not merely because he is a Negro, but also because he is poorer. He is poorer, not merely because he is a Negro, but also because he started and remains predominantly in a poorer section of the country, and because, having entered the industrial occupations later, the skills and competencies essential to advancement in industrial occupations are relatively less widely distributed among Negroes than among other parts of the population. It is not denied that being a Negro is a handicap, but it is not an absolute barrier.

The American creed makes differential treatment at any level, as a matter of public policy, impossible; what becomes a matter of public policy includes the Negro. That there are injustices and numerous denials of justice is a fact patent to anyone who knows what is going on. But that is not the point at issue; the important point is that they are recognized as injustices, recognized as something to be ashamed of, remedied, denied, or hidden. That is why there is no caste system really, and that is why there is no Negro problem as such. There are only the white man's troubled conscience and the fact that, for the complex reasons of a money economy, the benefits of modern civilization tend to go first of all to those who can pay for them in taxes, or in cash. There is no denial, there is only insufficiency of opportunity. The distinction is important. It cannot be stressed too often that the apparent static character of the Negro problem, where it appears as a "problem" in fact, is descriptive only of that part of our economy which is agricultural, where income increases slowly or not at all and where the surplus available for social reform is small.

The pointing up of racial conflicts and injustices is important in a study of both the position of the Negro and the state of American culture. But the frictions are a healthy sign. They indicate a many-sided contact between the two races. The frictions are an evidence of the fact that the Negro and white man live in the same community and quarrel over the

174   same values. As long as the two races are striving and dis-
agreeing over the manifold issues of living in the same culture, then it means that they are engaged in the painful
process of accommodation to each other and to the world.
The real danger would be if the Negro managed to live in a
vacuum where there was no friction between him and his
white neighbors; then there would be real danger of the developing of a perpetual caste system. It is desirable from the
point of view of the Negro that there should be friction at
many points, over many individual issues, in every part of
the country. It is desirable that nothing should remain static
until the issues over which the friction arises have themselves
ceased to trouble either the whites or the blacks. To want
peace when the contrasts are so great is to dream of an unreal
world. To expect either the white or the Negro community
to show neither anger nor hate, neither fear nor violence,
when their values are challenged and their aspirations are
frustrated is to ask for the impossible. It is not specific evils
that we must complain of—they are to be dealt with by the
police and public authorities. It is the general direction
which gives the evils their pertinence that is the significant
issue, and, from that point of view, the friction is a good
thing. It shows that the evils complained of are alive, trouble-
some, and impelling. They force men to do something about
them. They will do many wrong things about them, but, by
the same token, many right ones. Our argument here is for an
active rather than a passive policy in the matter, for the point
that there is no solution to the Negro problem, because there
is, as we said before, no problem with a big "P." There is only
the infinitely complex and essentially contradictory structure
of American culture, a universal credo sworn to by a folk
caked in old prejudices and living in a world of limited resources.

    In spite of its great merits and deep insight the study
under discussion all too easily follows the traditional pattern
of bringing out the Negro's ills and handicaps and proving

over again what has so often been shown: that the Negro occupies the lowest rung upon the ladder in American life; that he is poor and more disadvantaged; that, measured by any test, he has less of the goods of the world and fewer opportunities; he is the poor, the denied, the oppressed in our world—and all of this can be shown up by a series of statistical tables, setting up a comparison between the Negro and the whites in terms of income, property, education, health, and so on. But the very basis of the comparison is a dubious one if the purpose is to set the place of the Negro in a changing and expanding American culture. The comparison breaks down because the Negro and the whites did not start from the same base. The Negro started with nothing at all and with the handicap of the ways of slavery upon him and his white fellows. The true comparison is with the Negro himself at the time of slavery. If we wish to know the direction that the Negro is going, then it is best to begin at the beginning: Negro education and Negro health, Negro opportunities and Negro professionals, not in comparison with the whites of the present day, but with the Negro at the time of the emancipation.

It is important to note that, in the school attendance between the ages of five and twenty in the Southern states, the percentage had risen from 1.8 in 1860, to 64.4 in 1940 (*p. 942*). This is infinitely more revealing than the fact that the schools for Negroes are poorer, that the school terms are shorter, that the teachers are less adequately trained, than in the schools of the white children.

A similar observation can be made concerning the comparisons in the North with the total white community. It would have been more relevant to the issues in hand, if it had been stated in terms of the Negro as a recent agricultural immigrant, with all of the handicaps of an agricultural immigrant, to an industrial environment, and if the comparison in terms of place, opportunity, and achievement had been with the recent generation of Polish, Italian, and Russian

176   immigrants. The Negro might still have been proved under-
privileged even by such comparisons, but surely the gap at
any point would have been narrower than the one that is
revealed by a straight colored-white comparison. But it is
very doubtful whether the changes that have taken place are
measurable in terms of statistical techniques.

The milieu which makes the career of a Paul Robeson
and a Walter White possible represents a total change in
the temper of American life. The fact that those who defend
the poll tax are bitterly and raspingly on the defensive is
another illustration of the same point. For the thing important here is not the fact that the poll tax still survives, but
that those who uphold it should do so in screeching tones
and ill-tempered bombast, so revealing of their own insecurity
that they have to shout to convince themselves of their own
position.

Perhaps the most important change that has occurred in
the relation between the Negroes and the whites is that the
whites have lost faith in their own doctrines of racial superiority (*p. 1003*). The happy days when a Negro was a Negro
rather than a man, the days when the beliefs in the inferiority
of the Negro were supported by science, religion, and common sense, have passed away, and now he who upholds the
natural inferiority of the Negro has no authority to fall back
upon except his own self-avowed "prejudice," which finds
no support in the textbooks, or in the teaching of the church,
or even in the agreement of some of his own best friends.
The doctrine is not accepted any more by the people who
claim intellectual status for themselves, or by those who aspire to intellectual status; the scientists, the moralists, the
preachers, and even some of the politicians, are on the other
side of the fence.

The shortcomings of the Negro are now said to be the
results of an unhealthy environment, and those responsible
for the poor environment—the whites, of course—are also responsible for the shortcomings of the Negro. The Negro's

failings are the white man's fault. The shoe is now on the other foot. Instead of the Negro being deficient and, therefore, justifiably kept in a lower status, it is the white man's failure which makes a poor environment, out of which only handicapped Negroes can come. There may not be much comfort in this doctrine, but it gives the Negro a powerful leverage. The poor white man must now bear the burden of his own as well as of the Negro's failings. That this should have occurred in the United States, and in the South, too, is something of a paradox. But if the American community is going to believe in *environmentalism,* as it does, and as all of the social sciences of the recent past, even in some measure the biological sciences, have tended to do, then there is no real escape from the dilemma with which our conscience presents us. If the Negro is poor and handicapped, it is not his, but our, fault; the blame is on the white man and not on the Negro. That is a complete reversal of the older doctrine of Negro inferiority, and makes all of the operational techniques, so neatly fitting in a world of caste, unavailable when the caste system has lost its intellectual justification. From this point of view, it is the Negro who has the upper hand, for he has a moral claim, which a moral people cannot deny—certainly cannot deny with a good conscience. The white community in America has achieved a sense of guilt about the Negro because it has lost faith in the doctrines that made slavery and discrimination permissible and right. This is not a healthy psychological situation and may have other than beneficent consequences; but the ground has changed, and, in some measure, the roles of the races have been reversed, with the Negro as the accuser and the white man as the half-hearted defendant.

Should discrimination and racial prejudice pass away, the problem would still remain substantially what it is. The Negro would be allowed to vote, but, in the South, the rural Negro would in all likelihood be no greater participant in politics than is his equally poor white, neighboring sharecropper.

His opportunities for education would be little improved, his income would remain substantially the same, and, as a class, his role in the world would not be much changed! True enough, his theoretical opportunities would be greater and, in practice, some fortunate accident and opportunity would enable the gifted and the energetic to escape out of his milieu, but the basic issue of the failure of the American credo to carry over in universal terms would still remain true. The problem is greater than that of mere prejudice and discrimination; it is a problem made by the concentration of the Negro in a poverty-ridden section of the country, wedded to a crop of unstable and declining prices, burdened by the tradition of the spiritually impoverishing single crop, with practically no other outlets for new skills and no incentives to new enterprise. If that is the fact in the rural districts where most of the Negroes live, work, and die, it is not much different in the immediate situation in the urban sections in the South, and but little different in the North. An acquaintance with the milieu provided by the mill village in the South, which has become the spiritual as well as the economic grave of so many poor Southern whites, will reveal that it is not merely a problem of color, it is also a problem of economic opportunity and industrial diversity. It is a major question whether the poor white who has become a mill hand has, in the typical Southern mill village, improved either his economic or spiritual environment. The reviewer, for one, long since has taken the position that the shift from the mountains and the farms to the mill villages has impoverished and demeaned the opportunities of the Southern whites, even from the little opportunities made available by a poverty-stricken rural environment, and he sees no reason for changing that opinion.

To assume that the disappearance of prejudice would automatically improve the lot of the Negro is to assume that miracles take place in the workings of an economic system. That is also true, of course, in the larger cities; the rural Negro—like the rural white moving to a large city—suffers from the fact of his rural environment, especially when that environment is of the type represented by the rural South where the individual comes to town denuded of skill, enterprise, energy, and ambition, and where the opportunities are limited and the places crowded. If there were no race prejudice, the exceptional individual would escape and, in fact, does so now, but the mass would have to live, toiling in an environment poor in resources and sharing the very small yield in terms of income, and smaller surplus in terms of social benefit, that the local industry makes available. This is not an argument against the arbitrary and degrading impact of race prejudice but it is an argument against the assumption that the elimination of fear, which controls the Southern attitude toward the Negro, would of itself universalize the benefits implicit in the American creed. The Negro problem would merely be merged in the larger and more basic problem of poverty in a poverty-ridden section of the United States; that would be better, of course, but it still would be almost equally appalling.

It follows from this that the easiest way out of the hate, poverty, fear, and prejudice that gnaw at the bone and the flesh is the increase of opportunity, the diversification of interest, the multiplication of problems, the opening of new vistas, and the making of new difficulties. If the South grows richer, and if the rural environment becomes more diversified, then there will be greater opportunities for both the whites and the Negroes, and the burden of fear will be lightened for both races. Race prejudice cannot be abolished. It can only die out in time. And it can do that only by concentrating on other issues. If and when the South ceases to feel itself discriminated against, abused and exploited, it may cease to feel so proud, so self-conscious, so bitter, so "uppity." It may then become more urbane, more tolerant, richer in spirit and richer in goods, more secure in itself, and more unconcerned about the issues seemingly so important now, but in reality only an artificial wall against imaginary dangers—imaginary, but real in their influence and in the bitterness which they produce.

Unfortunately, there is no magic formula toward social felicity, not even in the preaching of the American credo. The human imagination is ingenious in devising subtleties of feeling and thinking that make the incongruous seem normal, and the unreal, real. The Southerner can be both a democrat and a practitioner of race discrimination in fact, even if he has a bad conscience over the matter. The way out is, not to concentrate upon the issue in hand, but to concentrate upon something else, concentrate upon opening up avenues for the good life for all of the people in the South, both white and black, and in time—in the long time—fears will diminish, memories fade, new practices and new attitudes replace the old, and the Negro will cease to be a Negro and become a man—just another Southerner, just another American.

on certain characteristics
of american democracy *8*

IN A WORLD BARELY RID of the threat of Nazi dictatorship in which the American people seem girded for the herculean task of spreading democracy across the face of the globe, it is important to ask, what is this American faith with which we would endow the people of the earth? Can it be described so as to make it acceptable to folk steeped in other traditions, and, if made acceptable, can it also be accepted? Is democracy a doctrine written in a book that may be learned by heart, or is it something that cannot be encompassed in any theory, incarnated in any constitution, or detailed in any system of law? Is democracy something that can be taught? Or is it something that can be learned only by practice, and is the practice itself conditioned by a historical process that cannot be repeated on order for any other people? It is really a question raised in response to the present effort to create democratic régimes in other parts of the world—by order from above, by laws copied from the experience of other peoples, by ideas that have their roots in a specialized historical experience. Can the lessons of one culture be passed to

Reprinted, with permission, from *Political Science Quarterly,* LX (September 1945), pp. 343–350.

182   another without losing the very essence of the lesson they would teach, the very meanings that give them substance?

The ethos that pervades any social system is a very private, a very unique, multiple of values. It is a summary—an unwritten summary—of all the efforts, strivings, success and failures of all the past that makes the present what it is. The ethos cannot be passed on. The practices which the ethos dictates have special meaning only in the setting where they have arisen. No formal declaratory statement of how democracy is practiced can make any other nation democratic. No machinery of election to office, no given system of law is adequate for the purpose. Democracy is a function of the past experience of a people and will differ as the ethos of the people differs. It may be true that there are democratic elements in any society, and that a certain genus of education might in time nourish and cultivate a democratic way of life even in a nominally nondemocratic community, but the emerging pattern of government would in some measure be encompassed by the traditional mores of the people who were being educated in the democratic way of life. If the new way of government proved incompatible with the peculiar ethos of the society where it was being developed, it would in the long run prove intolerable and unacceptable. Democracy beyond all other forms of government belongs to the people and must in some way fit in with a native slant and a native meaning, or it can have no meaning.

This is not an argument that no new lesson can be learned from a new experience; but, if the new lesson is not to prove ephemeral, then in some subtle measure it must be a continuation of the older lessons learned long since and embedded within the system of values that the people already have. If we would teach democracy to the peoples of the world, we must teach it on local rather than foreign foundations. The way of life must in the long run prove consistent with their inner sense of values. It must, in fact, by some magic appear to be and, in fact, be a continuation of their own past. The problem is subtle, difficult, and may prove beyond the competence of mere mortal men. But the lesson is clear—as clear as crystal. You cannot give peoples a set of permanent values which do not fit in with what they have already learned from their own old and painful history. Perhaps you can give a new slant to an old meaning, but no nation can be given a new set of values, new mores, a new ethos. If our task is not to prove futile, if our good intentions are not to turn to bitterness and taunt us with our failure, then we must seek in the basic experience of the peoples themselves the lesson of democracy we would teach them. Their history is as peculiar to them as our history is peculiar to us, and we cannot improvise a new system of values for other peoples, just as no one could improvise a new system of values for us.

American democracy is what it is. It is not commensurable with other democracies, and it is largely immune from exterior currents of thought and action. Much has been said about the easy spread of autocratic ideas and ideals. What has not been said is that autocratic practices came to the surface and achieved implicit consent only in those parts of Europe where democracy had not prevailed before. As a simple statement of fact, totalitarian theories found substantial root only in countries where democratic habits did not exist before; for democracy is a habit, a way of life, a process of social relationship. It is not fundamentally a theory of government; it is a method of government that derives its consent from each person governed—even from those who oppose the specific things that the government may do. One may in a democracy oppose all of the actual policies of the administration and yet believe in democracy, because the methods of achieving the defeat of the present administration are also democratic. In a democracy, he who has a concern has a voice; and the voice of each counts for one—and only for one. The rest is a matter of counting. The right to a voice, the personal conscience in expressing it, the freedom to utter an opinion—even a wrong one—and the honesty of the count are all essential elements of any democratic society. Underlying it is the belief that the experience of the many is more inclusive than the experience of the few; that the voice of the people is the voice of God; that what the people want is what they need. There is the further belief that no one knows better than the people themselves what they need at the moment. In a democratic society it is just as important to possess the right to be wrong as the right to be right; for in any society where a wrong opinion cannot be uttered it is not possible for long to utter a right opinion. In the long run, wisdom is tested by experience. No one can be sure that his own judgment is not in error, and he who has not the right to be wrong cannot long possess the right to be right. All of these elemental facts are true of every society where democracy is a habit, but American society contains elements that give the above special poignancy.

Ours is a social democracy. Neither class nor caste, nor special families dominate American life. We have no aristocracy. Those of our families that would draw an aristocratic mantle over them were born yesterday, and will have disappeared tomorrow. A list of the prominent leaders in American life would reveal that their fathers or grandfathers were farmers, peddlers, laborers, skilled mechanics, or lawyers' clerks who starved in boyhood, and achieved standing by the grace of good fortune, personal ability, and the wealth of a growing industrial society. The record will also show that many of the aristocrats of yesterday have today shrunk back into the mass and are indistinguishable from them; for in American social life the test of status is a test of immediate achievement. He who survives must do so by his own works. No one in America can long live on his past, or on the past of his fathers. What you do—that is the fundamental test of American life. There is a vertical flow in the United States that works both ways, and the movement upward of new elements is compensated for by a movement downward. While wealth may be important, it too is temporary. Many a wealthy family of yesterday is in poverty today, and the papers record, almost daily, the death in poverty of the scion of a wealthy father of a generation or two ago.

With the absence of class and social stratification goes an almost complete racial democracy. In the last century we have absorbed some thirty million foreigners, who came from all parts of the world. Literally every racial element in the world has gone into the making of the American community. Into the make-up of the American population have gone many thousands of English, Irish, Scotch, Italians, Poles, Russians, Danes, Swedes, Finns, Bulgarians, Turks, Armenians, Spaniards, Jews, Greeks, Germans, Chinese, Negroes, Mexicans, and representatives of every other racial and linguistic group in the world. In the same community, often in the same industrial establishment, there have been, and there are, representatives of twenty different racial elements. After the first generation they are all Americans—a curious kind of cultural absorption has pervaded the atmosphere, and has bred a new race out of the diverse elements of the world. While it is true that some elements have been more recalcitrant to absorption than others, it is also true that all elements have been proud of becoming Americans, and almost pathetically insistent in shedding the evidence of their origin. Intermarriage and a common public school system have done their work so well that in the United States, for more than fifty years, the source of origin has almost completely evaporated as a cause of separateness. While it is true that special elements can be pointed as a contradiction of what has been said, it is still true, however, that the process of absorption has been infinitely more rapid than the process of stratification. At the present rate of integration an American will, in the near future, have elements of so diverse a racial basis that separate identification will become meaningless. The Negroes have for [various] reasons been less readily subject to this process of physical incorporation, but anyone who would deny that it goes on, and at an increasing rate, is not really aware of the social process in American life.

Social democracy and racial democracy have gone hand in hand with religious democracy. There is more than religious freedom in the United States. There is almost a kind of reli-

186   gious inventiveness in the American community. Not only have the broad religious beliefs, brought over from the old world, had complete freedom to develop as they could, but an incredible number of American-born credos have risen and flourished. American ground seems to be specially favorable to new forms of faith—and, some of these new forms have become large and influential institutional groups. One need but mention the Mormon and Christian Science churches to make the point. There are, however, innumerable small sects. The city of Los Angeles is famous for the variety and the number of religious faiths that are to be found there. Not only has every religion been free to flourish and grow but every new religious form has found fertile ground. The conflict between the churches has taken the form of a competition for adherents. The denial of the completest freedom of worship is practically nonexistent, and the few voices of opposition have been lost in the general indifference to the issue raised. In the United States the worship of God is so varied that men profess their faith in every kind of temple, in every tongue, and in every form. The semi-hysterical public baptisms among Southern Negroes, on one hand, and the stately formal ritualism of the Greek Church on the other, are but bare elements of a scale that runs as wide as the human imagination.

Ours, too, is a political democracy in the specific sense of political organization. Foreign observers are often misled when they note the preponderance of two political parties. They should note that in both the Democratic and the Republican parties there are elements so diverse that under different conditions a great variety of parties could be constructed out of them. That they have not been is due to two very distinctive elements in American life. The first is the fact that local issues can be fought out locally, the party label being significant only in its national aspects. A conservative Democrat from Mississippi and a radical Democrat from New York meet only on the national issues. The second is that third parties in the United States have been fluid and temporary. They have lasted long enough to demonstrate that they really represented a considerable element in the voting population. As soon as that became evident, the larger and older parties have tended to absorb them by taking over their programs. That happened with the granger movement, with the prohibition movement, with the movement for old-age pensions; and these are but samples of a wide political process. The large parties, in spite of their seeming narrowness and definiteness, have really survived only because in the long run they have been open to groups as soon as these groups show sufficient importance to become a factor in winning an election. It is for that reason, in part, that in the United States there are at times numerous political parties. Our political parties are, in spite of their appearance historically, responsive to public demands—that has been their price for survival.

Part of this process is a kind of fluid economic democracy which has long pervaded American life. No one can understand the United States who does not understand that there is a persistent process of distribution of income that affects all groups. There is no economic interest that is not organized. There are large and frequently conflicting organizations of labor and innumerable organizations of capital, each seeking, and at times each in its turn successfully, to influence public opinion in its favor. There are groups in favor of the tariff and groups opposed to it; importers oppose the manufacturers; water transportation interests are in conflict with the railways; the railways oppose road transportation; and all of these may object to air transport subsidies. Agricultural interests are frequently in opposition to manufacturing interests, and agricultural groups may be sharply divided among themselves. The cane sugar growers are in conflict with the beet sugar growers, and both of these oppose the sugar importers. The fact is that there is a kind of divergence of interest in American life that is all-pervasive. Each of these interests has its own organization; each in its turn influences and on occasion secures public favor and governmental aid; and

188   each in turn affects the distribution of income of the American people. No one person, no one group, completely dominates the scene, and each group must be constantly on the watch to maintain its position. The effect of this upon the making of American democracy a sensitive and responsive instrument of public policy is great, indeed. It makes for lack of consistency in politics, but it also makes for freedom and for a shift of power as immediate needs, immediate pressure, and political acumen seem to require.

These various factors demand a kind of equality before the law, and a kind of weighing of the place of public interest as against purely private interest that gives the American judicial system and the American Supreme Court, in particular, a place in the scheme of American life that is difficult for strangers to understand. It also calls for a complete freedom of the expression of opinion. No such complex economic and social structure could survive unless each interest could make itself heard, unless each grievance found a voice, unless each group could influence public opinion and public policy. Without freedom of speech, press, assemblage and organization, American democracy could not function. It can be said that freedom in that sense is as available in the American community as can be expected in a social structure as large, varied and sectional as ours is. Occasionally and locally an attempted stratification of opinion takes place, but it has always been temporary and always localized. Freedom is essential to the American economic and public life, and both the conservatives and radicals believe in it for themselves, and, therefore, for others. But such great divergence can survive only upon an assumption that the end in government is not victory but compromise. That explains the good fellowship that follows a heated campaign for office, that is why no one assumes that defeat in a political campaign is the end of his program, that is why the day after election the preparation for the next election may be said to begin. With us democracy is a method. The end, if one may be said to exist, is to persuade the majority to our point of view, and if we fail today, we may succeed tomorrow. With us the majority is right, but only temporarily. We will be right tomorrow, for the time being, as long as we have enough voters. The American way is by compromise in little bits, by persuasion, by much talk and little bitterness; and if the next fellow is wrong today, we were wrong yesterday, though it is hard to admit. With us all political bargains are temporary, and all programs are for the day. No great battle is ever lost, and no great victory is ever won. When the day is over, and the new party comes to office, it continues the program that it denounced yesterday, largely because it would lose its adherents if it changed it. Our differences are about details of method and program; the basic ends are a good life and freedom of method in achieving it. These are so deeply ingrained as to be descriptive of what we call the American democracy.

a note on the economic interpretation of history

9

a book review

PROPERLY, the emphasis of Eric Williams' *Capitalism and Slavery* [1] is upon slavery and not upon the Negro. Slavery as an institution has its own special features, independent of the race enslaved, and may vary but little, regardless of who the slave is. This broad fact, that the institution takes precedence over the race most affected by it, has another and equally important feature, namely, that the cultural setting within which a problem develops has a reach beyond the people affected by it. The middle passage is horrible to contemplate. But the middle passage was as bad for the white indentured servant as it later proved to be for the Negro slave. The white servants were packed like herrings, each given but two feet in width and six feet in length for a bed, and sometimes kept beneath the deck for the entire voyage across the sea. What these white servants must have suffered on long voyages in small ships, insufficiently stocked with water, living on unrefrigerated food, subjected to the inevitable disease and the moral corruption, could not have been much less evil than what the Negro slaves endured upon their trip from Africa to the New World. Even the free, white, and paying passen-

190   Reprinted, with permission, from *Political Science Quarterly*, LXI (June 1946), pp. 247–253.

[1] Chapel Hill: The University of North Carolina Press, 1944.

ger fared miserably on these crowded ships, haunted by a thousand unknown dangers.

Mr. Williams writes of slavery with the indignation proper to a child of the American and French Revolutions, and, at the same time, with a strongly flavored faith in the economic interpretation of history, given strident enthusiasm by a visible notion of Negro nationalism. All of these things may be good in themselves, or even in combination, but they provide an inadequate framework for an objective study of the history of slavery. Slavery is what it is, and the history of man is replete with the record. But it is not what the child of the belief in "equality, liberty, and fraternity" thinks it is. Nor yet is it what one raised in the doctrine of a "classless society," or on the assumption that malice is a tool essential to the preservation of status, thinks it is. In any society where slavery has been institutionalized, the issues between free and slave labor become infinitely variable, and it is often a question of where slavery ends and freedom begins. Stated this way, it is better to speak of a slave society rather than of slavery, for the effects of the labor system—slave or free—permeate the entire social structure and influence all of its ways. If we are to speak of slavery, we must do so in its larger setting, as a way of life for both the master and the slave, for both the economy and the culture, for both the family and the community.

Slavery in America, as a system of labor, the author points out, had economic rather than racial origins. African labor was economically available. It was within reach at an acceptable price. It proved, in the tropics, more resilient than either Indian or white labor, and within nearer reach than labor drawn from either India or China. The fact that the labor drawn from Africa was black was incidental. It might have been yellow; it might even have been white. The labor was drawn from the available sources, and under acceptable conditions of price and survival value. But, in spite of Mr. Williams, the Negro had survival value. He endured the conditions of labor in the heat better than the Indian. The

Indian died out, in fact. The Negro endured it better than the whites, because, for reasons not moral but physical, he outworked the white man. The tropics in this hemisphere are a sort of Negro empire—not by accident, but because the Negro did well in them, did better, in fact, than his master, and, in the long run, the master went his way, mainly to the grave, and the Negro has inherited the earth. That is a truer and, it seems to this reviewer, a more accurate way of stating the meaning of Negro slavery in the West Indies and in the American tropics than Mr. Williams here uses.

Historically speaking, the Negro has inherited the tropics because he could inherit them. He had the competency needed for the effort. The white man was merely a temporary instrument in making the achievement possible. The white man, for his own short-term interest, started the process of enticing the Negro to slavery, into a world which ultimately was to belong to the Negro. The white man served the Negro well—better than he had planned, in fact. But that too is only a part of the way history works itself out. The consequences are what they are, in spite of the immediate plans and purposes men strive for.

In this instance, a great migratory movement was initiated under duress. The duress under which it began has long since passed away, but the immigrant and his children have remained. In the sum total of it all, the Negro race has been given an additional large share of the face of the globe for its own. It received this territory as a kind of unplanned gift; but there is nothing unusual in that. It is, in its own nature, no different than the process which has occurred as a result of the allurement which led millions of Europeans to labor in American mines, fields, and factories, and then within the century to become the backbone of American democracy, and the source of the movement that twice returned to Europe to save it from forced conquest. That, too, was unplanned and unforeseen. The result is one thing, the immediate purpose is another.

Objectivity must rule the historical judgment in apprais-

ing a process so vast as the migration to this hemisphere of
millions of Negroes as slaves. The immediate purpose was
"economic." It was greedy, narrow, selfish. Let the devil, if
you must, have his full day of unrestrained malice and conspiracy, lust and cruelty, and let us say that all of the history
of the slave trade and slavery was motivated by nothing at
all but evil intent. Say it if you believe it, but that would be
stretching the matter a bit too far. The result has been moral.
It has proved a good thing for the Negroes in the long run.
They have achieved status, both spiritually and materially, in
the new home to which they were brought as chattels, and
the final judgment upon the process must include the last part
of the story as well as the first.

Mr. Williams endeavors to prove that whites will do as
well as the Negroes in the tropics. The fact remains that, after
four hundred years of experience, the Negro is the chief occupant of the tropics, and the increasing occupant of them. The
example of Cuba, given by the author, that the Canary Is-
lander and the poor Spaniard dominate the tobacco industry,
while the Negroes dominate the sugar industry, is not valid,
because sugar is grown on the coast and tobacco is not. The
same holds true of the example from Puerto Rico. The white
jibaro lives in the mountains and has devoted his energies to
coffee and tobacco. The sugar plantations in Puerto Rico on
the coast are still largely Negro. The insistence of the author
upon the equal fitness of the whites and Negroes in the
tropics leads him to clutch at straws in the argument. He says:
"similar white communities have survived in the Caribbean,
from the earliest settlement right down to our own times, in
the Dutch West Indian Islands of Saba and San Martin,"
quoting Price.[2] But Mr. Williams neglects to quote from the
same author the following: "As regards the future, Saba, in
spite of its large proportion of whites is clearly turning colored, as are almost all of the islands of and borderlands of
the Caribbean. No matter how greatly the altitude or the

[2] A. Grenfell Price, *White Settlers in the Tropics* (New York, 1939).
p. 91.

trade winds may mitigate the tropical disadvantages in favor of white settlers, the whites cannot compete with the prolific families of the negro. . . . The negro possesses greater immunity from tropical diseases. . . ." In fact, Price concludes that even in the most advantageous conditions in the tropics the whites, in the long run, tend to succumb. Of San Martin, which Williams uses as an example to show white survival, Price says that, owing to disease and isolation, the "people degenerated almost to the animal level." Even of the Germans, in Seaford, Jamaica, cited by Williams as a shining example, the very source he uses says, ". . . the German communities in the Seaford region have deteriorated as a result of negro competition and will inevitably be absorbed by the negro population." Of the Queensland experiment, of which Williams speaks with such assurance, as indicating that whites can do equally well in the tropics as the Negroes, it needs to be pointed out that the Queensland area is "peculiarly favorable to white settlements," that this region is marginal, and, most important of all, "the penetration is so recent that it provides no proof that the tropical climate will not cause degeneracy in later generations."

But the question is not the validity of the emphasis Mr. Williams chooses to place upon the stray examples of white survival in the tropics, but the straining for evidence of such survival. What after all is the point at issue? It would, if Mr. Williams were right, deny the easy adaptability of the Negro to the tropics. It would deny him the greater vigor given him by an immunity to some of the tropical diseases, such as hookworm and malaria, and would deny the four hundred years of experience that the Negro has not merely survived but thrived in the tropics—at least in the American tropics—because he is superior rather than inferior to the white man in that respect. Such long-range examples of persistence of type are not accidents and were not politically conditioned. It seems to the reviewer that Mr. Williams would have done better to accept the greater fitness of the Negro for the tropics and acclaim the fact that that fitness has given to the Negro an additional and highly successful habitat in the tropics—a habitat which he is even now expanding at the cost of both the white remnants and the Indians of certain tropical regions, for instance, the Choco area in Colombia, where the Negroes at this date are encroaching upon the Indians.

The Negro's position, insists the author, marks the triumph of economic and not of geographic conditions. Why be so positive? It may well have been the triumph of both. It would have made little difference to the Negro if geography had something to do with it, and it may explain the present physical thriving of the Negro. Is human experience of four centuries of no value at all when set against a fixed idea that only economic forces are the ruling factors in shaping human destiny? When Bolívar wrote, as he did frequently, to Santander, begging him to set free some thousands of slaves and dispatch them to him as soldiers because in the tropics his white men, drawn from the mountains, were dying like flies, and saying that unless he could secure colored troops his campaign would be a failure—was that, too, economic? Or is the fact that on the Mamore-Madeira railway, which at a terrific cost in lives was built by people brought in from many parts of the world, only the Negroes have survived along the tracks and have, to all appearances, made a happy adjustment —is that too, not geographical, but only economic? What is there to be gained from such monistic theorizing about the forces of nature that shape human destiny, except the satisfaction of having supported a dubious point?

Negro slavery was a fact and a tragedy. But its causes may have been many rather than one. That would not change anything about slavery except the explanation of it. It would not prove the Negro inferior, nor the white superior. No one knows anything about the measure of inferiority or superiority in the moral sense, and prejudice weights every other measure. Surely a scholar like Mr. Williams might stop arguing an irrelevant matter as if it were important to the issue. The only ones who proclaim Negro inferiority are those who

196   assume their own superiority and that constitutes no evidence
of the point at all. In fact, the very enthusiasm with which
Mr. Williams rises to the challenge presumes that he takes
the charge seriously. Is it not about time that we accept the
historical record for what it is and go on about our business
of explaining the issues as they arise? A book such as this is
not a political pamphlet. It is a serious study, and it is a pity
to spoil it by bending the argument to prove an irrelevant
theme. The author himself cites the complaints of the whites
brought into St. Christopher after the abolition of slavery—
that they wanted to return home because "if we continue
much longer in this injurious hot climate (the West Indian)
death will be the consequence to the principal part of us."

In his enthusiasm for an economic explanation, the author
would whitewash the middle passage by saying that its horrors were "exaggerated," and lighten the labor of slaves on
plantations because it did not "differ fundamentally from the
exploitation of the feudal peasant, or the treatment of the
poor in European cities."

The freeing of the Negro, James Somerset, by Judge Mans-
field is minimized because the judge limited himself to saying
that "the case was not allowed or approved by the law of
England" (as if that were not the question at issue), and
any attempt to take note of this decision as evidence of a
moral change is condemned as "poetic sentimentality translated into modern history."

It is hard to be a child of the Renaissance and a high priest
of economic interpretation at the same time. If slavery was
merely economic, and if economic forces are the only conditioning factor in shaping human institutions, then why all of
the indignation and the sarcasm? Why the appeal to moral
forces, to justice, and to humanity? If slavery was just an
economic institution and abolition was merely a new form
for the working out of changing economic forces, then the
abolitionists were mere dupes of the new masters of the
economic life in England. If all of this is true, then one has
no right to be indignant at slavery or slaveholders, or to re-

joice at abolition, or to prize freedom, or to give value to any code. All of life is a kind of automaton, a predestined pattern, dictated by an immutable law, inescapable in its impact, and unyielding to any human effort. Man is a mere tool for the working out of a plan, untouched by any ethical bias, unflavored by kindness, unenlightened by wisdom, and indifferent to justice or mercy. Destiny is implacable, the human will of no avail, and all strivings mere reflexes of the economic demon that dooms man forever to its own indifferent and unmoral ends. The law, the code, the prophecy, and the faith, the moral strivings for justice and decency, are witless and useless.

Even Mr. Williams cannot take all of this. He would claim that the Negroes have had a few friends, but why should they or anyone lay such a claim upon an unethical, unsentimental universe? Friendship is sentimental, and sentiment can, as Mr. Williams asserts in a hundred places, have no place in history. The Negro has had no justice; but why claim something that cannot exist in a universe where justice would be impossible, for only economic forces determine what men do? Mr. Williams, in fact, repudiates all of the values of human life, all traditions, all the tenacious notions of right, good and fitting, all of the ideals and beliefs that men have stood and died for. These are not just something imperfectly achieved, they are nonexistent. Man is not merely a fallible animal in Mr. Williams' sight; he is just a cog. He is duped to serve the false gods of some ethical faith, which is not only nonexistent but, in the nature of the case, nonexistable. The law of the economic interpretation of history has ruled ethics out of the pages of history, and where it survives it is some misguided sentimentalism that would force itself upon our attention, something we must repudiate in the name of reason, science, and research, plus a doctrine of the economic interpretation of history.

Now, such an extreme position is neither science nor history. It is merely a new theology—not even a good theology because it is uninspired, it has faith in nothing but a verbal formula. It would rule Christ out of the Christian church, Lincoln and the idea of national unity out of the Civil War, Roosevelt and the concept of human dignity out of the battle against the Nazis. There is nothing in the world but a blind force which fools people into playing moral roles—fools them! The role they play is inconsequential in the affairs of men, and the shape of the human drama would not have varied by a single line if all of the conscientious labors to affect the way of man across the face of the earth had not taken place at all. Man has nothing to do with history. The game is played by a blind and invisible hand, and, like a puppet show, he is present without participating. He is just merely there.

It is a pity that a good book is spoiled in the making by an acrid vehemence that makes Mr. Williams deride his teachers, and to attach folly or worse to those who disagree with him, as if by some strange magic he had laid wisdom by the heel all by himself. Now, there is some wisdom in charity, even to those who are in disagreement; there is some presumptive value in the recognition of human fallibility—a failing common to all mortal creatures, even the writers of books. There is no absolute evaluation of human experience, for even a great scholar knows only a very little and may not understand the little he knows. Facts are easily acquired by industry and diligence. The meaning of the facts, all of their meaning, is beyond the ken of any scholar—perhaps beyond the ken of mortal men.

the prospect
of violent revolution *10*
in the united states

THE WORD "REVOLUTION" is something with which to conjure American public opinion at the moment. The Reds base their strategy on the certainty of revolution, and the ultra-conservatives represented by the National Security League and the Congressional Committee headed by Representative Hamilton Fish are actively concerned with its possibility. American business, watching the working out of the Soviet's Five-Year Plan, has qualms and apprehensions of its own.

But the prospect of revolution is not a new phenomenon in America. It was vocal before the Great War, when the I. W. W. and the Socialist Party had a publicity value unknown even to present-day Reds. The hysterical fears that gripped such public officials as Attorney-General Palmer, after the Bolsheviks came to power, made the revolution seem imminent indeed.

If it did not take place in those days it was not due to any lack of advertising. The mere whisper of discontent was pounced upon as evidence of deep-hidden conspiracy. It did not occur then and it seemed for a while that the terror or

199

Reprinted, with permission, from *Scribner's Magazine*, LXXXIX (May 1931), pp. 521–525. The essay was written at the height of the depression when there was much talk of revolution.

hope, depending upon the point of view, had ceased to be real. But now, with the depression on hand, with unemployment on the increase and with the middle class discontented due to the break in the stock market, it seems to many earnest people that the revolution is here, is on its way, will happen tomorrow.

But such a revolution has not taken place and a social revolution has not occurred in any industrial country—not in the United States, not in England, not in Germany, not in any place where modern industry absorbs a large proportion of the energies and the interests of men.

We have had revolutions in France, and then the series that followed in their wake all over Europe. More recently we have had revolutions in Mexico, in Russia, in Turkey, in China, in Italy (if that be a revolution), in Bulgaria, in Hungary, in Bavaria (the short-lived Bolshevik revolution there); but we have had no revolution—no serious attempt at a revolution—in any industrial nation.

That is a strange phenomenon—even stranger when it is remembered that the doctrine of social revolution was evolved within an industrial environment and promulgated for the abolition of capitalism and the social evils it generates. In the face of this promised revolt against capitalism and in spite of the harassing fears of those most addicted to witch and heresy hunting, to the searching out of agitators and their more or less gentle crucifixion, nothing of the sort has taken place. In the face of such a fact we must look for the reason for the comparative peace and quiet that industrial nations, including the United States, have enjoyed in a century of social upheaval and catastrophe in agricultural countries.

It may be true, and I think it is, that the theory of a class struggle is rooted in animistic theology. This theory, around which such mighty intellectual battles have been fought, has as its background the universally accepted antithesis between absolute good and absolute evil, dramatized for all believers as a mighty battle between God and the

devil. Their repudiation of theology and theological con-
structs did not enable the theorists of the social revolution
from Marx down to escape the impact of this common underlying assumption. It was so deeply rooted that thinking outside of the limits of this antithesis was impossible. It may
be an irony of fate that the socialists and the revolutionists
repudiated the drama but unconsciously retained the motive
about which the drama was postulated. God and the devil
were denied; but uncompromising conflict between absolute good and absolute evil was retained. The theological
drama was shifted from heaven to earth—but the motive was
the same, God and the devil, good and evil had become
Labor and Capital. The actors were now human beings,
whereas they had been "spiritual" ones.

No theory of the class struggle could have been conceived
in a world where the older theory of the theological struggle
had not existed for centuries, and had not absorbed the
"spiritual energies" of hundreds of generations. It was possible only because people believed in a demon, and the
transfer of fear and hate, of hope and adoration, from the
next world to the present, was a comparatively simple matter and helps to explain the rapid spread of socialistic doctrines, of feelings of despair and hope over so wide an area
in so short a time. This, too, may account for the "religious"
atmosphere of revolutions—the hymns, the songs, the prayers,
the slogans: "You have nothing to lose but your chains, and
a world to gain." All of this is not said in derision. It is said
in admiration of the simple, childlike faith that has inspired
thousands of men and women in the last fifty years to give
the best in them to save the world from evil—the all-
embracing evil, "capitalism"—and to establish "heaven upon
earth."

The taking over of the absolute separation between good
and evil made it inevitable theoretically that the outcome
should end in cataclysm. No compromise is possible between
God and the devil on any issue, and the division of society
into two forces completely separated and divided, and repre-

202   sentative of two different absolutes, made the acceptance of
a sudden and violent revolution the only way out in theory
—and if you grant the premises, in fact.

In an agricultural country the evil largely arises from
the concentration of land in the hands of a few. The "Lati-
fundista" of Mexico was a visible, immediate and present
source of evil. The destruction of the one implied the destruction of the other. The death or disappearance of the lord
of the manor made the division of the land a possibility—a
possibility that could be envisaged, that could be seen. The
revolution was over in Russia when the Maujie took over the
land of the land-owner, or in Mexico when the *peon* divided
the large estate.

First you killed the owner, then you took his land, then
you took his cattle, and the revolution was over. So it happened in France, in Russia, in Mexico. There was a simple
objective, a simple remedy—all people could understand the
evil, all people could visualize the remedy. Not only that, but
the evil was immediate in the sense that it lived by direct
physical exploitation. The relation between wages and income for the master was direct. The owner lived in a non-
competitive world. "Unit cost" was beside the point. He was
not concerned with efficiencies, he had no machinery, he
knew nothing about stimulants except the whip—whether
in Russia or in Mexico. That was where the class struggle
did apply, or seemed to; that was where personal exploitation
was visible and felt; that was where immediate hate was
directed against an immediate object and the hate could be
quenched by blood.

A revolution is possible in an agricultural country and is
apparently not possible in an industrial one. I mean a violent
social revolution. That does not mean that violence, sporadic
violence for immediate ends, is not possible or even sometimes essential. It does not mean that we may not have and
may not need the tragic lesson of despair and folly, of heroism and faith, of martyrdom. But such violence is something
different from a social upheaval that moves a whole nation—

millions of people at one time—for one objective in a great cataclysmatic urge that seems to have no bounds.

A profound social revolution needs a scapegoat—someone who embodies the evil, embodies it and symbolizes it. In Russia it was the Czar; in Mexico, General Diaz. In each little place it was the Czar's representative; in Mexico the *Jefe Politíco*. That scapegoat serves many ends—emotional and practical. All evils derive from him—all power is concentrated in him—all good will follow his downfall. Such a scapegoat is non-existent in an industrial community. Political and economic supremacy are not synonymous. True enough, they frequently seem to coincide, but they are not synonymous at all times. And in a democracy, and all industrial nations are democratic, political and economic powers may overlap, but they are not embodied in one person at one time sufficiently long to make possible a concentration of hate to an extent which makes blood the only means of removing him. Instead of having one scapegoat for all evils and at all times, an industrial community tends to have many scapegoats, each at a different time and if at the same time, serving different and frequently opposing ends.

The point is, I think, clear enough. There is not one evil in democracy, but many. There is not one master in industrialism, but many, and they do not impinge everywhere at the same time, upon all classes and in the same degree. Industrialism is so decentralized in form and surely in fact, that political concentration to the extent that was possible under an older feudal agricultural aristocracy is non-existent. That in itself changes the complexity of the social situation. That alone would make a social revolution in the United States—a violent revolution—difficult.

But this fact does not stand alone. Industrial experience makes for many classes, and not for a class. It would be absurd to deny the existence of profound struggles between different social groups, or, if you will, classes, in the United States. But that is not a class struggle in the older sense, against the background of which the older theory of revolution is postulated. We have our struggles between big and little capitalists, between industries, between the lower middle class and the upper middle class, between one industrial group and another, between the country and the city, between farmers and workers, between workers themselves.

One needs to know the more or less primitive agricultural community that has provided the battle-ground for the social revolutions of the last century to realize how homogeneous its experience is, as compared to ours. The *peon*, the *moujik*, the French peasant—each in his place—lived a life that had a rhythm between himself and that of his fellows. Not only was there a common relationship between master and *peon*, but a common physical and emotional rhythm, a common set of tools, a common relationship to the seasons, a common relationship to the soil, all of which bred a basis of psychological and emotional structure that could be welded into one force, that could be forged into a unit of activity in the face of a common enemy.

No such experience unites our people, not merely in the different social groups, not even in the same industry. If you doubt this, think of the difference between the railroad engineer and the track laborer. It is not merely a difference in income, it is a psychological difference bred from different experience, a different relationship to the social, economic, and, perhaps most important of all, to the technological world in which these two men are working. They become different people because they do essentially different things.

People have often described the fatalism of "primitive" life—and one might add of agricultural life. One who has watched the relationship between a master and a *peon*—absolute command, and absolute obedience—a fatalism that arose of a class difference that had no bridge—a difference as in Mexico which was of race, of culture, of clothes, of food, of habitation, of social aspirations—anyone who has seen that will understand what I mean by saying that it was essentially a fatalistic world where change could be envisaged only in terms of a cataclysm because it involved a total change—the very foundations of the world had to topple before the slightest improvement could be made. The existing social structure was encrusted hard and could only be broken. It could not be mended and it could not be bent. It is from that hard setting that the theory of social cataclysm is derived.

But ours is essentially a world of compromise. The very divergence of experience makes compromise inevitable. The struggle for compromise is frequently bitter and bloody, and the attempt to compromise is often defeated. But from the mere fact that in an industrial society differences are graded and groups are varied, changes and compromises are effected in parts and patches, in groups and places, in specific details without at one swoop changing the whole world. That perhaps is as significant a fact in shaping the social psychology of industrial society as anything that one can pick on.

But a world of compromise is a world of converging values —of valuations—of individualism. There is no individualism in the Mexican village. There was apparently none in the Russian Mir—that is illustrated by the ease with which commands are obeyed and orders executed, even today, in the remotest village in Russia, and why even in Mexico the very phrase *Supremo Gobierno* carries a flavor which is totally unintelligible to one bred in an industrial world. It isn't fear, it is custom, it is habit, it is the conditioned obedience to command. Industrial experience does not provide such a basis for common obedience, for common faith, for common idealism.

Ours is an individualistic world. Good or bad, right or wrong, such it is. We work, not for our city, for our block, for our community, not even for our family. Increasingly we work for ourselves. One needs only to be conscious of the people about him to realize how lonely our life has become, how isolated, how self-centered, how "unsocial." It is not the basis upon which to construct a universal ideal in some utopia. There may be occasional agreement upon some specific object, but that is never unanimous as it is in the

206 Mir, or in the Pueblo. Agreement in general has become impossible. A Mexican Indian in trying to convey the public opinion of the village upon some matter in dispute remarked: "Say the children, say the women, say the men, says the whole village." He left no one out. Such general agreement has become impossible among ourselves.

Social revolutions have presupposed a community—people living together for a long time, having common interests that are permanent, common attitudes that are inbred, common ideals that arise from a common experience and the possibility of a universal rage. We drift from city to city, from industry to industry, from East to West, from North to South, from job to job. Our friends change, our neighbors change, our stimuli change, and the "Elks," the "Masons" do not provide an adequate substitute. We will continue to move. That is in the nature of industrialism: new industries, new raw materials, new tools, new power. We have no community and cannot have any. And without it a revolution seems impossible, or at least extremely unlikely.

But this constant movement has a peculiar effect upon the faith of the mass. It stimulates on the one hand "individualism" and on the other hand "cynicism." If you wish for an explanation of the practicality of American life, here it is. The struggle for adjustment is so great that compromise with the world about you is essentially an instrument of survival. But you cannot compromise over and over again without losing the pure faith in the ideal. We are "cynical" because we are so practical, we are so practical because our environment keeps shifting under our feet, and the effort to keep a foothold in the world makes cynics of us. The phrase "What is your racket?" has wider acceptability as an attitude toward people and their motives than one ordinarily assumes. To promise the utopia to people in that state of mind is a rather futile gesture, and only the innocent indulge in the exercise. The peculiar floating character of our world has changed the social set and with it the psychological make-up of our people. Their very life of compromise makes them incredulous.

It makes them selective. The general credulity of an agricultural community is an ideal sounding-board for any doctrine.
But an industrial community is rather different, as the
churches have discovered. The people are selective. They
pick and choose. They have to live in this world of ours. But
they pick and choose not only jobs and professions, but books
and magazines, they pick out their special favorites on the
radio, and in the movie, and in the newspaper.

Universal education has strengthened and fostered this
selectiveness, this individualism, this "cynicism." There is no
"instinct of the herd" in an industrial society. There may not
even be herds. And we have long suspected that there are
no instincts. Education is a good thing, of course; at least so
we all believe. But whether it is a good thing or not it is as
essential to industrialism as are letters to the alphabet, and
eyes to see the light with. Reading, writing, and arithmetic
may not be the rock upon which capitalism is built, but they
are so essential that they are increasing everywhere with the
machine. The information, ideas, suggestions poured in upon
one are so numerous, conflicting, and varied, that cynicism
is a natural and perhaps a healthy by-product, perhaps their
most important by-product. After all the "I'm from Missouri"
attitude is but a popular version of the scientific attitude of
mind. The general result of all of this is simple enough. It
makes for a competition of loyalties, ideals, plans, cures,
promises. The divergence of experience in the physical and
social world is made still greater by the divergence in the
intellectual by-product that it brings forth. The world ceases
to have unity, uniformity, faith, so essential for the establishment of heaven upon earth, or the reaching of it in the
beyond.

A common faith becomes impossible, differences of opinion inevitable, and in a democracy desirable. Not only does
incredulity increase but volubility as well. Where we used
to have one prophet we have a thousand, where we used to
have one faith we have hundreds. It is, perhaps, no accident
that in the United States, where experience is most divergent,

where common-school education is so widespread and individualism is so rampant, we should have so many religions. We will follow no man's creed but our own, and go to no heaven but the one we build. But that is not a good ground for a profound social upheaval. And it should be remembered that all profound social upheavals have occurred in countries where the mass of the people were not only agriculturists, not only confined and rooted in communities, not only followers of some common faith, but credulous because they were illiterate. There has been no social revolution in any country where the mass of the people could read and write, and one of the reasons is that reading and writing make people vocal and voluble. They acquire opinions, and still more, they acquire a desire to express them. The quiet patience of the agricultural community which harbors its pain, sorrow, and rage for a final outburst in some sudden upheaval is here taken out in talk; the more schooling, the more talk; and the more talk the less likelihood of a revolution.

The individualizing process of industrialism has generated in addition to cynicism a peculiar sense of social consciousness. This is certainly clear from the many and varied purposes that animate men and women in modern society. The impact of industrialism has destroyed uniformity of experience, but it has not destroyed a sense of responsibility for the outcome of individual experience. The very disappearance of a universal panacea has increased interest in the immediate difficulty. In part this is due to the spread of individual responsibility. The individualizing process has torn woman from her traditional role and given her a share in the industrial process. It has done for her what it has done for men—made her self-sufficient, purposeful, resourceful, cynical, selective. But a combination of physical and traditional circumstances—family, responsibility, children, greater leisure, greater interest in the humanities—has made women the bearers of the public conscience to an even greater extent than men. The activities of women in social organizations give increasing evidence of that fact.

Whatever traditional reasons have made them conservative, industrial culture has made them aggressive and purposeful, and the right to be counted politically has made them effective in helping shape public policy and public opinion. The full weight of the participation of women in public life is difficult to measure. But it is increasingly effective. No revolution is possible in the United States against the will of American women, and one would be gloriously optimistic who believed that such support would be available. It would be less available than that of the men in each particular instance, and for that reason more effective in the shaping of the changes in particulars by which our whole society seems to shift from position to position. The power of women to reform the world in little ways is the source of their power to make a revolution difficult. No revolution has ever taken place in any country where the women of the land had an equal voice and more time than the men to determine the range of public policy.

But this whole process of individualization is but one way of describing the "democratization" of industrial society. What is important about democracy is the fact that it provides channels for a grievance. That is its basic contribution to political technic. The channels need not be direct, they need not be immediately effective—they need only to exist. Their mere existence guarantees that they will ultimately prove effective when public pressure makes the groove deep enough. So long as the individual feels reasonably certain that he is counted in the final judgment, so long does the grievance lack the poignancy that makes blood the essential element in the solution of a problem.

As a by-product of the democratic process comes a certain sense of give and take, of "sportsmanship," that would have been and was impossible in a crustified and hardened feudal world. The congratulation of the successful candidate by the unsuccessful one is but the repetition of the passing of the silver cup to the winning team, for a year. The psychological process involved is not essentially different in each of these cases, and is possible only because no issue involves all of life, no battle is eternally lost, no cause ever hopelessly defeated, no promise absolutely unkept. This is, after all, part of the give and take, part of the "compromise," part of the "cynicism," of valuation—you today and I tomorrow—that is true in business, in politics, in sportsmanship. We have therefore a mobile world, literary, vocal, cynical, compromising, aggressive, and individualistic, with shifting values—and changing group loyalties, with political play (like the football game), a source of method as well as a source of power and hope. In such a world, a social revolution is not conceivable.

the social function
of trade unionism *11*

OF THE GREAT CHANGES occurring in our time public attention
has mainly been attracted to those social movements that in
historical perspective will probably appear as of lesser significance. The Socialist, Communist, Nazi, and Fascist erup-
tions, now so widely visible, may prove secondary manifestations of a deeper rift which has remained, if not unnoticed, at
least until recently not fully appreciated. The popular upheavals, so compelling in their sweep as to seem cataclysmic
in their import, are of passing significance because they rest
upon general doctrine subject to modification as the fashions
in the prevailing ideas change. If this dependence upon
ideological formulae is a certain evidence of inner debility,
their use of force to pattern the social design, dictated by
the formula, assumes a competence to model and freeze man
within some preconceived mold which is contrary to experience. The fantasies of a fertile imagination, under whatever
name, are not strong enough to hold the protean flux of the
people of the earth in an ideological strait jacket; and the

Reprinted, with permission, from *Political Science Quarterly*, LXII
(June 1947), pp. 161–194. This essay provided the background idea
for *A Philosophy of Labor* (New York: Alfred A. Knopf, 1950; London:
Jonathan Cape, 1964, under the title, *The True Society*).

use of force toward that end means, as it always has, that the role is temporary, the end violent.

These vast, but in their nature secondary, movements are merely symbolic of an underlying drift of the economy, which involves a natural, or rather organic, clustering of men about their work. This fusion has been going on for a long time, largely unplanned, responsive to immediate needs, irrepressible but inarticulate concerning its own purposes—because on the whole the trade-union movement did not know what they were. The lack of an "ideology" kept the movement from being obtrusively vocal, obscured its significance, and permitted other more self-conscious and more immediately political groups—the Communists, Nazis, and Socialists—to look upon it with a certain commiserating tolerance or to cast direct aspersion upon it, as something of no great importance. But its very lack of ideas made it strong, enabled it to concentrate upon immediate ends without wasting its energies in a futile pursuit of the "will-of-the-wisp." It could therefore go on generation after generation, with many failures in between, gradually accommodating itself to a changing industrial environment and, without challenging the political or moral ideas current at the time, nay while even espousing and defending them, gradually acquiring place and power within the community until suddenly it dawned upon men that a new *force*—not an idea but a force—had come into being. This force represents a change in the very structure of the economy and is of such a nature that it has compelled a new distribution of power within the communtiy. It is a force potentially so great that the balance of contemporary society itself is involved.

It must by now be clear to the reader that the reference is to the trade-union movement. The emphasis is upon the fusion of men, either in their respective trades or in industries, and upon movement. There is nothing static about it; and to call this profound social process, that has now for a century and a half been of more or less public concern, a problem to be solved is a quaint commentary upon our insulated optimism. It is still true that books are being written upon the labor problem—a problem to which the authors, by implication, have a solution. But the trade-union movement is not a problem. It is a process giving rise to innumerable conflicts because it has incalculable consequences. Its influence is felt at every point just because it affects every phase of modern society. The trade-union movement—movement—is not soluble. There is nothing in modern political or social technique that can write *finis* to this flux—or even give it permanent direction.

It is no more a soluble "problem" than was the rise of the middle class. As we look back upon the centuries of conflict which record the slow, patient, unconscious, but continuous, and at times violent transition from a preponderantly feudal to a preponderantly middle-class, commercial and industrial commonwealth, it is perfectly clear that there was nothing the older society could have done that would have prevented the newer design from taking shape. If there was a "problem," it was to find a way for the changes, or the metamorphosis, to occur with as little violence and destruction as possible. And so it is with the trade-union movement.

Though the trade-union movement is essentially conservative because it is concerned with the detail, the immediate, it is profoundly revolutionary in outcome. What is involved is broader than any political platform or party program immediately envisioned. Likewise, in proper historical perspective, the rise of the middle class was more broadly significant than the French Revolution, the Reform Bill in Great Britain, the revolutions of 1848 in central Europe, or the hundreds of other political upheavals recorded in history from the period of the Reformation down to our own time. It is in this sense that the Communist movement in Russia, the Nazi upheaval in Germany, or the socialization projects in the contemporary world are merely incidents in a wide drift. The issues at stake have been obscured because, in a world where verbalization has become something of a public mania, the verbal utterance endows the conscious and deliberate project, and therefore the thing of secondary significance, with a seemingly primary importance.

IT HAS been reported on the "grapevine" that the late President Roosevelt inquired of Philip Murray, the leader of the Congress of Industrial Organizations, what was the basic difficulty in industrial relations, and that Murray replied "insecurity." This simple word "insecurity" if translated into a phrase "individual economic insecurity" is from a special angle descriptive of our modern "industrial epoch." What the Industrial Revolution did to the individual, and especially to the individual laborer, was to disrupt his society, tear him loose from a traditional family and communal mooring and throw him upon his own resources. The timeless custom of being a member of a community, of belonging to a landed estate, of carrying on one's work in a family or a cottage industry, of being identified with a guild, of having a "mystery," in short, of being interlaced within a society as a moral person and having a specific "status," wore away more or less rapidly and in varying degrees. Man, for the first time in his history, was individualized to an extent he had never been previously. There had been unfortunate "masterless" men before, or itinerant tinkers or scholars; but here, for the first time, man in general was made independent. If he could get a job, he could live by himself, without a family, friends, guild, or craft. The complex technological and economic changes which wrought this disintegration—social, economic, political, and personal—are too well known to need detailing here. But the long-run consequence of this loosening of the moorings was unforeseen. As the process spread, it tended to embrace larger and larger sections of the community and more and more elements of the population. The individualization embraced not merely men, but women and children, old and young, skilled and unskilled; and it spread through most sections of the community so that a society of traditional "status" melted away and became increasingly composed of isolated, equal, and independent persons who for the first time became responsible only to themselves and irresponsible for the well-being of anyone—even of their closest relatives. The atomization of society had been set in motion, and it was never completed, even in the most industrialized societies, for there is no absolute consistency or logic to a social movement, except in theory. But its effects were sufficiently deep and broad to characterize an age and to lay the foundations for a series of conflicting social and political upheavals of which we, in our own time, are the unwitting heirs.

This broad consequence was symbolized by the increasing substitution of a money for a real wage. As the payment of an individual wage to an individual laborer—man, woman, or child—steadily supplanted the acquisition of an income, mainly in kind, that supplied an entire family, the atomization of society was accelerated; for a money wage made children independent of their parents, made the old and young equal to each other or made the younger better than their elders, made it possible for sons to lord it over their father, and made even daughters competent to abandon the family roof and live "independent" lives. Hordes of individual men, women and even children drawn from different towns, and from different countries, were thrown together in crowded urban slums to find, as individuals, the way to the good life that had formerly been provided by the family, the church, the guild and the community. The isolated individual—free, irresponsible, and independent—dominated the scene. (Pittsburgh was once described as a city of lonely, single men—lonely, but free, independent, and equal.) Man was free, if he had a job; independent, because he could leave it; and equal to his fellows, because each had an opportunity to be measured by his competence to earn a living. Equality for the worker took on a peculiar twist—to earn a money wage. It came to mean equality for competitive strife; to secure a job and hold it proved to be the test of all else and the very condition of survival itself. A kind of free-for-all became the prevailing rule among men, and the social and economic milieu was sufficiently fluid to make room at the top for many who had the energy, competence, skill, or shrewdness to swim with the tide and outstrip their competitors. But that was for the exceptional, the fortunate, the strong, and the ruthless. The mass of men found the going hard, the life a lonely one, and the vaunted freedom and equality something of a burden.

THIS broad social trend fitted into a prevailing theory of politics that endowed the individual with inherent and equal rights, privileges, and immunities, that presumed each to possess all of those moral and intellectual traits which would make him the best judge of what was of the greatest interest and use, and that ascribed to each a certain inner light with which he could discern the fine distinctions between good and evil, right and wrong, and take that course which was best for him and therefore for society. The economists merely strengthened the existing predisposition to an extreme individualism by saying that economic relationships between men, if free and untrammeled, would result in a kind of competitive harmony, where each man would get his just due and each in turn, even if unconsciously, would be helping to work out a natural harmony that was represented by all men working individually, each for his own interest. What the logic of the theory imputed was that each man was sufficient unto himself, that the self-sufficient individuals were equal, and that among such equal individuals only a competitive relationship could reveal the natural harmony the design embodied. Government therefore rested upon each individual and was derived from his consent; morality was completely personal, for on the principle of "pleasure and pain" only the inner man could be an adequate judge of what was good or evil; and, in economics, the principle of gain and loss made each man the best judge of his relative role in the harmonious scheme.

This body of doctrine endowed atomization of society with

a kind of moral purpose. The breaking down of customary and ancient "mysteries" that had clustered men together in small groups about some commonly held value, belief, or function was described as a good and progressive sign; and in its extreme form it may be said to have taken on the proposition that that society was best in which organized social relations and responsibilities were least. One need but recall certain avowed implications of Malthusianism and the "tooth and claw" perversions of the theory of the survival of the fittest and the currency gained by such doctrines as those embodied in Herbert Spencer's *Man Versus the State*. The theoretical justification for individualism seemed to lie in the fact that man was related to the government vertically, each by himself, and to the society horizontally not at all. If this is too strong a statement, then he was related to the society through his immediate family which was, however, merely an extension of his own personality.

In those circumstances it was natural to assume that that government was best which governed least. If true harmony was to be found in the unimpeded competitive relationship between men, no other conclusion could be drawn. The trend of events cast doubt, not upon the theory, but upon the compromise the theory had accepted, that is, that that government was best which governed least. Men looking about the world as it developed under the early impact of the Industrial Revolution began to question not its implicit beneficence so much as what seemed to them the needless suffering and evil resulting from the perversion of the government and the abuse of the powers it had. If that government was best which governed least, then to anarchists like Proudhon that government was best which governed not at all, that, in fact, removed itself from the scene and permitted these self-sufficient, morally competent individuals to work out the natural harmony uncorrupted by legal interference. That was one solution of the difficulty.

The socialists offered another one. They accepted the whole theoretical formula from Locke, through Ricardo to

218   Darwin, plus Hegel. Individuals were still equal; but, through
the control of the government, some of them, the propertied
ones, here called the bourgeoisie, oppressed the propertyless,
here called the proletariat. The class in each case is composed
of individuals, and the ideal remains individual felicity. "To
each the full product of his labor" is purely individualistic
philosophy with a new bias. But here, under the new version,
that government is best which governs most, for in fact it
now governs as much as is needed to keep the bourgeoisie in
their possessions and the poor in their poverty. The implied
notion in the socialist doctrine that the state will ultimately
wither away is understood to mean when the time comes that
all men are truly equal. The notion of the equal endowment
of each individual is thus the essential prerequisite for each
variation of this underlying formula that would explain the
process of industrialization and its impact upon modern
society. We thus have three solutions to this problem—that
government is best which governs least, that government is
best which governs not at all, and that government is best
which governs most. Most of the social movements of the
last century and a half in the Western World are in some
measure a quarrel over this argument—the degree of governmental responsibility for individual felicity.

THE current, however, was not all one way. There is no simple
logic to a broad social trend; and while the theory and the
public policy were mainly concerned with either fostering or
alleviating certain consequences of the increasing atomization of society, another and unheralded movement came into
being which denied the theory without repudiating it and,
where it could, counteracted in its own way the process of
atomization. The persistent individualization and isolation of
the individual that resulted from the Industrial Revolution
made men not merely free, equal and independent, but, by
destroying the social texture into which their lives had been
woven, made them economically helpless and morally adrift.

The element of personal insecurity and isolation lay like a pall upon all men—not merely the workers. Men had known insecurity previously, but not as individuals. They had in fact known it throughout the ages—pestilence, drought, war, and earthquake—but insecurity was collective. The community or the family or the city was involved. Men had their fortunes and misfortunes in common. Now, however, something new had come to bear upon the destiny of men. Misfortune came to be personal, and frequently the causes thereof were invisible.

More to the point, however, was the personal helplessness of the individual worker in the face of his employer. The reduction of all resource for life to a money income made the holding of a job imperative; and in the new circumstance the job was in the hands of an employer to give and to take away, without warning and even without explanation. As the Industrial Revolution became more inclusive in its effects, more and more individuals were cast into complete dependence upon the job; and as business enterprises grew larger and larger, the personal contact between the worker and his employer grew less and less, and the element of possible reasonableness and moral identity between the two became less and less. A new phase in the structure of the economy had come into being—numerous individually helpless persons, each impersonally dependent upon a common employer, and none individually competent to assert either moral or economic influence upon shaping the conditions of their labor or even to influence their retention of the job they had. They were equal in their helplessness.

What they had in common was their employer, the industry they worked in, the hours they labored, the bench or the machine they worked at, the wage rate they received, the foreman who ruled over them, the materials they worked with, the whistle that called them from their beds in the morning or brought a halt to their labors. In addition, they had each other in common. They worked together upon the same bench, inside the same mill, or mine, struggled with the same refractory materials, and were dependent upon each other's cooperation. He who failed in the assembly line, or delayed the flow of materials, affected the entire group. Something new had happened. The process of atomization which had gathered these individuals from many places by the inducement of an individual money wage, and the theory which asserted that each man stands and falls by himself, had now thrown them together into an interdependent relationship where the growth of a sense of identity became inevitable. Men were so physically grouped together in the industrial process that they discovered a moral dependence upon each other and a basis of common faith, interest, and objective.

Their individual helplessness was apparent to each. Their collective strength was to be discovered. But the fact that it could be discovered lay in the psychological identity that common association and common individual dependence upon the same outside source of power had provided. Their common association and experience gave them a common language—the language of the craft, the job, the shop, and the industry. They shared the infinitely variable talk about the job—interesting in its repetitious monotony because it detailed the daily round and gave them a vocabulary locally meaningful. The common employer acted as the catalytic agent that crystallized them into a self-conscious group. The atomization consequent upon the payment of an individual money wage was in time to be defeated by the fusing of men together functionally, and this functional coalescence became the organic basis upon which the trade-union movement has grown and which, in fact, made it inevitable.

The original organizer of the trade union is the shop, the factory, the mine, or the industry. The agitator, the labor leader, merely announces the existing fact. This is true in spite of the many instances of workers refusing to join a union. The process has gone on for so long a time, over so wide an area, that it must be looked upon as a natural consequence of the spread of modern industry. The trade-union leader not merely symbolizes the existence of a group already forged but also expresses its grievances derived from the common experience. The hours of labor, the conditions under which it is done, the rates of pay, the securities in the job, are defined by the job and the market conditions under which it exists. The union represents the spontaneous grouping of workers, thrown together functionally as individuals, for the manifestation of that moral identity and psychological unity which men working together always discover, discover because they need it and could not live without it. There is nothing new about this. The fact that it takes the form of a trade union is a historical accident, conditioned by the type of relationship the machine imposes and the doctrine that facilitated the assembly of the men in the first instance. The individualization and the insecurity derived from a competitive market, in which labor was a commodity like any other, made collective action the only means of asserting the moral status of the individual. The trade union, as visible evidence that man was not sufficient unto himself, always existed on a local basis originally, was generally unpremeditated, had no long-range plan, was often "provoked" by the breaking of some unwritten rule which had grown up in the relationship between "master and man," and had only immediate and specific ends.

THE trade-union movement represents a return to an older and socially "normal" way of life on the part of the men, skilled and unskilled, who do the labor of the world. If the historical record has any meaning, then we must assume that a sense of identity among men engaged in a common craft, trade, industry, or occupation is an organic relationship to the function. Men functionally identified develop a sense of their part of the social universe which is peculiarly their own and which they, in fact, can share with no one else. How otherwise explain the fact that the guild for traders, craftsmen, and artisans is a seemingly universal phenomenon? There were guilds in China at least a thousand years ago; in India we know of them in 600 B.C. They were prevalent in ancient Japan, were widely scattered and of long duration in the Islamic world, existed in Greece and in Rome, and were common features of town life in the Europe of the Middle Ages and beyond. These guilds lasted for centuries; in some instances, as in India, perhaps for millennia, and in parts of the world they still persist. They seemed always to carry with them the same sort of group responsibility, special distinction, social or religious identification, that set them apart as a group—sometimes little groups, as must have been the case with the 1,100 guilds in Istanbul in 1640. But, large or small, these groups had some authority, distinction, and recognizable personality. Their position in the sight of the law varied from time to time and place to place, but there are long periods when they had corporate standing, when their decisions were considered as part of the law—or at least when the judges took their decision into consideration. They owned property and had claims upon the property of their members, if they died intestate. They settled disputes among their members; dealt with questions of hours, wages, equality, apprenticeships, admissions to the craft; and controlled many, if not most, of those things that are an essential part of any trade subject to the vagaries of a market. Membership became in some instances hereditary so that the descendants of the same family continued in their father's trade and profession. At times these guilds were under strict control of the state—as was the case in Rome after the fourth century—at other times they shared in the control of the municipality—as they did in Liége after 1384, when the 32 guilds formed the City Council and retained power for almost three centuries. In so far as we can see, everywhere they seemed to seek objectives remarkably similar. They tried to control the labor supply by defining the conditions of entrance into the craft. They controlled wages, hours, prices, quality, tools used; they sought equality for each member; they protected their members from undue competition and from injury; they strove for security and for a stable monopoly market. Membership became a privilege, often hereditary; or, as in India, often identified with a given caste.

We have said enough to indicate that for ages before the Industrial Revolution labor in other occupations than in agriculture—and in agriculture, too, it was organized about a manorial court—was associated labor; and the association, or guild, always carried with it a sense of craft, mystery, status, conformity, honor, and responsibility. Every guild had its particular saint, its niche in the church, its special festivals, its peculiar customs, powers, and laws. Generally democratically administered, it enforced its decisions by collective action, strikes, boycotts, ostracism, and seemingly political influence as well.

The changing condition of the market—the difficulties of maintaining the rules of a limited monopoly implicit in the guild structure, the increase of the business classes, foreign commerce and the developing use of machinery—made the guild organization increasingly precarious. But its final abolition by legal enactment in France in 1776 and 1791 and in England in 1814 and 1835, and later in Germany and other European countries, marks a revolutionary departure from the historically "normal" relationship among men functionally grouped together. The theory of self-sufficiency and individualism, as applied to the worker, ran counter to historical experience. The early appearance of the trade union in spite of legal opposition, as well as its survival in the face of innumerable obstacles, was the reassertion of the moral fusion of men physically associated in labor. The need for devising a vehicle that would express the identity of the group proved imperative. The older functions performed and needs satisfied by the guild now reasserted themselves in a different organization.

The role of the new trade union was different, because the structure of the economy within which it was establishing itself had greatly changed. The older small-scale proprietary and family organization that had been the dominant form of business and of commerce was being modified, especially

after the middle of the nineteenth century, into a nonpro-
prietary, impersonal and corporate form, where the owner
—that is, the owner of shares—and the wageworker were
almost equally divorced from immediate moral responsibility
for the enterprise from which each made his living.

THE nature of trade unionism, then, has been conditioned by
the structural change within the economy. In terms of both
theory and practice, labor is considered impersonal, pecuniary, and fluid. A man is hired for the job by the day or even
by the hour. Not only is he free to leave his job, but the doctrine of competition and personal advantage made it theoretically advisable for him to do so if a "better" job was available.
He had no moral responsibility to the employer, to the enterprise, to the craft, to the body politic—only to himself, and his
advantage was measured by pecuiary returns, that is, the
price of labor. Thus theory fitted a substantial body of actual
experience. The enormous migration of labor from rural to
urban communities, and from foreign countries as well, the
high labor turnover, the persistent sampling of different jobs
by workers, in their search for a better niche, the ebb and
flow of employment with the economic cycle, the periodic
change of occupation in seasonal industries, the shifts in employment resulting from technological improvements, all
induced a feeling of insecurity, a habit of wandering, and an
essential moral indifference to any given job. This does not
deny that there were numerous cases of stability and identity
with job, business, or skill. But the over-all feeling was one
of insecurity and instability.

This change in the relation between the worker and the
job was only part of the structural change. The other and the
equally significant one was a similar change in the relationship between owner and the thing he owned. The millions of
stockholders—and sometimes the hundreds of thousands—in
a large corporation have ownership without knowledge, without direct responsibility or moral commitment; and if they are

dissatisfied they sell their holdings and buy into another enterprise. They are like the worker who seeks a better job, who
gets tired working in one place, who stands in line waiting
for employment or who scans the news advertisements to see
if a good opportunity is opening in some other place. We
thus have a double fluidity—both of labor and of ownership—
and a double moral irresponsibility. In each case the controlling motif is pecuniary.

The proprietary ownership by the individual, the family
or the partnership, where the living to be gained was conditioned by an insistent attention to details, by personal concern, worry and skill, by the fact that the owner was really
personally responsible, has thus given way to a fluid, impersonal, nonmoral relation to the industries from which people
draw their livings. The structural change represented by the
corporation is not merely its size, its great wealth, its impersonality and its pecuniary commitment. It is in what it has
done to ownership. Under the corporate form, ownership is
not only impersonal but also fluid. The purchaser of stock
has an ownership of which he can divest himself at a moment's notice, and he measures the prospect of profit in ways
that bedevil the subtlest of psychologists or economists. He
and the other stockholders own the industry, but they are not
acquainted with the managers; they do not even know the
names of the board of directors. They make no decisions affecting the enterprise; they feel no direct responsibility for its
operations; and they would be incapable of expressing a
sound judgment upon its multitudinous problems if called
upon to do so. The industry is operated by the managers in
the name of the owners, the managers themselves owning
little or no stock in the industry; and while the managers are
in fact responsible to the owners, whom they do not know,
in practice they report to the board of directors who again
may or may not be skilled in the problems of the industry.
These directors are in fact, even if not in theory, selected by
the managers to be elected by the owners, and their chief
duty as directors is to approve the policies asked for by the

management and submitted to the stockholders, for whom the directors act.

This anomalous and unlooked-for outcome, where both owners and labor have no spiritual identification with their source of livelihood, is not durable. It is not possible that a society shall continue which requires that the mass of the folk who make their living through ownership or labor shall have no concern with the source of their livelihood. The difficulty is upon us, even if its recognition has lagged behind the facts.

In its essence, trade unionism is a revulsion against the social atomization, on one hand, and the divorce of owner and worker from their historical function as moral agents in industry, on the other. If there is any meaning that can be derived from the persistent grouping of men about their tools or within their industry, it is the very clear attempt to reassert human experience, namely, that work must fill a social, a moral, as well as an economic role. The vacuum created between the job and the man has proved intolerable; and it cannot be filled by higher wages, shorter hours, better conditions of labor, music in the shops, or baby clinics. Man has to belong to something real, purposeful, useful, creative; he must belong to his job, to his industry—or it must belong to him. There is no way of permanently separating the two. What gnaws at the psychological and moral roots of the contemporary world is that most urban people, workers and owners, belong to nothing real, nothing greater than their own impersonal pecuniary interests. To escape from that— the most profound tragedy of our industrial society—is the great problem of our time. For the worker the trade union has been an attempt to escape from this dilemma.

There is still a failure to recognize that the trade union, as well as the corporation, represents a structural change within the economy. It is not a reform movement; it is not a political party; it is not revolutionary in intent; it is not a legislative activity. It may at times contribute to all of these; but it is none of them. It is the formal expression of the socially inevitable grouping of men in modern industry, just as the corporation is a new way of organizing capital for industry. The trade union is the opposite side of the medal. Where you have corporate industry, there you have labor unions. As long as industry and commerce were small and proprietary the very nature of the trade union was different.

MONOPOLY is the child of competition. Monopoly, or a persistent tendency toward monopoly, is the logical consequence of a free market, either in industry or labor. There are many areas where monopoly is incomplete, or only incipient. There are few areas in our society where the effort to escape the insecurities of the competitive market has not set in motion tendencies which, if unchecked—or perhaps even in spite of legal prohibition—may in effect achieve monopolistic results. This is true of the trade union. Trade unionism is often monopolistic, restrictive, arbitrary, often at war within itself, costly, and in contradiction of all the theories of a free and unrestricted market. So is the corporation. If ownership is going to be divorced from direct responsibility, be impersonal, pecuniary, and fluid, but increasingly represented by powerful corporations, labor which is also fluid, impersonal, pecuniary, and deprived of responsibility is going to be organized into powerful unions, paralleling the organization of corporate industry and doing for the worker what the corporation does for the owner—attempt to protect and secure his pecuniary interest. If "management" represents the "owner," that is, the fluid stockholders, then "leadership"—no good name has yet developed for this function—represents the worker and attempts to protect and secure his pecuniary interest. There is, however, one great difference between the role of the "fluid" owner in modern industry and that of the worker: the worker still has to be physically present on the job, or in the shop, or in the factory. It is this physical presence of the worker in the shop, as well as the continuing emphasis upon an impersonal pecuniary interest, that explains a major part of the trade unions' activities. To the worker pecuniary stability—a regular income from good stocks and bonds in the owners' sense—depends upon the security of the job. To make the "job" secure has been, and has remained, the largest item in trade-union policy: to make it secure, first, and to force it to yield a high pecuniary reward, second. That these ends may be incompatible, that a high wage and "job security" may in any given case prove destructive of each other, is a bit of economic wisdom that is hard to learn.

The drive for individual economic security is implicit in almost every trade-union demand. The current demands for an annual wage and for health, old-age, and unemployment benefits to be derived from a tax upon production are merely newer phases of an older drive. Nor can this new development be separated from continuing pressure for the closed shop, the checkoff, seniority, and the hundred other items, each of which is considered one more brick in the wall that would stem the tide of insecurity. In making the union the chief means toward these ends labor has created an institution of great power and expanding influence. From the small beginnings of a local union came the growth of other similar locals, and these in turn federated into national or international organization embracing all of the plants in an industry. The industry-wide organization was dictated by the needs of defense against the impact of a free national market. The drive in each instance may be local and individual but the sum of these local movements means a change in the relationship of man to his work and of men to each other.

The organization has increasingly replaced the individual; and, if the movement continues, there will be no individual bargaining left, and by implication no individual power, and little freedom of occupational choice within the economy. From the union's point of view, industry-wide organization became an essential of survival because it was the only means of protecting the organized worker, as well as the organized plants, from the competition of lower wages and prices. But the growth of trade unionism tended to strengthen the trend toward monopoly, by making it more difficult for the smaller concern with its lesser capitalization and higher production costs to meet the standard imposed nationally by the union. Thus, in its attempt to protect the "job security" of its members the union has tended to strengthen the very power of monopoly to which it presumably is opposed. It has, in an expanding cycle, imposed a standardization of rules, methods, wages, and conditions of labor. The unions not only have taken over or encroached upon many of the functions previously enjoyed by management—such as hiring, firing, promotion, setting of wages, shop discipline, admission to the industry, training for the job, influencing the introduction of new machinery, and affecting policies of sanitation—but also have acquired a whole series of controls and disciplines over their members, which in effect have changed the relationship of the individual to his job and his "freedoms."

The worker cannot enter any job he wants to; he cannot even learn any trade he wants to because apprenticeship may be limited. His career in the job he does enter is circumscribed by seniority rules; the amount he can earn is defined for him; his freedom of movement is restricted by the fact that he may not be able to enter another industry, or the same in another place, and by the fact that if he leaves he may lose his seniority and his rights to promotion and higher wages. He cannot leave his union even if he wants to, because if he does he will lose his job. He must carry out union policies, even if he objects to them. His freedom of criticism and of speech is restricted by the fact that local leaders are in a position to do him injury in ways that he cannot escape, or for which he cannot find redress, because recognition of these grievances has not as yet become part of either the written or the common law. He has little influence over the policies of his national union, and that usually only through his own local. The union's constitutional requirements for elections of local officers may be inadequate; conventions for the election of general officers may be rare, and the delegates seated may not always be those chosen by the local.

These grievances may be unusual in the mass, but they are not rare instances. The expenses of the administration may be audited by the delegates to the convention, that is, by a committee appointed by the president from the members who are part of his machine. The officers of the union have, in certain instances, as is evidenced by repeated court proceedings, used their power for personal aggrandizement at the expense of either the employers or the workers. The organization exercises police powers in certain jurisdictional strikes and hires, or entertains, as was recently testified in court, "two thousand men" to keep the "wrong men" from entering the job. Violence, though a decreasing feature of labor controversies, is still not unknown either in strikes or in jurisdictional disputes. In addition, the worker is taxed by the union not only for admission into it by an initiation fee, but by monthly or weekly dues which he must pay, with or without his consent. In his efforts to regain security and "social identity" in an unstable economy and atomized society, the worker has raised a powerful and growing institution that increasingly restricts the industry he works in and the life of those who earn their living at it.

The essence of the conflict is union power because, without it, the union could not survive. The necessary logic of the situation requires that power be increased. This conflict over power within the economy has society-wide implications; for power is conditioned by an essential function and is evidenced in its use. And so it has been in this instance. The search is always for greater security, and the method is always increased power to set up standards of economic life that will stabilize the job, and by implication the economy. The effects have been an increasing limitation of freedom of action and an increasing trend toward equality of income.

The older range of competitive freedoms is incompatible with the trade union, and equally so with large-scale industry under monopolistic control. The free market of the economist, by constant pressure for lower costs or a secured price, tends toward monopoly. The free market for labor, by constant pressure for pecuniary security—the same kind of security business seeks—leads in the same direction, toward monopoly. This monopoly may not soon become "perfect," but the tendency toward its perfection is always there. Historically, the ideal of a free competitive world where each man by himself is a representative of the implicit harmony of the whole, has proved self-defeating. Both labor and capital, when given the choice, have "escaped from freedom" and bartered away their privileges for the hope of security.

WITH these basic structural changes in the economy a new pattern of industrial relations has developed. Collective bargaining has become the immediate instrumentality for adjusting the day-to-day issues between labor and management; and the question raised over and over again is whether collective bargaining is compatible with the protection of the consumer, the maintenance of "full employment," the increase of production, the continuance of technological improvements, the narrowing of the swing between deflationary and inflationary tendencies, the defending of "job security," and the protecting of the individual against the loss of those "freedoms" so essential to a democratic way of life. All of these issues, basic to our times, are now involved in any attempt of the individual worker to achieve "industrial economic security."

[The] trade-union movement is a vast and growing phenomenon. . . . The Wagner Labor Act, passed in 1935, facilitated and speeded the growth of organization; but the readiness to organize was already there. If the movement, instead of being bitterly and violently resisted, had been permitted to follow its natural course, unionism would have grown more slowly over the last century, and would have had time to mature without the legal protection provided by the Wagner Act.

Whether slowly or rapidly, these new organizations of workers, functionally related, have acquired disciplinary power and influence over the lives and activities of their members; and, as they grow larger and more embracing, they tend to circumscribe and define the rights and privileges of men who are, under the law, equal to each other. There has thus come into being a new issue hitherto unsuspected: the rights of the worker within and against his own organization. The fact that over three hundred cases of seeming infringement of civil rights have already been taken to the courts by union members against their organizations is an indication of the power of a labor union to interfere with a member's right to bid for a job, or with his right of free speech, or with his right to see an accounting of how his money has been spent by the union officials. These questions are bound to become more insistent as the unions become more embracing; and a whole body of new law and tradition will in time have to come into being to protect the worker against arbitrary abuse of the powers that mere organization makes possible.

If membership in a union is essential for an opportunity to work, and if every union has its own rules of admission, apprenticeship, dues, initiation fees, promotion, wages, retirement funds, and social benefits, then every union becomes in fact a differentiated order within the community endowing its own members with rights and immunities shared only among themselves. It must be added that these organic structures are of such a nature that it becomes difficult or impossible to leave them because the penalities for desertion are severe—the loss of a job, the impossibility of securing other employment, the loss of seniority and of the right of promotion, and the surrender of accumulated retirement, sickness, and old-age benefits. Consequently, a new system of human relationship has come into being which profoundly changes the very substance of a free society associated with a free-market economy. The gradual extension of collective bargaining, with the explicit commitment to a single bargaining agency, with a tax upon the worker collected without his consent through the checkoff, with union security established in one of its many forms, so that the worker must in fact end by being a member and paying his dues, means that we have the outlines of a new social design, where status rather than contract is the governing rule. The fact that in theory, anyway, this status is voluntarily assumed makes little difference in practice, for the penalties for not accepting the "voluntary" status become unavoidable. This institution is now to be found in a vast number of industries, occupations and professions— from barbers to steel workers, from musicians to airplane pilots, from chorus girls to sailors. Skilled and unskilled workers, professional and learned occupations, small and large plants, highly mechanized and semi-mechanized industries are being incorporated into and made part of this pattern. Nor is there any immediate end to the process in prospect; and, if the history of the trade-union movement means anything at all, we must assume that restrictive legislation, or other opposition, which proved ineffectual when the movement was new, will not bring a halt to the process now, for the growth of trade unionism is responsive to an organic need —that men who are grouped together functionally must have an instrumentality to express their common identity and interests as moral persons.

It is noteworthy that these stratifications have been justified and defended in the name of freedom, equality and justice. But the freedom, equality, and justice here spoken of have a functional, rather than a political or civil, context. Out of the individual worker's attempt to achieve "individual economic security" has come the gradual remolding of industrial society on the older pattern of status. The very forces of industrialism that destroyed the older order have laid the basis for the new one. Membership within a social group, so natural to man, was inevitable again when the workers were congregated into industries where a common setting made the strangers of yesterday the companions of today. The word "brother," used in common parlance by the unionists, is not just an accident. It spells out the common dependence imposed by the machine. And once thrown together and given this organic relationship, all that has followed in the structure, form and impact of the trade-union movement became inevitable. The last hundred and fifty years are a strange interlude in the history of man in the Western World—a period in which man was "freed" from one type of an age-old association and after a lapse gradually re-identified with another one. If there is anything to this view of the matter, the system of "estates" now being developed is a necessary and logical outcome of the Industrial Revolution and satisfies both a social and a psychological need of man.

THIS trend is of so wide a range as to make possible in the foreseeable future an integration of the greater part of the working and professional population. A new type of group identification and loyalty is being developed, a new kind of discipline is being accepted, and a special kind of union power is making itself felt. These broad shifts in structure, loyalty and discipline are on the whole peculiarly unconcerned with ideological formulae, are but little influenced in their actual behavior or policies by "radical" doctrines, the "reactionary" union being just as self-centered, dogmatic, exacting, and "revolutionary" as the "radical" one. Their historical significance lies in their impact upon social structure, and not in their public utterances.

One consequence of the spread of trade unionism has recently challenged public interest and concern—that is, the power of a single strategically placed union to disrupt the workings of our complex economy and to cast a shadow over the social structure as a whole. A national strike by the United Mine Workers, if it were to last long enough, would throw millions of workers out of their jobs, bring transportation to a halt, cast cities into darkness, stop our ships from plowing the seas, and condemn the citizens of thousands of small and large cities to starvation. This great power, accruing to one or a few men, is greater than that previously exercised by one person or group. It is greater than was claimed by the head of any state; and it was evidenced only in special areas as a result of a total war. This implied threat over a total society—for it would in addition affect our defense as well as our ability to carry on peaceful international relations—is in its nature absolute power. It is a consequence and not an intent of the original effort of the individual miner to find security and stability in what has for him been a very unstable and insecure economic order. One would suspect that even the leaders were but dimly aware of the threat to the nation as a whole contained in their ability to call a national strike.

There are many strategically vulnerable spots in our economy. A national railway strike would be of the same order as the one just described; a power strike that would still the power houses of the nation, and sometimes the strike of a small fraction of the working force of a great industry—the switchmen on the railroads—would have like effects for the nation as a whole. Similar powers are concentrated locally. The few tugboat men in the harbor of New York City could deprive it of food and coal; the 1,000 lathers could bring all building to a halt in that great city and throw thousands of other workers out of their jobs; while the milk-wagon drivers can endanger the sick in the hospitals, and elevator operators in the large public office buildings can disrupt vast national and international operations. The exercise of power under these conditions becomes irresponsible and in practice intolerable. But it needs to be repeated that the impact of these new powers is a consequence of organization and not of the original purpose. We have here a curious outcome of the free market that began by describing labor as an impersonal, fluid, pecuniary, unmoral commodity. The fact that the laborer was denied the morally associative relationship, which he needed, forced him to construct an instrumentality that in the long run has accumulated enough power to disrupt the very society of which it is a part.

The willingness of labor leaders to use this power lies partly in the fact that the significance of the power they hold has not fully dawned upon them, and partly in the definition of the situation: the balancing of a national union against a national industry. But even more important is the description of the issues at stake as profits on one side and wages on the other. This makes possible the cataclysmic and disruptive pattern of behavior, when no agreement can be reached. That the argument should take this pecuniary form is a hangover from the day of a presumptively free, impersonal, and fluid market for both labor and owners, when it was believed that in each seeking its own advantage, it would help achieve the implicit harmony. But the very existence of the corporation, the trust, the cartel, and the national or international union is evidence that the free market has been greatly circumscribed. That the ideas which it generated, and the motives which it sanctioned, are still operative on both sides is made evident by the fact that it requires such a dramatic threat to the society itself as that represented by a national coal strike to call to mind that the structure has now so changed that even the language of an older day no longer applies.

The description of trade unionism as "business unionism" is merely indicative that the workers adhere to the philosophy of the free market seriously enough to act upon it, that is, to get every bit of pecuniary advantage out of the situation that the "traffic will bear." They wanted more wages, more benefits, shorter hours of labor, less responsibility, less work, more security. They wanted an increasing share of the total product of industry without commitment to a greater responsibility for providing the product because, as they understood it, that was the "moral" and economic ethics of the time. Get as much as you can, give as little for it as possible. They attempted to operate in a "sellers' market" to enjoy the extra pecuniary advantages of a "monopoly." The issue is not really their emphasis upon increased pecuniary reward for their labor; it is the insistence that this increase should go hand in hand with a lesser concern for the sources of production that made the increasing return possible. This divorce between a moral commitment to the thing worked at and the insistence that it provide an ever larger income has defined the situation now laden with catastrophic consequence for the economy itself.

One need not impugn the motives of the workers or their leaders. The "morals" of competitive business have lent themselves to the perversions of "getting rich quick," to the notion of "making money" and of "having a good job," "good" meaning easy and highly remunerative. The trade unions may not have taken over all of the implicit value judgments of the free-market economy, or been aware of all its sanctions, but they took over those that they understood and that they could use. The real danger in this situation lies, not in wanting an increasing share of the product, but in refusing to be responsible for producing the increased share. It lies in demanding an income from an industry without assuming a morally responsible relation to the industry. It lies in behaving in fact as fluid, impersonal ownership behaves which flows from industry to industry as the market dictates from hour to hour or from day to day.

EVERY activity of the trade-union movement could be shown to be a denial of both the theory and the practice of a purely free-market economy. We have here a reassertion of the necessary "sociability" of man, of the dignity of the human being as a laborer, and the insistence that man must in some degree be identified with his work, must be attached to it, and must have an attachment for it. Every discussion of shop rules, of efficiency of work, of the definition of a grievance, or rights and duties, obligations, and expectancies, carries by implication a concern about the industry; and the feeling, so evident in a thousand past references to "this is my job," is but a pathetic restatement that the work and the man belong to each other.

The dramatic character of strikes, boycotts, mass picketing, and public riots has obscured the less dramatic but continuous instances of cooperation between organized labor and management, and of the role of trade unions in creating a sense of identity with industry—through regulating discharges, promotions, layoffs, apprenticeship, and the introduction of new machinery. Even if the activity has been restrictive, it has been so on the assumption that the industry is of concern to the union and to the workers. One could cite various attempts to specify responsibility and to set up systems of cooperation between labor and management. But these are merely straws in the wind; they are the less important because they are often overadvertised and deliberate. The important thing is the evidence that the union, as representing the workers, insists upon behaving as if it had a permanent stake in the industry. The quarrels over the division of the income are indicative of that fact. The very strikes, from this point of view, are a healthy and morally promising sign. If the workers are going to quarrel over the division of the income, then they must in time become concerned over the production of the yield over which they quarrel. The attempt to persuade the general public of the justice of their demands by laying before it laborious studies that purport to show that the industries are in fact able to raise wages, and that the demands of labor are neither excessive nor unjust, is but another bit of evidence of the same inner compulsion. It is in some measure a way of easing a bad conscience, or of establishing a moral right to larger immediate income from an industry which is presumed—even if not asserted—to "belong" to the workers as well as to the owners.

This is merely a generalization of the oft-repeated statement of workers on strike—"This is my job." It is a different way of asserting an identity with the source of one's livelihood. And the claim that wages could be raised without raising prices—even if made for "propaganda" purposes only—is of the same order. It establishes a recognition of the fact that there is a relationship between wages and prices, and therefore between wages and the cost of production, and therefore with production itself.

The most significant of the many recent bits of evidence

of this sense that the industry and the union are interdependent comes from the demands for an annual wage and for social benefits to be drawn from production. It is perfectly clear that an annual wage can be derived only from a stable and profitable industry, and such an industry can be maintained only if the workers take their share of responsibility for keeping it both stable and profitable, that is, if they share with management some of the burdens of reducing costs, improving quality, and increasing production.

By far the most important of these manifestations was the dramatic request by John L. Lewis of the United Mine Workers that for each ton of coal mined five cents be set aside to establish social security benefits for the miners. The demand involved a shift in avowed policy on the part of the miners—perhaps greater than the miners themselves had in mind—for it presumed that in the future the miners were to have a permanent interest in production, and it presumed that the worker instead of having just a day-to-day wage contract would now acknowledge a lifelong stake in the mines. If the union is to build a system of social security for its members—health, old-age, and unemployment benefits, hospitals, and a hundred other items envisioned in a broad social program to be derived from production—then interest in production must become a matter of primary concern with both the workers and the union. A conscious lifelong stake with accumulated benefits is something of a different order than a daily wage; and the texture of the total relationship is involved. It is in fact an avowal, even if an unconscious one, of a moral responsibility for production and for the industry from which the miners are to draw the substance of their lifelong security.

There is peculiar irony in the failure of the mine owners to recognize this demand as an offer to become concerned for the welfare of the industry upon which the miners proposed to build their life's interest. But the older definition of the situation persists in both ownership and management, as it has so long persisted among workers and their unions, and apparently continues among the proprietors even when there is evidence that the workers are prepared to redefine their position, that is, to move consciously from a negative to a cooperative relationship.

Social security institutions cannot be built on a conflict situation. If the workers wish to construct a system of security to be derived from a tax upon production,[1] then they must become interested in the factors conditioning production. One of these conditioning factors is the provision of capital, which in turn involves ownership. Only upon ownership can permanent responsibility be developed. The funds accruing to miners from the tax upon production would presumably have to be invested; and the industry that provides the funds upon which the security is to be built becomes a logical outlet for at least a substantial part of the funds it provides. What is really involved is the extension of the interest in the industry to include a growing participation of ownership in the industry. There is, in fact, no other equally satisfactory basis upon which lifelong interest and responsibility can be built.

It is predictable that this pattern of industrial relations will become a conspicuous feature of union-management relationship and that it will involve the investment of the funds, in part at least, in the industry from which funds are originally drawn in the first place. The process has already begun. It will be long in maturing. It took over a century for a free market to dominate the economy to a degree that it pulled a large section of the activities of men in the Western World into its orbit; though even here it never completely embraced all of the economic activities of the modern world. It may

[1] The miners could have asked for a share in the profits, say five per cent, which would have made the demand consistent with profit-sharing notions of the past and from the industry's point of view would have for all practical purposes represented an addition to the tax burden. They chose, however, to stake their demands upon production instead, and unconsciously at least gave testimony to interest in the daily output and performance. It is at that level that the real issues in modern industrial life are to be found and not in quarreling over a division of the profits. Profits, which are an end product, are no substitute for a concern about the means of production.

take just as long for the newer process to achieve a similar impact upon the mass of men. But the older division between labor and industry is breaking down, and the growth of a life-long integration between the worker and his job is visibly here, even if it takes generations to complete itself, even if it never fully embraces all men laboring for a living.

For their own members the trade unions have reestablished the older head-tax dues, now collected as a matter of course under provision of collective agreements or, during the war, under sanction of the government. As a result, the unions have become repositories of large and continuously growing funds. They have in fact, like the insurance companies, become semipublic savings institutions. The miners are supposed to have $15,000,000 of such funds now in hand, and one of the clothing unions under a similar provision is said to have $27,000,000. It is logical and necessary that some of these funds should go back to the industry from which they are derived, for the very reason that a permanent concern for the industry's welfare can rest in the long run only upon a participating ownership.[2] It thus opens up a new source of industrial investment from semipublic agencies at the very time when a tendency to equalize incomes and reduce the great fortunes makes it less likely that great private funds will continue to be available for such investment.

IN BROAD outline the nature of the present drift of the economy is now visible. A system of contract made almost uni-

[2] The legal restrictions imposed upon the investment of fiduciary funds may place serious difficulties in this development. Should that be the case it would be an interesting example of one institutional requirement impeding the growth of another one, and it would force the unions to become heavy investors in government securities, would still further divorce them from an active concern about the industry, would shape their interest in government tax policies, would greatly influence their political ambitions and would lead to what in fact might become an attempt on the part of the unions to "capture" the government to protect their holdings of government bonds. One would hope that there might be enough wisdom in our democracy to permit water to run downhill rather than to force it to run uphill.

242   versal as a result of the Industrial Revolution has unwittingly evoked a reaction that has reestablished an older system of "status." This unforeseen structural change is wide in its reach, affecting the Western World and all areas where similar influences have shaped similar human relationships. The industrial machine has acted like a vortex drawing men about it, casting them into a special mold, endowing them with special needs, interests, and powers, and giving them a permanently organized relationship to each other, to the industry, and to the society itself. In the process the pattern of the society has in fact been modified. The metamorphosis is reflected in a not only dual but contradictory movement— a gradual disintegration of the older pattern to fit the needs of a free market and the reintegration of a new pattern to escape the evils consequent upon the free market. These opposing tendencies went on together and at the same time. The first unions came into being almost with the first industries, as is evidenced by the bill passed in 1800 in Great Britain defining union activities as a conspiracy. The change is by no means complete and may well continue for a long time.

While this underlying social reorganization has been occurring, a great many political movements have drawn their inspirations from [it,] and, misconceiving their own importance, have attempted to stem, direct, or ride the storm it has generated. The battles and the passions, on the whole, have been about side issues, because the nature of the social change was not visible and was not understood. In outline what is now perceptible is a society functionally organized, with men identified and integrated with their industries in a responsible relationship, with men confined in broad groups, having special rights, privileges and immunities that these groups make possible, and suffering from the special limitations and restrictions that are the natural outcome of such integrated relationships. One of the most important changes implicit in the growth of these organizations is the re-establishment of a proprietary interest on the part of the unions in the name of the workers in the industries from which the workers draw their living. At least for the worker, the day of fluidity, impersonality, and irresponsibility is drawing to a close. If he is going to have a pecuniary interest, he will also have to assume the moral responsibility that a pecuniary relationship has always involved, responsibility for the property he owns, the work he does, and the quality he produces for the rest of the community.

There is nothing in law, morals, or public policy which is contrary to the growth of proprietary interest by the workers through their organizations as a result of the changing relationship they have with the industry and the cumulative savings that are now accruing to them on an ever-increasing scale. It is not likely that these savings institutions—for so may the unions be considered—will ever own all of modern industry. But increasing ownership is a seemingly logical next step and with it increasing responsibility. These changes, implicit in the growth of the trade-union movement, carrying as they do growing concern with the nature and the role of the industries at which men earn their living, and implying a lifelong relationship to these industries, require the assumption of a reorganization of the educational system to make possible the intellectual and creative identity of the men at work with the industries in which they work. A new system of industrial education already envisaged in many incipient efforts both in industry and in trade unions is bound to be part of the process.

What is presumed in this development is that the union will gradually assume a role in the modern corporation by buying into it. This change-over will perhaps raise as many difficulties as it will eliminate. It will re-establish in fact a society of status—the "estates'" of an older day, with all of the restrictions upon personal mobility and personal freedom. But in a measure it has already done that. It will raise issues of civil rights and of the relationship of a democratic government to these new powerful semipublic corporations. In a measure too these already exist—the corporation versus the state, the cartel versus the state, the national union versus the state. The question of the relationship of these large bodies to each other and to the government will, of necessity, become the major source of both common and written law, the major problem of public policy. A matter of grave concern will be— as in a measure it already is—the relationship between the union-proprietary corporation and management. The problems of efficiency, of technical change, of free decision, of corruption, pull, pressure, and interference are all bound to plague management. But there is no reason to assume these difficulties are insurmountable, or that they will create graver conflicts than those the industrial system has weathered in the last hundred and fifty years. Presumably the growth of proprietary ownership on the part of the unions will be slow and their part in the directorships will long remain a minority share, long enough if fortune is on their side for these new owners to acquire the necessary insight and restraint to accommodate them to the complexities and exactions of modern management. And it will prove something of a trial, but perhaps not an unwelcome one, for management to find itself responsible to a corporation where ownership and responsibility are united rather than divorced, and the organization of foremen and other "managerial personnel" is in fact narrowing the gap between management and labor.

THERE is a seemingly normative quality in the latter parts of this essay—though the effort has been to stay within the visible trends and their obvious implications. There is no program of action suggested. This is the seeming outcome of the drift of our time. The present economy cannot rest for long on a system of fluid, impersonal ownership and fluid, impersonal labor. Labor in fact has already ceased to be in many instances either fluid or impersonal. If the presently implicit outcome is not in the cards, what is the alternative to what is here taken to be a nonenduring structure? The obvious alternative is state ownership—socialism, communism, state capitalism, expropriation, confiscation, revolution, or what not. But state ownership and control, under whatever guise—and the essence of the thing is the same regardless of the name it gives itself—is essentially a political solution. By its very nature a political solution is unstable. The rift between the organic groups in industries and the government will continue, as it has continued between the unions and the corporations, and between the unions and the government. To maintain its hold the government—just because the solution is unstable and political—will be forced to develop a series of policies or techniques arbitrary in their nature and dictated by political considerations.

All of the charges made against the Nazi and Communist management will be made in time against any system of government control. Industrial life is too complex, many-sided, subtle, and changeable to be handled by political dicta and for political considerations. The end result of any such system would be unstable, because the state can operate only through repression; and, in the end, either the organic groups now in unions will destroy the state or the state will stifle the industries and ultimately destroy them. Those who manage the industries must remain free in a functional relationship, or the industries will in the end prove inoperative. That is a lesson that folk bred on general theories find hard to learn; but a little acquaintance with the complexities of a modern industry, even a small one, will sober most men not wedded to an ideology.

The present drift is responsive to a technological organization of energy. Men have been massed into large industries in highly concentrated areas, in great corporate units because the form of the development of modern industry has been conditioned by a technology based upon coal, iron, and a system of railroad and sea transport. It is because the available energies are concentrated, the means of transport elaborate, and the basic structural materials and energy expensive and limited that we have the present form of economic organization. As long as there are the conditioning technological bases of modern industry, there will be large factories, masses of people in large cities, national industries and national unions as a natural consequence. It is however possible —and there are many signs in the air—that the movement toward decentralization has been going on for some time and is increasing. Such inventions as the automobile, the radio, television, the Diesel engine—especially of the present efforts to adapt it to fuels available on the farm—the development of plastics, the spread of the chemical industries in small units to areas where the raw materials are available, the use of windmills for the harnessing of electricity—an invention long in the making and now in use on a small scale [3]—the rapid spread of hydroponics, the freezing unit in which foods can be stored indefinitely—these and many other contemporary developments, not to mention the prospects of atomic energy, indicate the possibilities of a reversal of the last hundred and fifty years' trend toward concentration. If this should be the new development, and it would be imperturbable self-confidence to deny its possibilities or even its probabilities, the trend toward centralization and bigness implicit in the body of this essay would be reversed.

If within a reasonable time the typical industrial unit becomes small—say, employing less than five hundred people at the most—if it is located in the country, if the available energy and technology make possible short hours of labor, and the local plot of land provides alternative opportunities for employment during off hours or slack seasons, and if in addition the wide distribution of energy in homes is cheap through the newly developed Diesel engines or the electric windmill, so that skilled craftsmen can use power tools on a small scale in their own homes instead of in a factory, then it is predictable that a very different economy will be structured. Such a change will reduce the role of the national and international market, and reduce the importance of the modern corporation and the modern union. It will favor proprietary ownership

[3] The writer has himself seen small, two-paddled windmills used to generate enough electricity to light a small house and charge a battery for the radio in places as far apart as the Yaqui country in Sonora, Mexico, and in the Argentinian Chaco.

so essential to moral and personal identity with the work which man does and will again re-identify the laborer with his job on a very different basis than that implied in the growth of the trade union.

The interesting and baffling prospect to contemplate is that within the next two or three generations we may well see the growth of the powerful union-proprietary corporation, overhanging state ownership, and decentralized industry with its return of man to the smaller, more intimate social unit, and closer to the soil, all developing at the same time. I would wish to assume, or perhaps confess a hope, that, of those three possibilities, it will be the last that will come to rule the lives of men and give them back that sanity and sense of values which man can find only in the intimacy of personal association within small groups about a common task, and in close contact with the infinite perplexities of the soil.

12 group responsibility

AFTER SEARCHING the history of the labor movement in the United States for an answer to the question of how to discover the means of group responsibility to society, Professor Randall found that "there is no solution." [1] He qualified his generalization by saying that "no elaborate formula can be applied to the concrete material any more than there ever is a 'solution' to the complex human problem." [2] If there was no "solution," he saw that in an industrial society certain issues could not be avoided. Labor would somehow achieve a "reasonable equal status with minimum and possibly maximum" income arrived at through a graduated income tax. An industrial society must guarantee stability and security for the worker. Labor is determined to have a secure and equal position in society. [3]

There is a certain prophetic quality about this; it was

Reprinted, with permission, from John P. Anton (ed.), *Naturalism and Historical Understanding: Essays on the Philosophy of John Herman Randall, Jr.* (Albany: State University of New York, 1967), pp. 262–273.

[1] John Herman Randall, Jr., *The Problem of Group Responsibility to Society* (New York, 1922).
      [2] *Ibid.*, p. 269.
      [3] *Ibid.*, p. 224.

written in 1922 or earlier, when American labor was weak
and when the air was filled with recriminations between the
A.F. of L., the I.W.W., the New Unionism, the Socialist
Party. The author saw no Marxist "solution"; the American
people would stand for no more "post offices." [4] In the
United States, whatever was achieved would have to be by
agreement with the owners of industry. There would have to
be effective provisions against unemployment; [5] the industrial society must satisfy the chief aim of labor. Whatever
was accomplished would be done slowly. We did not really
know enough about the complexities of our society, and every
undertaking would have to be of an experimental character.
The chief value of the labor movement was its educational
influence upon the development of group responsibility.[6]
Education for "group responsibility" to society was "not a
wholly impossible task." This was certainly a modest and
conservative demand for a labor movement that had elements
of brimstone and fire about it, and spokesmen who talked
about the panacea of Whitley Councils, the miracles hidden
in the "New Unionism," the utopianism of a Eugene Debs,
and the Revolution of a "Big Bill" Haywood.

Forty years have now passed since these modest hopes
for an education of "group responsibility to society" were
written. How much evidence is there that the trade union
movement has become more aware of its "group responsibility
to society" or to itself? So many contradictory things have
happened in our society since 1922 that it is more hopeless
to seek for a "solution" now than it was then. The word "solution" suggests a prospect that is probably misleading when
used in dealing with a social phenomenon. It assumes a degree of control over the consequences of our deliberate activities which, I think, lies beyond human reach. If the word
"solution" is not usable, then perhaps "problem" ought to be
discarded as well. If one has a "problem," then presumably

[4] *Ibid.*, p. 263.
[5] *Ibid.*, p. 264.
[6] *Ibid.*, p. 250.

250   there is a "solution" given in the formulation of what is called a problem.

The labor movement is a movement of labor, a process, a drift, a continuing change which may produce many specific issues, like demands for higher wages, shorter hours, better ventilation in the factories, or protective devices against machinery. But these are all specific things and can be dealt with in different ways. They are mere incidents in a movement, a process, a drift. To the drift itself there can be no "solution" because it is not a problem. The labor movement is a human response to a changing material universe. It is an effort to maintain a "society," a very human need among men in a mechanized world which as it grows destroys an older society organized about the house, the village green, the church, the handicraft—a society where men could feel "at home." "At home" here has the very specific meaning of feeling that you are master in your own house and control the tools you use.

It is this inherent desire to control the tool, the machine, that explains the labor movement. It is a reassertion of the superiority of mind over matter, of the dignity of man, of the power of the human being to convert the material environment to social ends. The labor movement is a continuing manifestation of this inherent desire for self-identity: to be part of a community, to have standing, to play a role, to be a recognized member of a society. The contrast between the older and the new society is not defined in these terms by either the proponents or the opponents of industrialism. They see the issues as good or bad, as desirable or undesirable, as legal or illegal, as moral or immoral. In fact, however, the changing community is all of these things at the same time—on occasion more moral, on others less so; on occasion visibly good, and on others visibly bad. A historical process of many generations involving millions of human beings (there are now nearly eighteen million members in the unions of the U.S.) of necessity has all of the characteristics of history itself—it is both good and evil.

If this is the character of the trade union movement, it is broader than any code, precept, rule, formula, theory, or educational doctrine. What has been happening in the industrialized parts of the world in the last two hundred years is comparable in scope to what occurred in Europe between the Renaissance and, say, the middle of the sixteenth century. Today, we in the Western world are living through a profound reconstruction of society in all of its phases. Urbanism and individualism go together in the Western world. So, too, do mechanization and unionism go together. They are but the opposite sides of the same coin. They are indivisible. The large corporation and the large union are kindred institutions that belong together and could not exist apart. The modern labor leader and the modern corporation manager look alike, dress alike, have approximately the same income, drive the same kind of a car, talk the same language, and have similar goals.

This is obviously an overstatement—only some labor leaders have arrived at this position. But give them time. That is where they are going and nothing will stop them—nothing, except a reversal of the centralization of industry. For the centralization of industry has made necessary the centralization of labor, and both of these, the centralization of government.

When we are talking about education for group responsibility we are speaking in the context of a highly fluid world. We are in the United States dealing with a population that in the last hundred years moved from the farm to the city. Farm labor is only about 10 per cent of that engaged in all other employment.

The matter of fitting into a city-wage-labor-factory-union relationship became a primary burden. Accommodating the farmer—with his independence, his individual self-management, his very special sense of value-ownership of his own farm, his love of his animals, his house, his equality with his neighbors, his sense of being "[monarch] of all he surveys"—to a small apartment on a narrow street, a factory job, and the factory whistle as the guideline of his daily existence, was a major complication in the movement from the farm to the trade union. The difficulty is still with us. But man must have a moral reason for his work; he must have some identity with it. That is what the union has provided. It has given him freedom and status within the factory, and therefore in the community at large. The union has given the farmer who became a wage-hand citizenship in the society of the factory. In that sense it has "educated" him to play his part in the large community—and provided him with a sense of "group responsibility to society," in so far as he has it. I say, in so far, because he obviously has it only partially. But one could ask the question of whether he has it in a lesser degree than other elements of the population.

No group, not even the church, stands outside of its own time, place, and milieu. To expect a labor movement that embraces many millions of human beings to rise above its own time is to ask for something that cannot be had. The trade union movement cannot be either much better or much worse than the totality of the society where it has its being. It is predictable that its members will have a full measure of both the good and the bad current among the men and women who are their brothers and sisters, uncles and aunts, teachers and foremen, employers and governors.

There is the additional fact that in the United States a large part of the labor force had to make the transition not only from rural to urban, but from foreign to American. The worker and his children, in millions of instances (we had some fifty million immigrants between 1820–1920), learned to accommodate to a new urban environment, a new language; new motives, values, and ideals. All of this is part of the story of why and how American trade unions came to be what they are. It is as characteristic of them as of any other mass phenomenon—pioneering, westward migration, the gold rush, prohibition, and gangsterism. Its history is part of all of these elements in the American scene—and more cannot really be asked of it than what the environment both offers and expects. The expectancies in the American environment are themselves elements of change and adaptation in our enormously fluid society.

The transformation over which the "machine," automatic or otherwise, has presided has no visible terminal ending. The direction of the drift is recognizable by the marks it has left, by the temporary goals it has set, and by the body of law it has given rise to. It has done this very much the way a river leaves bench marks along its banks, or the way an ocean tide shapes its beaches. I put it this way because what has happened in industrial society was necessary to its growth. An industrial society goes hand in hand with urbanization, with faster communications, more widespread schooling. It involves a breakdown of the family and the support it has given to the weak and fallible human being whom it has cherished, served, and protected. It also goes with the breakup of the face-to-face community. The stranger becomes your neighbor, your traveling companion, and working partner at your elbow.

This is what the industrial process does, has done, and continues to do on an increasing scale and with increasing speed. This is "natural." So, too, has the response to this sudden wrenching of the individual from his customary moorings been natural. At first, the individual did not understand what had happened to him and reacted rather slowly to the isolation in which he found himself. His response was slower, too, because he had no philosophy that fitted his new situation or explained his direction. Whatever philosophy there was seemed indifferent to his state of isolation and helplessness. It did not confront the reality in which he found himself, and had not been developed to explain his condition. The individual worker, the stranger among strangers, without a family to care for him in illness, or to bury him when he was dead, had no explanation for what had happened to him.

What had occurred was the coming of the machine and the cutting of the social roots that made life meaningful. The individual must belong to something, to someone; someone must belong to him. He must "own something"—something that defines him as a moral creature. The union was the unwitting response to this situation. I say unwitting, because the justification given for the efforts to organize the unions were of another order. They were for shorter hours, for higher wages, for more safety, for a grievance committee. True enough. These, however, were mere incidents in an effort to re-establish a moral universe, a place where man had a place recognized by all, a home among neighbors, a feeling of mastery over the tools he used to earn the bread he ate. These were the real though unspoken issues in the initial organization of the trade union and have mostly remained unchanged. Group responsibility to the community requires as a preliminary the adaptation of the individual to the industrial environment.

The gradual conversion of the original farmer to an industrial laborer has taken many forms. One of these is the drift towards egalitarianism. It is probably true that a monetary economy must of necessity be "hell bent" for equality. The emphasis upon money is an emphasis on consumption, and an industrial society operating for profits tends to emphasize the acquisition of gadgets. With or without trade unionism, increased wages would have been a prerequisite of a gadget-manufacturing society. Making "money" has only this route to travel. It must spread the product among those who produce it. The trade union, however, added something to this inherent drift. It added the idea of minimum standards, of equal pay for equal work, of limits on hours of labor, or a right to a voice in furthering the process, and of recognition to a right in the job.

Let's look at the egalitarianism which forced itself on the machine-made society. One effort has been to set minimum standards of income. This has been done in many ways. We now have a federal minimum hourly wage. Every trade union tries to set its own minimum. The bakers, hatmakers, bricklayers, teamsters, miners—they all have their minimum wage. The theory of a minimum has spread beyond the organized union. It has contributed to a growing egalitarianism in our society. What has been happening may be seen from a few figures.

The lowest 20 per cent of income-receiving families had an increase of 125 per cent between 1935–36 and 1956, while the upper 20 per cent had an increase of 32 per cent. The total share of all family income of the lowest group rose from 4.2 to 6.1 per cent, while that of the highest group fell from 51.5 to 43 per cent. These figures are pre-income-tax, which reduced the gap still more.[7]

The same tendency shows itself in other ways. The wage rate of the unskilled laborer has tended to rise faster than that of the skilled. The skilled craftsman falls in a bracket with some professionals. The two highest wage-brackets include telegraph operators, boilermakers, electricians, locomotive firemen, plumbers, structural metalworkers, brakemen, railroad conductors, compositors, locomotive engineers, printing craftsmen. They are classed with teachers, artists, professors, writers, and chemists.[8] This tendency toward a minimum wage, toward national standards, toward reduction of differentials between skilled and unskilled, between craftsmen and professionals, between lower-income groups and upper-income groups, is evident in industrial nations everywhere. It is part of the drift from the eighteenth to the twentieth century, wherever the machine has become the major tool employed by man. These changes include old-age pensions, sickness insurance, unemployment benefits, social security. Institutions established by the state, the trade unions, or corporations take on services that were performed through the ages by the family and the parish. The pensions and medical care now provided may be more "efficient," but psychologically and morally they are no substitute for the necessary identity within the community. The only alternative, though "inefficient," is the union.

[7] Lloyd G. Reynolds, *Labor Economics and Labor Relations* (New York, 1959), pp. 535–536.
[8] *Ibid.,* pp. 482–483.

Obviously, neither caprice nor the labor agitator has brought these millions of human beings together into unions, either here in the U.S. or in other industrial societies. Because we are a society recently constituted and not yet fully formed, this gathering of men into unions has special features. The fifty million immigrants that we absorbed between 1820 and 1920 are still short of complete involvement in the new society. How long will it be before the Irish, the Jews, the Spaniards, the Germans, the Italians, the Polish, have lost all recollection of where they came from and become so welded together as a people as to know and have memories only of the United States? Surely, this will not be in our generation nor the next. And as long as this is true, everything in the U.S., including the trade unions, will have the character of a culture in the process of self-identification. The trade union movement with its violence and corruption is after all part of the American scene.

Part of this scene is the fact that there are nearly eighteen million workers in trade unions. They have grown from between four and five million in the 1920's to their present place in American society, where they embrace over one-half of all the manual workers outside of agriculture. Of the 30.6 million classed as manual labor in 1956, slightly more than half were in unions, while of the nineteen million white-collar workers, only 13 per cent belonged to labor organizations.[9] Increase in union membership from white-collar workers and the service trades will probably be slower than it has been from blue-collar occupations. White-collar workers and intellectuals are less prone to organization in trade unions, but there is no reason to assume that they will remain unorganized. What has occurred in the aviation industry, in the theatre, among musicians, is likely to occur in other fields.

What is involved is the way of life in an urban society, where a worker earns his living by tending a machine, or by occupying a chair among a thousand draftsmen in an engineering firm. How does he acquire status, moral identity, in "a

[9] *Ibid.*, pp. 3–37.

society" where he is known, or where he has rights and an opportunity to voice them? How and where does he acquire a sense of "ownership"—the feeling that this is *"my* job," *"my* factory"? The union, with all of its imperfections, is the only available institution which has, and the only one which probably can provide, this kind of feeling of "belonging," of having a "place," of being part of. To be able to say that this is "my job" is as important as it used to be to say this is "my home," "my family," "my town." If the individual is not to become completely vagrant, disillusioned, and destructive, he must identify with something higher than himself. The only thing available to him in the machine-made world is "his job," and his job can only be "his" through an institution which belongs to him. The only one in sight is the union.

This is not the place to go into a lengthy discussion of the wider meaning of identity with the surrounding material and social environment. But one way of explaining the destructiveness of our teen-agers, the young people invited to a house party who demolish the house, is that they have no attachment to the world about them. They do not identify with it. It is not theirs. The union has helped save the worker from this complete isolation. At least the job is his. Seniority, featherbedding, and other devices have been devised to protect a man's security, status, and dignity in a world that machinewise is indifferent to human values. This is especially true when men confront automation and sudden industrial changes. Whether or not in the long run these changes really mean an ever-narrowing place in producing, distributing, and providing the material goods that satisfy man's needs for food, comfort, and pleasure, they do mean that many men will find their jobs gone.

A man without a job in an industrial society is a man without a reason for existence. He can no longer provide for himself and his family. Whatever footing he had found against the tide has been swept away. He has become a creature no longer needed among men. If he disappeared, he would not be missed. For most men brought up in the Western world—

in the ethic of an individualistic society, in the belief that idleness and godlessness are synonymous and that a man is what he does—to do nothing is to be no one: not to exist. I submit that man reared in a world where hard work and ambition were major virtues will find this change unacceptable. Fortunately, these changes, though they may be sudden in the life of the individual, take much time before they envelop a whole society. It took a hundred years or more for the first industrial revolution to make its way in western Europe and the United States. It will take a long time for the second one, with cybernetics and automation, to make its way.

How many years will it take to replace the current equipment, to train people, to develop a sense of the necessary interdependence of resources, skills, suppliers, distributors, and users of the newer machinery to achieve a substitute for what we have now? Will it require a hundred years? Fifty? Surely, it cannot all get done in twenty-five years. Surely, the commitment to help industrialize the new nations will call for a great deal of effort, time, equipment, and capital. What I am trying to say is that automation cannot overtake us in a week, a month, or a year. We cannot know what alternative activities may be generated that will provide meaningful employment for many or most of the people who are being thrown out of jobs. Time is important, for we could not deal with the issue if it came like an earthquake. If the change arrives quickly, too quickly to accommodate our present institutions, then centralized government will become more centralized and men will be put on the payrolls as soldiers are—but with less meaning to their existence. But if the new industrial revolution comes slowly—twenty-five, fifty years—the union may prove a flexible-enough institution to make a meaningful readjustment for the individual. A feasible adaptation really means the provision of stability for the workers in an increasingly changing world. What the unions have done about giving the worker a sense of security is a matter of record. A part of this effort has taken the form of developing pension funds.

These funds are a by-product of the union's search for protection against those incidents in the life of man which in a non-industrial society were provided for by the family and the parish. Accident, sickness, old age, like birth and death, were looked after by relatives, friends, and neighbors. The individual's house was his hospital, his old people's home, his unemployment insurance, his childhood nursery, and his funeral home from which, when the time came, he was carried to the family grave. Only in an industrial society where men are hired for wages by the hour, the day, or the week could it be said that there was no place for the individual in his days of distress. In the new factory-dominated town no one had either a formal or moral responsibility for him. This is why first the union and then the pension funds were initiated. The funds were characteristically enough described as fringe benefits, something in addition to wages. They would pay for vacations, for a doctor, for unemployment benefits, for care in old age, and, finally, for a pension to the widow and children. These fringe benefits differ as widely as do the unions and employers.

There are broadly three kinds of funds. Those managed by trustees named by employers, those managed by employer-union committees, and those that are uninsured and managed by the union itself. In their origin, fringe benefits seemed like an innocent venture. John L. Lewis demanded and secured five cents on every ton of coal; more recently the International Longshoremen and Warehousemen's Union in San Francisco signed an agreement which would increase the contributions to the pension funds in proportion to the freight handled. Whatever the basis—and they differ from contract to contract—these payments have grown to massive funds set aside for the sole purpose of providing for various needs, including health, sickness, unemployment, and old-age benefits. They add up to many billions. The corporate funds, those managed by trustees appointed by management, have risen to fifty-five billion dollars and are described as the fastest growing capital accumulation in the country. The funds in the hands of employer-union groups and those managed by the union directly are much smaller, but growing. In addition, the unions have increasing sums accumulating from dues. The Teamsters Union alone has an income of some twenty million dollars a year from this source.

These funds set aside for various pensions, and derived from employer and employee contributions or union dues, deserve careful study. When set aside for pension purposes, the companies divest themselves of ownership in these monies. They no longer belong to the corporations. They do not belong to the workers. The latter are only entitled to specified fringe benefits provided in a contract. The funds do not belong to the banks where they are deposited, nor to the managing trustee, who is a hired employee of a fund. They belong to no one. Here is an increasing body of capital invested in industrial and government bonds to which no legal person stands as an owner. It is certainly predictable that the unions will claim increasing participation in shaping the investment policy of funds set aside for the protection of their members.

The smaller sums managed by employer-union boards occupy the same legal position—it is money that belongs to no one. It is managed jointly, through a trustee paid for his services, and similarly invested. There are, in addition, the large and increasing amounts derived from union dues. The $20,000,000 of the Teamsters Union annual income make a hundred million within five years. How much in ten, twenty, fifty years?

The workers have become the beneficiaries of increasing amounts of invested capital, and the labor organizations are owners of large and growing investments managed by the union—a role the labor leader did not expect and is not prepared for. For the ordinary trade-unionist, capital and wealth have always been mysteries he did not understand and not infrequently considered tainted if not unholy.

Sudden wealth has given rise to occasional misuse, sometimes dishonesty, by labor leaders unprepared for the role of trustees of funds belonging to the corporate body. There were no rules because there had been no experience. The management of money on a large scale is not an art easily acquired.

The question raised by this new wealth is broader than this or that labor leader's integrity. Experience and the law will ultimately deal with dishonesty here as it has sought to deal with it in other areas of money management, as, for instance, in insurance. The more difficult matter is the impact this new role is going to have upon the labor leader, the union, the relation between them, and the relation of the unions to the industries in which their members are employed.

The labor leader brought up to be a soldier fighting a battle against his employer now finds that he has another role. He must be a banker, like the leader of the Amalgamated Clothing Workers, or the United Mine Workers of America. He must be an investor, and so the A.F. of L.-C.I.O. and the International Ladies Garment Workers Union appoint investment counselors. He must operate an insurance company, or sit on a board of such a company. He must decide whether to promote a housing project for his own members or put the union's money in mortgages in expensive hotels, or golf courses in Las Vegas. He must consider whether to place the union funds in government bonds at 2½ per cent and then pay 6 per cent for money needed in a housing project, or decide to buy common stock that will yield him a better income. He must decide whether to buy the majority stock of a company to keep it from failing, as did the Hat Makers Union, who wanted to save the jobs of 325 of their members, or buy a block of stock in Montgomery Ward during a proxy fight, as the Teamsters Union did, and force a contract upon a nonunion manager.

The labor leader is suddenly a businessman, a broker, a builder of a hospital, the organizer of an elaborate health and medical service. As the union has expanded and grown in membership and wealth, the labor leader has found himself in many public roles that hitherto belonged exclusively to the businessmen, bankers, political figures, and men of the highest public standing. The fact that David Beck, president of the Teamsters now serving a sentence in prison, could be named head of the Board of Regents of the University of Washington, is a revealing instance of what has occurred and is occurring on a widening scale in our community.

What happens to the relation between the leader and the rank and file under these circumstances? To the relations between the local union and the national union? To the character of the bargaining relationship between the union and the industry? Between them and the government, at the local, state, and national level? What happens to the ownership of property when corporate bodies of millions of workers are holding, through contractual rights in pension funds, or through direct ownership of common stock, mortgages, and government bonds, an increasing share of the active capital used in our economy? And what bearing have these and many similar developments upon the question of group responsibility to the community?

Clearly, what was hitherto a private interest has become a matter of public concern. The unions have ceased to be private institutions that could carry on in secret. In a way undreamt of fifty years ago they have become public institutions, not only because of their sizable wealth, but also for reasons of public policy. The Wagner Act, the Taft-Hartley Law, and other legislation have not only given the unions rights they did not previously possess, but made them subject to public scrutiny. It is no accident that the United Automobile Workers set up a public review board to which an individual member, an officer, or the local can appeal against arbitrary treatment by the national executive board. Responsibility of the group to the community is here made manifest by the maintenance of civil rights inside of a large corporate body. When the unions become sufficiently powerful to effect public

policy, their activities become a public concern. The question
of public responsibility becomes more sharply defined and
the direction discernible. It is not an easy matter, but neither
is it a hopeless one. The growing practice of continuing consultation and negotiation between labor and management is
a step in the right direction.

Questions of group responsibility may be difficult, but
one need not be overly pessimistic in areas where public
opinion can make itself felt. It is more doubtful where the
labor leader has lost his bearing, his sense of direction. Is he
a labor leader or banker? What is the role of the union leader
in an affluent society, where most people graduate from high
school and in increasing numbers from colleges? What is the
language one uses to distinguish the separate roles of the
employer, the worker, the labor leader, and the management?
This perplexity could make itself felt, perhaps painfully so,
in a situation where the management of an industry, whose
majority stock is held by a trustee for a union pension fund,
was bargaining for a new contract with its own employees.
And such situations are likely to become ever more frequent.
For the unions, through accumulated dues, through various
pension funds, are increasing their stock ownership in American industry.

The process is a long one. But there is no hurry. Our
largest corporations are only a little over half a century old.
Give the unions another fifty years and they will, at the
present rate of involvement, loom large among the owners
of American industry. This is inevitable if we assume a continuation of the present norm in union-employer-government
relations. The problem of responsibility cannot be worked
out in a vacuum—a propertyless working class is a moral
anomaly which in the long run is historically intolerable. The
unions are destined to become larger owners of industrial
shares. The visible outcome is joint responsibility of labor
and management to the larger community. Public opinion
would in the end set the standards and the expectancies.

What automation will do to this trend is hard to predict. One thing is clear. In the United States, whatever difficulties arise will be resolved in a manner conformable to the politically possible in the American milieu. And the politically possible contains a substantial and growing element of "corporate" responsibility. It has already impressed itself upon our society in a measurable degree through the growth of the trade union movement.

the
university seminar movement *13*
at columbia university

THE FORMAL BEGINNING of the University Seminar movement [1]
at Columbia University can be dated from March 8, 1944,
when nineteen members of the Faculties of Philosophy and
Political Science sent a joint letter to Dr. Frank Fackenthal,
then Acting President, suggesting the establishment of a
series of *permanent* seminars. This proposal was in some
measure the result of many years of heart-searching discus-
sions, first by the Woodbridge Committee, appointed by
President Butler some years before the Second World War,
and later by a special committee under the leadership of Professor Philip C. Jessup.

Professor Edgar G. Miller describes the activities of this
second committee in the following words:

> In the winter of 1940–41, the world was in as much a mess
> as now, and the University was terribly worried. President
> Butler asked Jessup to ask the University to get conscious.
> The point of view on which that original thinking started was
> that the university scholars as individual scholars were con-
> tributing heavily to the world. Here on Morningside Heights
> our concentration of special knowledge, and adding New

Reprinted, with permission, from *Political Science Quarterly*, LXVIII
(June 1963), pp. 161–180.

[1] There is a widespread feeling that the present name is misleading.
These new institutions are not properly seminars. It has been suggested
that we call them Fellowships, Academies, Institutes, or what seems the
most generally favored name, *Collegia*. If adopted, then they could be
described as the Collegia at Columbia University, and each separate
association would then be the Collegium on the State, Religion, Professions, and so on.

York City, was pretty hot. Was there any way of bringing this specialized knowledge, apart from individual efforts, into focus on problems presented to the University and to the world? The technique was the problem. Butler appointed a committee with no name. It became the program committee on the University project. It met for over a year, trying to find out a method of focusing details transcending any one department or discipline, or any one conceivably wise man. We flunked the project completely. There was a dream that we could add a new function. Creation, preservation, and transmission of knowledge was the University's job. If we could only create something to focus these things and transcend the lines. It was a dismal failure, but with indirect values all around. About six years ago the Faculty of Political Science dreamed up this seminar thing—the best answer available. The problem that originally sparked the whole thing—the ability to focus on a problem—is really the reason for the seminars.[2]

It is interesting to note that an outline of the University Seminar idea was made before this committee by the member of the faculty who in 1944 drafted the letter to Acting President Fackenthal. Mr. Fackenthal deserves the greatest credit for this development at Columbia.

The letter follows:

COLUMBIA UNIVERSITY

IN THE CITY OF NEW YORK

DEPARTMENT OF HISTORY

March 8, 1944

Memorandum to: Mr. Frank Fackenthal
From the Undersigned:

Professor William L. Westermann	Professor Wesley C. Mitchell
Professor Harry J. Carman	Professor Ralph Linton
Professor James T. Shotwell	Professor Arthur W. Macmahon
Professor Horatio Smith	Professor John H. Randall
Professor Robert L. Schuyler	Professor James Gutmann
Professor Horace L. Friess	Professor Philip C. Jessup
Professor Herbert W. Schneider	Professor Leo Wolman
Professor John A. Krout	Professor Joseph P. Chamberlain
Professor Schuyler C. Wallace	Professor Frederick C. Mills
Professor Frank Tannenbaum	

[2] From the mimeographed Report on University Seminars for 1950, p. 5.

The undersigned, in response to your letter of February 15, 1944, wish respectfully to submit the following proposal for a series of permanent seminars within the Faculty of Political Science. These seminars are conceived of as being, in effect, permanent, independent organisms within the Faculty cutting across all departments and calling for cooperative participation from scholars in various fields. It is proposed that in addition to the existing facilities for study and research provided by the Faculty of Political Science and by the other faculties through courses and seminars given by individual professors, the University announce the establishment of perhaps no more than half a dozen seminars devoted to the study of some of the basic institutions continuous in human society, such, for instance, as the state, war, the organization of labor including the history of slavery, crime, or such ever-present issues as conflict between church and state, friction between urban and rural areas, or the human family. Each seminar would, therefore, be devoted to the continuous study of one of the basic human institutions. These institutions are more comprehensive than any course or any department and reach beyond the present organization of any faculty.

The professors grouped in this type of seminar could be considered as the continuous, intellectual servitors of a permanent institution. It would be their privilege and their task to explore the history and unravel the complex and manifold influences of such an institution. An example perhaps would illustrate the point. Crime, for instance, is as eternal as human society. It has been part and parcel of human development and its ramifications touch every phase of the social structure. A properly staffed seminar on crime would include as a minimum the following personnel: the historian, sociologist, psychiatrist, educator, political scientist interested in municipal problems, lawyer specializing in criminal law, anthropologist interested in crime amongst primitive peoples, and specialists concerned with judicial administration and police and penal administration. Even so the list is probably not complete. It is obvious from the above that the institution of crime is bigger than the Department of Sociology.

Another instance would be a seminar on slavery with which some of the signers of this memorandum have had experience. Slavery as a system of the organization of labor has been a practically continuous institution in the history of man. A proper seminar in this field would include an historian, economist, political scientist, sociologist, lawyer interested in the civil law, anthropologist, and perhaps others. It is again obvious that the institution of slavery is greater than the Department of History or the Department of Economics. Another illustration would be the history of the state, which ordinarily falls within the province of political science or philosophy. But a seminar on the history of the state that would attempt to study the ramifications of the state as an institution would include a philosopher interested in political theory, an economist interested in taxation, a political scientist especially interested in the civil service and bureaucracy, a geographer, an historian, a lawyer interested in public law, and probably one interested in international law. Again the list is obviously incomplete. Again it is clear that the institution of the state is greater than any department or than any professor in any department.

We have probably said enough to indicate the type of organisms we wish to see established in the Faculty of Political Science. Our reasons for wishing to see them established are too obvious to require much elaboration. But we should like to point out that it would achieve one of the things long sought for—cooperation between the departments of the Faculty of Political Science, as well as with other departments in the University. It would, for the purpose of those seminars, obliterate the departmental lines and throw the emphasis from a "subject" to a "going concern." The seminars themselves, which, as we indicated in the beginning, ought to be limited to perhaps half a dozen, should be very carefully defined both in terms of the pertinent and permanent issues around which they are organized and in view of the available personnel in the University. It is not proposed to abolish, reorganize, or in any way interfere with the traditional and habitual procedure either in the Faculty of Political Science or in the different departments. The only thing that is proposed is that interested members within the departments group themselves together in the service of one or more of these continuing study groups.

1] The seminar so constituted would be not only interdepartmental, but also interfaculty and might even include people completely outside the University.

2] These seminars would be permanent and have an organic existence of their own regardless of personnel changes in the faculty.

3] The seminar would draw its students either by direct registration or by the professors bringing some of their own students into it for special purposes.

4] The seminar would be administered not by a department or by a faculty as such, but by those faculty members who make up the seminar.

5] The seminar would have from year to year the same name and in time develop its own traditional status within the faculty and the University.

6] The seminar would in time, and the sooner the better, develop its own publication either from seminar papers or from articles contributed by the staff, and we could project into the future a series of publications under the auspices of a slavery seminar at Columbia University or the seminar on crime at Columbia University or the seminar on war at Columbia University.

7] This in time would give the seminars personality and character not only within the University, but in the outside world and serve to attract students from different parts of the United States or from different countries who, being especially interested in one of the major institutions to which one of the seminars is devoted, would come to Columbia to do their serious work in that seminar, regardless of the faculty or the department in which they are registered.

8] It is foreseeable that a student coming to Columbia to take his doctoral degree in the Law School would really write his thesis on some aspect of the law of slavery and have it published as one of the series under the auspicies of the seminar on slavery at Columbia University.

9] Instead of writing his thesis by himself in some corner in consultation only with his professor, he would really be writing it in the face of criticism of the entire group of those in the seminar who are interested in that institution.

10] In time to come it might even be possible that this seminar serve as the examining board for the doctoral dissertations written in that field.

To recapitulate the argument: the proposal assumes that it is the function of the University to so organize its energies formally as to devote part of them to a continuous research, study, analysis, and interpretation of a number of the more important and eternal institutions. These seminars, though permanent within the faculty, involve no reorganization of the faculty itself or of the departments. It is only projected that certain members in the departments will devote part of their energies to the seminars because they are already interested in those institutions. It is assumed that these seminars would be self-governing and call for no elaborate overhead administration. It is assumed that in the long run the personnel within the departments might be strengthened with a view to strengthening one or another seminar. It is assumed that a seminar would have a historical perspective without losing a current concern for current issues in human life. It is assumed that graduate students would be able to do their work within these seminars for their degrees. It is assumed that the seminars would develop their own traditions and character and their individual reputations in the world and have their own regular publications. It is assumed also that such a harnessing of the energies of some members of the staff within the University would stimulate intellectual cooperation within the faculty, influence the teaching, vitalize the student's interest in his graduate work, attract students from outside of the University and from other parts of the world, who would become votaries of one or other of these institutions, and would lead both by writing and through the training of personnel to a more direct participation of the University in resolving the many issues that afflict our contemporary world.

This letter was circulated among the members of the University family by George B. Pegram, Dean of the Graduate Faculties. The proposal was widely discussed and, in the end, formally approved at a meeting presided over by Professor Austin P. Evans. In 1945, the movement was set in motion with the establishment of five University Seminars.

UNCONSCIOUSLY, perhaps, the University Seminar movement has a theory of the integration of human experience, as well as its own notion of the structure of knowledge that is different from that which underlies the organization of the University. Our Faculties of Political Science, Philosophy, and Pure Science, and our professional schools as well, are compounded of departments which rest upon the assumed existence of "disciplines." The discipline is conceived of as some unique body of knowledge—practical and theoretical—which is sufficiently self-contained, pure, isolated, and independent, so that it can be studied meaningfully by itself. The University, in building a separate department for each unique discipline, and then grouping them in faculties or schools, becomes the depository of all knowledge without violating the essential separateness of each discipline.

In contrast, the University Seminar movement sees society organized in many continuing institutions, enriched by experiences peculiar to themselves, and possessed of knowledge and wisdom derived from their own associated existence. The church, the trade union, the corporation, the state, organized crime, the military establishment, the educational system, are separate professional orders, with a logic uniquely different, and shared only by the initiated in each separate order. These permanent groups, going concerns, and institutions are the constituent bodies of our society. Each perennial group, going concern, and institution is a structure of knowledge, experience and practice. The University Seminars aim to encompass all of these elements by building an academic fellowship in which they are represented. The University Seminar, therefore, reaches for membership into all disciplines and activities pertinent to the objective—the understanding of the behavior of a going concern.

AS CAN be seen from the following table, the five University Seminars organized in 1945 have now grown [as of 1953] to thirteen.

The University Seminars have within the last two years expanded beyond the Faculties of Political Science and Philosophy in which they were first developed. It seemed for some time that they might not lend themselves to other fields. But we now have a vigorous University Seminar on The

272 Theory and Practice of Organization Management initiated in the School of Industrial Engineering by Professor Robert T. Livingston. Professor L. C. Dunn, of the Department of Zoology, has organized in the biological sciences a seminar on human variation. Though not at present formally included within the University Seminar family, it is still part of the same development.

Seminar	Founded
The State	1945
Peace	1945
Religion	1945
The Renaissance	1945
Rural Life	1945
Content and Methods of the Social Sciences	1947
Labor	1948
Population [3]	1949
The Professions	1950
Education	1950
Organization and Management	1951
Communication	1951
Human Variation [4]	1952

This year there are 280 people attached to our Seminars. Of these, 193 are members of the University faculty, 42 are drawn from 21 other institutions of higher learning, and 45 come from 31 different nonacademic activities.

THE University Seminars are independent bodies, authorized but not administered by the University. Functionally, they are attached to the University through a subcommittee and chairman chosen by the Joint Committee on Graduate Instruction.

The University also provides for the expenses of these new institutions, and gives academic credit to students ad-

[3] In abeyance, 1951–52.
[4] Not formally grouped within the University Seminar family, but part of the general movement at the University.

mitted into the University Seminars. The Trustees have created the honorary title of University Seminar Associate for
members drawn from beyond the Columbia family.

BEYOND these limited administrative connections, the University Seminars are voluntary and independent associations.
No pressure to join is brought to bear upon any member of
the faculty. Membership is based upon invitation. The time
and energy devoted to this activity are an addition to the
academic responsibilities that faculty members carry. Nor is
there any remuneration for the time given to these fellowships, and members of the faculty have devoted many hundreds of hours to these new academic bodies. The University
has not actively fomented the growth of these associations.
They have developed spontaneously in response to the interest and needs of members of the faculty. Some one or more
members of the faculty become concerned over an issue
which they feel can best be dealt with in cooperation with
others. A small committee may be formed for the purpose of
surveying the field to which the proposed University Seminar
is to be devoted, and to discuss the available personnel from
which the original membership might be drawn. If the conditions seem propitious, the question of formal establishment
of the group as a University Seminar is then raised with the
chairman of the subcommittee in charge of the University
Seminars.

The question of acceptability is dependent upon the following conditions.

1] Are the issues to be examined perennial in character, and
of such significance as to justify the establishment of a
permanent group within the University?

2] Are the questions raised best to be dealt with by drawing together specialists from many different academic
disciplines and, where feasible, from nonacademic activities as well?

274   3] Is the membership of the proposed group likely to guar-
        antee the highest standards of academic competence
        and scientific objectivity?

If these broad conditions are met, the University Seminar
receives formal approval, and is listed in the University an-
nouncements; it can draw on the small amount of financial
support provided by the University, and have its outside
members given Trustee appointments as University Seminar
Associates.

From that point, the newly associated scholars are completely on their own. They elect their own chairman, who is
theoretically reelected annually. They determine their own
future membership, and their own program. They decide how
often they will meet, how they will work, and whether or not
they will accept students, and what the qualifications of such
students shall be. They pick their own secretary, usually a
junior member of the University faculty, who may receive a
very small stipend out of the funds provided by the University.

CONCERNED as they are with the many-sided incidence of
perennial institutions, groups, activities, or issues, the University Seminars choose their members so as to satisfy their
special requirements, and they may have as many different
disciplines represented as they have members. If the group
so desires, it invites professors from other universities. Most
of our University Seminars have active participants from
neighboring institutions of higher learning.

In addition to participants from other academic institutions, the Seminars draw members from many nonacademic
activities.

The theory on which the Seminars rest recognizes no
sharp divisions between the academic and nonacademic
world. It assumes that all the many facets of any going concern are equally important, and, if possible, all should be

represented. The "practical people"—the judge, the district attorney, the policeman, the prison warden—are as important to a continuing study of the many-sided activity known as crime as is the sociologist, psychologist, jurist, or professor of criminal law. Only by bringing face to face all who are professionally involved in these matters can the issues be seen in their totality.

The academic and nonacademic members are invited to permanent membership, for only by continued association over many years can these varied bodies of knowledge and experience be merged into a common language system without which understanding is not really feasible. It requires long informal association between men variously trained and attuned to different preoccupations before they can communicate to each other the essence of their own insight.

THE University Seminar is an independent universe. Its boundaries are limited only by its horizons. It is confined only by its own intellectual commitments, and these change with time and changing personnel. It has only one reason for being: the desire to understand the workings and to unravel the hidden mysteries of a continuing activity which we call an institution. The group is held together by the experience of supporting one another's curiosities, and deepening one another's insights. Each member already knows a great many facts about the institution, and many of them spend their lives in research, or in finding their way in the maze of conflicting pressures and contradictory choices which we call practical life.

The University Seminar is neither a research institution nor a board of directors. It is an intellectual fellowship which deals with ideas rather than facts—if such a distinction has any meaning. It wants to know why the research workers want these particular facts rather than others, and why certain conclusions are to be drawn from the facts when they might yield many others besides. It is concerned with meaning, direction, drift, purpose, value. The facts are plentiful; their many-sided significance is often hidden. That is why the membership drawn from every context is needed, and that is where it is useful. Nor is the University Seminar a board of directors drawing up plans and making decisions. It is concerned about why the plans were drawn, and the decisions made, and their many results and implications. It plays the role of evaluating the practice and policy of the institution in the light of the given ends and purposes.

The University Seminar is not an educational project. It is, however, an educational process, an associated way of learning among mature scholars who teach each other. Many specific riddles that need to be unraveled may arise in this process. Each riddle in turn may then become a project, just as buying a dinner or renting a room is a kind of project in daily living. But the dinner and the room are incidents in a life, and so the projects that may arise are incidents in the life of this kind of intellectual fellowship.

Neither can it be said that the University Seminar has a particular method. Each facet of each institution, as it is studied in turn, calls for its own method, and each member adds to the skill, competence, and variety of methods available. The Seminar has as many methods at its disposal as it has members, and each possible combination of members and their special gifts, training, and experience.

This was noticeable, for instance, in one Seminar when the question under discussion required a broad knowledge of languages. It was soon apparent that the group had among its own members the ancient and modern European languages, and a goodly number of Middle and Far Eastern languages as well. The Seminar could bring to bear a breadth of bibliographic knowledge upon the point in question that no single worker or group of workers in one discipline could hope to master, short of much hard labor and months of time —if then.

The method and the project are both incidents, both by- products of a process of continued associated inquiry.

Though the University Seminar is not primarily a research institution, it may stimulate a great deal of research either by its own members or by other groups, and if it is not primarily a board of directors making decisions, its very existence has long-run policy implications. It draws into a common language system and a related body of ideas (if and when these things come to pass) all the available knowledge and experience of the institution which it is studying. Such an outcome cannot be a project, a purpose, or an aim. It can only be a hope, an ideal, a something possible—but possible. Even the approximation to that kind of communication among active people, all of whom are devoting their lives to dealing with the incidence of a given institution, must have wide practical influence.

WE HAVE had sufficient experience to recognize that the University Seminar has a special role in relation to the visiting foreign scholar. Ordinarily, the foreign scholar, if he is not invited to teach a class, has few, and usually formal, contacts with members of the faculty. He may be invited to an occasional meal, or may be asked to give a lecture or two, but unless he has some close personal friends he finds himself isolated and with little opportunity for intimate communication with his temporary associates. His position is improved if he has a class of his own because it gives him students to work with, and greater occasion to deal with the members of a department. But even then it is a rare person who finds himself adopted into an intellectual family.

The situation is different if the foreign scholar finds himself a member of one of our University Seminars. One instance will illustrate the point. A Swiss scholar, brought over by the Rockefeller Foundation to a university located some two hours distant from Columbia, was invited to attend a

278   meeting of one of the University Seminars. He was sufficiently interested to ask if he could come again. He returned
to the Seminar regularly for the entire academic year, paying
his own expenses, and never missing a single meeting. He
fell into the mood of the group, took an active part in its
proceedings, was asked to act at least one evening as the
leader of the discussion, and proved himself a useful member.
He had, in fact, found intellectual companionship and accommodation, and soon partook of the friendly informality which
characterizes these groups. When the time came for him to
return to his own country he remarked privately that this
contact was the most important, as well as the most useful,
thing that had happened to him in the United States. He had
become a participating member of an active intellectual fellowship. His presence was useful to the Seminar, and very
meaningful to him. On his return to Europe he wrote about
the Seminar and about the issues the Seminar dealt with. In
some ways, he had so partaken of our activities that he had
become one of us, with much benefit all around. Most of our
University Seminars could absorb two, probably three, foreign scholars each academic year.

A very similar experience can be cited for a visiting
scholar from another part of the United States. In this instance, he had come to Columbia on a one-year appointment.
He was brought into one of our University Seminars, in
which he became an active participant. At the end of the year
he moved to another institution in a neighboring state as
head of a research institute, but he has maintained his membership in the University Seminar and rarely misses a meeting. On leaving the University he wrote a letter to the effect
that this regular, friendly association in an intellectual
activity was the most important event in his year at the
University.

In some way this drawing in for a period of time of scholars from beyond the immediate reach of the University, or
from foreign countries, could if broadened become some-

thing of great value to the intellectual life of Columbia, and
to scholars in foreign lands and distant American universities.

WHEN first established, it was assumed that these associations
would prove highly stimulating and effective teaching institutions for specially chosen graduate students. On the whole,
this hope has not been fulfilled. The reasons for this are many,
and would deserve careful analysis. The older classroom is
but a continuation of the chapel, with the preacher in the
pulpit, and the congregation down below. The ordinary seminar is an adaptation of the same structure to more advanced
students, with the professor at the head of the table. But in
our University Seminars there is no teacher. There are instead between fifteen and twenty-five mature scholars, equal
among themselves, and there is little place for the student.
He finds it a little embarrassing, and the professors feel
restrained.

This was particularly true in the early days of the University Seminar. In one instance, when it was suggested that
students be admitted, a distinguished member of the faculty,
with a national reputation as a teacher, threw up his hands
and said, "Mercy, no. We don't want them to see us flounder."
For exploratory, tentative, intellectual floundering is characteristic of the process of integration between men drawn
from different disciplines and varied spheres of life. It may
take much time before they learn to talk to each other rather
than at each other. This is facilitated if the gatherings acquire
a relaxed, friendly mood, when members begin to call each
other by their first names, when they can laugh with and at
each other. Eating together is a great time-saver. It helps the
process of integration and identification within the group,
and eases the strain of difference.

All of this, however, does not make it easier for students.
One or two students, if carefully selected, can be absorbed,

but as many students as there are faculty members would in most instances prove a hindrance to the main purpose of the group. It is, however, not desirable that graduate students, who stand to gain so much by contact with their elders under the stimulating conditions of a University Seminar, should be excluded. Teaching is one of the purposes of the University, and a major function of the scholar. The University Seminar has its indirect influence upon teaching by its impact upon the teacher. But the University Seminar itself should be able to do this directly, at least upon a limited scale. In the few instances where students have been admitted, the experience has been a profitable one.

Any considerable number of students would require some arrangement for supervision. We already have the power to give academic credit, and we have the experience in the University Seminar on Religion with students who have successfully worked on doctoral dissertations. It has been our hope that the doctoral dissertation would come to be written in response to a need of the University Seminar, and, so to speak, in its presence. In view of the experience with the Seminar on Religion this seems feasible, and useful to both the group and the student.

In this and in other instances, it is possible to foresee that the Seminar groups could be appointed as the examining committee on the doctoral dissertation. In view of the fact that at Columbia University the doctoral degree in Religion is given under the auspices of an *ad hoc* committee, it would not be impossible, if it seemed desirable, to transfer this power to the University Seminar. In fact, the entire field of the relation between the students and the University Seminars is wide open and can develop in many different directions. Much will depend upon the degree of permanent financial support the University Seminars will find. An effective graduate student program will call for a permanent and paid skeleton staff which is not now available. But these are matters for future growth, which cannot be diagramed at the moment. One thing is clear, however; it would be a real loss to the usefulness of this new institution if it were to remain without students.

WHEN first organized it was contemplated that each University Seminar would develop or acquire its own publication medium. The Seminar on Religion and Health and the Seminar on the Renaissance have been able to use existing quarterlies. *The Journal of Religion* and *The Journal of the History of Ideas* have been vehicles for some of their work. In the first instance, the papers from the Seminar on Religion were published annually on two different occasions by taking an entire issue of *The Journal of Religion*. This was financed from the small fund at our disposal. *The Journal of the History of Ideas* has published many of the papers read before the University Seminar on the Renaissance. The other University Seminars have not been so fortunate. The need for publication is real, and the Seminars would be more productive if the means for publication were at hand.

The University Seminar on Organization and Management has two unpublished manuscripts ready for the printer. The University Seminar on Rural Life has at least one such volume. The University Seminar on Labor has raised a small fund to prepare a volume in honor of its retiring chairman, Mr. Arthur E. Meyer, to be based upon its very excellent minutes. There is at least another volume that should be developed out of these minutes, but someone would have to be given free time and secretarial assistance to collate and work over the material.

The same thing is true in the case of the University Seminar on Peace. Here, lying unused and unknown, are seven years of excellent minutes, containing the record of the best thought of a group of teachers of international law, history, politics, economics, and so on, on the question of how to organize the peace. It would require a year, possibly two, of someone's free time to do justice to this rich body of material.

In fact, the record of most of our original Seminars ought

to be examined. How fruitful such a project can be is illustrated by the history of the first five years of the University Seminar on Religion and Health prepared by Professor Horace L. Friess. This was made possible by a small grant for assistance from the Rockefeller Foundation. Certainly such a review of the history of the University Seminar on the Content and Methods of the Social Sciences would be of real value.

This does not begin to exhaust the question of publication. We have no full record of the papers and books published by members of our University Seminars that have grown out of the work of the Seminars. Even less have we a record of the way these groups have influenced the writing activities or the thought of its members. An accidental remark by a former member of the Seminar on the State will illustrate the point: "I have published four papers on the history of Roman bureaucracy which would not have been written but for my membership in that seminar. In fact, it led me to change my basic research interest in the History of Roman Law." Another member acknowledges that two of his recent books would probably not have been written but for membership in these fellowships.

OUR University Seminars are, as we have noted, free from administrative tutelages, and can adapt themselves to new situations as they arise. Thus, the Seminar on Religion was for two years organized into two separate groups, on Religion and Health, and on Religion and Democracy, with some members belonging to both. This same Seminar has discussed the desirability of designating a committee from its own members to make a study of some special problems that have arisen, but which are too technical for the group as a whole to deal with. The committee would report back to the larger group. It has also been approached from outside the University with a request that it undertake a special job of research and evaluation for some groups interested in religious phenomena. It declined the invitation after considerable discussion, but there was nothing to have prevented it from doing so except its own sense of appropriateness in the light of its membership and program.

A similar offer in a very different field was made to the Seminar on Organization and Management. The Seminar on the Content and Method of the Social Sciences has, through a special committee, signed a contract with the Office of Naval Research. The Seminar on the Renaissance has been asked to take over some of the activities of the American Association of Learned Societies after that body disbanded its Renaissance Committee.

In the light of its structure and organization, the University Seminar can, if its membership so desires, assume a multiple of different shapes, and take on varied responsibilities within the wide range of academic tolerance.

THE traditionally wide administrative tolerance that characterizes Columbia University has permitted these groups to develop with a minimum of official meddling. In return, the University Seminars have brought to the Columbia campus many distinguished scholars from other institutions, and men of affairs from varied walks of life. These associates have discovered grounds of identity with Columbia. In doing so they have enriched our own intellectual life, and our fellowship with the larger community beyond the Columbia campus.

It is here, perhaps, that the University Seminars have their greatest promise of future usefulness. We are really building an edifice that embraces not merely Columbia University, but all of the other institutions of higher learning in the Metropolitan area, and the community at large. We are bridging the gap that has so long divided not merely the different disciplines, but the academic and nonacademic worlds as well.

There is an additional service that our fellowships are rendering to the University which deserves special mention, and this is the communion made possible between the younger and the older members of the academic staff. Our Seminars, though perhaps not often enough, include not merely the older and more distinguished scholars in the University, but a sprinkling of instructors and assistant professors. It has been difficult in a large University to bring the younger men into intimate and continuous contact with their elders, where the conditions of friendly equality prevail. This we do, and the results in mutual respect, friendship, and understanding that grow out of these associations are of great value to the individual members and to the University.

THERE are certain self-evident conclusions that can be drawn from our eight years' experience that bear upon the question of intellectual cooperation among men trained in different disciplines and engaged in varied nonacademic activities.

1] The most important of these is the essential condition of *permanent association.* It takes a long time for intellectuals to get acquainted with each other. It takes a longer time for them to understand each other. The primary requirement is for a complete breakdown of formality, and of the artificial barriers inside which intellectuals tend to live. Intellectuals can think aloud in each other's presence only when completely relaxed, when the atmosphere is friendly, and when differences of attitude, belief, and perception can be revealed without any sense of diffidence and hesitancy. It is essential that associates may be free to hesitate, fumble, retract, and make many new starts. Otherwise there can really be no gradual intellectual overlapping, so essential to the development of a common language, and a mutual insight. Time is the essence of the matter, and, given time enough, the group will grow into a true intellectual fellowship. And only in an atmosphere of fellowship can we hope for the stimulus essential to the flowering of the human spirit.

2] The second lesson to be drawn is that this fellowship of the mind comes easiest and most fruitfully when many men are working together on the same issue but from different angles. All facets of the question must be presented and considered, not once, but over and over again.

3] The issues to which the group is devoting its time must be of major significance to the members, and of sufficient complexity to challenge their best thought and their deepest concern. The questions studied must, as all real questions do, change under their hand, and in a measure always remain baffling, contradictory, and just beyond complete understanding.

4] The group must feel completely free to follow its own bent, it must be responsible only to its own academic conscience, and it must be untrammeled in organization, method, and membership.

5] It must be based upon voluntary association, where membership is a privilege, and where the only compensation is the sense of intellectual growth, and the esteem of one's equals in a common intellectual endeavor.

6] Finally, it must be sensed as a lifelong companionship, as something that will always be there, exacting the best one has to offer, and returning the best in fellowship and intellectual stimulus. If it is recognized merely as a temporary group it will neither evoke the best from its members nor return full compensation for the effort.

IT IS difficult to foresee the future developments in a movement as many-sided and flexible as this one which has grown up at Columbia University. But one can perhaps hazard a guess at the broad drift implicit in these voluntary groupings. It is within the range of the probable to say that the University Seminars will in time grow into independent collegia inside of the University—independent in administration, program, membership, and finances. They will also be different because they will not merely bridge the formal disciplines and schools, but gather under the same roof scholars from other institutions, and many men from the active world, who will bring their practical experience to enrich the collegium of their choice. But the collegia, because of that, will have some bit of wisdom and use to add to practical people who spend their lives in mending the structure of any living institution.

implications
of an educational movement *14*

THE EDUCATIONAL ENTERPRISE that we call the University Seminars is a regional movement among scholars of over 150 colleges and universities between Boston, Ithaca, New York, and Washington, centered at Columbia University because that is where it originated. In addition, it counts among its 1,600 participants some 300 from the nonacademic world. Members now come regularly from as far as the Universities of Texas, Minnesota, and Michigan, and the movement boasts of a branch in the University of Padua in Italy and an organized correspondence group in Japan. Among its participants are scholars from many countries and from all the continents. It is a movement rather than a project, program, or plan because it responds to an inner impulse to expand. It is not something that is being organized; people do not have to be persuaded to join. Its growth is spontaneous and how large it will ultimately be no one can now say.

When I say that it is a movement, I am thinking that twenty-two years ago—specifically in 1945—we began with five collegia on Peace, Rural Life, Religion, The State, and

This essay was written especially for this collection. The previous essay, "The University Seminar Movement at Columbia University," is an early statement of purpose; the present one is an effort to trace the progress of the Seminar movement.

288   The Renaissance. Those have now grown to 47 separate continuing groups that meet regularly, at least once a month
during the academic year, and are established about such
varying themes as Africa, South East Asia, China, Japan,
Biomaterials, the Use of Language, Human Maladaptation
in Modern Society, Technology and Social Change, Early
American History and Culture, and so on.

The individual Seminars divide like a cell—where you
had one, you now have two, where you had two, you now
have four. As a rule these Seminars do not die, they continue
year after year with the same people.

When I say that the movement grows spontaneously, I
mean that literally. A colleague walked into my office one
day and said: "I have been a member of the collegium on
The Renaissance for seven years, it is now time we had one
on Classical Civilization." And when I asked if anyone else
is interested, he tells me: "Yes, I have talked to a number of
colleagues and they all think the way I do." The only question that remained was whether the new collegium should
be in ancient or classical civilization. After some talk it
became clear that ancient civilization was too vast a field
for one Seminar. Some time later I heard that the collegium
on Classical Civilization had invited the entire Department
of Greek and Latin to join—and it did. To the question of why
the Department had been invited, I was told by a friend that
"we never meet as a Department except at examinations and
that is not an auspicious occasion. Now we can pick each
other's brains, and behave like an intellectual fellowship."
This year, the University Seminar on Classical Civilization is
planning to publish a volume in celebration of its tenth
anniversary.

One day I received a letter from the chairman of the
University Seminar on Modern China in which he informed
me that, after a full discussion, the members of his collegium
had decided to establish one on Japan. He further told me
that those who knew both Japanese and Chinese would belong to both Seminars, that they would regularly exchange

their minutes and hold joint meetings as seemed desirable. They had also chosen the chairman for the new Seminar. The chairman was leaving for Japan on a grant and the inauguration of the new collegium would have to wait until he returned. Now, the Seminar on Japan is a distinguished institution in its own right with members from a dozen universities and colleges, and participants from public and private bodies involved in Japanese affairs. And, as one young scholar who was going off to a midwestern institution told me: "I have been elected a corresponding member of this Seminar. It is a great honor."

While writing about the Chinese Seminar, I might add that in 1966 a group of scholars came to see me because they wanted to establish a collegium on Traditional China. I asked if they had consulted with the one on Modern China. Yes, they had. In fact, some of them are members of the Modern China Seminar and expect to continue in it. But Traditional China, going back for thousands of years, required a separate scholarly community of its own. Thus the original Seminar on Modern China has thus provided the impulse for the emergence of two others.

What has emerged from the movement is a new and permanent addition to our system of higher education, with subtle overtones that it carries within itself the elements of change, perhaps profound change—the reshaping of the modern university.

The University Seminar organized about a complex, an area, a historical period, a going concern, is not bothered by disciplinary distinctions. It can take in anyone professionally involved in the field under discussion, regardless of the special facet he devotes his energies to, and he does not have to be a member of the Columbia faculty, or of any faculty for that matter. He does not even have to have a professional degree. Some of the most useful members of the collegium on The Renaissance came from the rare book trade.

Another example of how the collegia come into being illustrates their spontaneity. A young colleague, a chemical engineer, came to see me. His immediate interest was the surface of the blood. He was deeply concerned with bio-materials. Something like a dozen specialists and sciences were involved. He wanted to be able to carry on a continuing dialogue with others working in this relatively new and exciting field. The new collegium on Biomaterials is concerned with the "structure and concomitant function of living materials and the synthesis and assessment of artificial substances which functionally emulate living materials." When I attended the first meeting of the group on Biomaterials, I did not understand a single word. That was not surprising, for this was a highly technical field. What was surprising was the repeated interruption of the speaker by one or another member with "I do not understand the meaning of that word," or "would you please explain how you arrive at this concept." A few days later, I received a letter from a distinguished cardiologist at Johns Hopkins who said that "for some years I have wondered how I could get together regularly with two or three specialists to discuss those important matters. Now, thanks to you and Columbia, we have brought together fifteen."

The University Seminar Movement assumes that in the work-a-day world knowledge and experience become synthesized in clusters of organized activities rather than in departments. Some such synthesis is essential to any ongoing social system. The institutional orders within which man has his being would otherwise malfunction and deteriorate. In practice one might conjecture that human institutions can only carry on by weaving together the strands provided by knowledge and experience. A sense of direction and value derives from this synthesis; otherwise policy makers would work altogether in the dark. Considerations such as these have influenced the election of participants in the University Seminars. They are drawn from areas relevant to the themes of a given collegium. A few figures will show how these ideas have been translated in the election of members.

In the forty-five University Seminars in session in the

academic year 1966–1967, there were 1,381 participants. The Columbia faculty contributed 522, the faculties of other institutions of higher learning 517, and the noncollegiate world 342. As an illustration: 5 came from Amherst, 17 from Princeton, 5 from Cornell, 9 from the Cornell Medical School, 17 from Harvard, 4 from MIT, 58 from New York University, 25 from the University of Pennsylvania, 30 from Yale. But 46 out of the 150 colleges and universities had three or more members of their faculty in the University Seminars, the rest one or two each. So much for the academic contingent. Nine governmental institutions had staff members who take part in the Seminars: the United Nations was there with 31 participants, the Federal Government with 21, and the rest with fewer members. This theme repeats itself for nine separate labor organizations, through the presence of some of their leaders. In all, 62 business firms had members of their managerial groups in our Seminars: IBM had the largest number—over 20; one or more came from Standard Oil of New Jersey, American Telephone and Telegraph Company, Chase Manhattan Bank, Columbia Broadcasting System, Equitable Life Assurance Society of the United States, General Electric Company, McKinsey & Company, Mobil Oil Corporation. Participants from 14 separate foundations and 47 institutes and societies were counted as members of these collegia. Our collegia also had in 1967 participants from religious orders, publishing houses, magazines, newspapers, hospitals, and museums.

What gives the Seminars their special character within the academy is that they are holistic and cooperative by the logic of their being, instead of divisive and isolationist like the departments. A University Seminar aims at seeing whole the complex it would unravel and tries to encompass whatever knowledge and experience is available for that purpose. This is an ideal that is probably never reached, but is of necessity always aimed at, otherwise the effort to recognize the full incidence of any ongoing concern must falter.

Evidence of the holistic character of the University Seminars is best shown in the disciplines they gather together about any issue to which they are dedicated. The collegium on Genetics and the Evolution of Man contains physical and social anthropologists, demographers, blood group serologists, hematologists, and related medical specialties, mathematical statisticians, geneticists, as well as occasional psychologists, sociologists, medical geographers, and linguists. Another example is the Seminar on Studies in Contemporary Africa. It counts among its participants educators, historians, political scientists, economists, musicologists, art historians, archaeologists, linguistic specialists, economic geographers, sociologists, anthropologists, as well as representatives from the School of Law, Business, the Foreign Service, the Science Foundation, the United Nations, institutes, and the American mining industry.

This desire for seeing things whole is furthered by occasional joint meetings of two and sometimes three collegia around some issue that overflows any one Seminar—thus a meeting to honor a distinguished Buddhist scholar brought together the Seminars on China, Japan, and Oriental Thought and Religion. The Seminars on The Development of Preindustrial Areas and on Studies in Contemporary Africa held a joint meeting; so did the Seminars on The Theory of Literature and on The Problem of Interpretation (Hermeneutics). There is no set boundary to the search for understanding. The University Seminar on Genetics and the Evolution of Man had joint meetings with the Rockefeller Institute, the Sloan Kettering Institute for Cancer Research, the New York City Medical Association (Genetics Division), and the Columbia University Department of Biology.

The holistic character of the collegia dictates the choice of members. A collegium will invite those whom it needs regardless of their status. Individuals are chosen for their competence and represent only themselves. No member is sent by a department, school, business, or foundation. He is there for his personal merits. This gives the collegia a flexibility they could not have had if members were delegated by departments or institutions. To maintain this flexibility and independence the University Seminars pay the fare of scholars from distant colleges. If the members were official representatives of other institutions, the collegia would lose their flair and excitement. They are an oasis where the academician, the practitioner, and the policy maker can meet outside the pressures and demands that burden the contemporary university.

These considerations raise the question of the relation of the University Seminar to the Department, the Institute, the School, the University as a whole. Columbia faculty who now take part in the collegia number about 600, and at the present rate of growth, half of the Columbia professors will participate in this activity in the next few years. As the collegia have no retirement, membership tends to be for life. Increasing numbers of emeriti who have long left their academic posts, their government jobs, their business, continue as active participants in these groups. A member of the faculty who has moved to another institution returns once or twice a month to the Columbia campus to carry on with his former colleagues as if he were still in his original place. This, of course, holds true for participants from other institutions. Some years ago, a Renaissance scholar who moved from Princeton to Cornell found it easier to move from the department than to give up the collegium he had participated in over a number of years, and he returned monthly to his Seminar meeting. A businessman came from Boston over many years; when he retired from business he moved to Pennsylvania but he continued to come. A Judge of the International Court at The Hague returns to the collegium at least once a year when he comes to the meetings of the Assembly of the United Nations. A former Undersecretary of War, now returned to his professional career, writes to ask when his Seminar is going to meet, as if he had not been away.

All of this is evidence of a new loyalty to an intellectual community developing on the campus. These loyalties are to a growing institution that belongs only to itself and is not bound to department, school, or faculty. Evidence of this growing institution is cumulative. Participants serve on program and membership committees, act as chairman for an entire year or more, vote on the admission of new members, write papers, in some cases vote on the admission of students, join together to prepare a volume for publication, argue over the rules that ought to govern the fellowship. When on rare occasions a Seminar suspends its meetings, members keep calling up to ask when the gatherings will be resumed. The Seminars themselves rarely disband and when they do they tend to come back into existence, as happened with the Seminars on Population and on Religion. Members identify themselves in public as Associates of one or another of these collegia and acknowledge in their books their indebtedness to the other participants; at MIT membership in a University Seminar was cited as one of the merits justifying a promotion.

A new academic grouping is being added to the ancient house of learning. This addition differs from the older units in many ways. It is voluntary, cross-disciplinary, interuniversity, and intercommunity. Its members consist of academicians, policy makers, and practitioners who are meant to be associated with each other for the rest of their days, and many of whom attend more than one Seminar. These repeated gatherings of so many scholars from such a variety of disciplines has led Professor Aaron Warner to remark that in no other university in the United States or, for that matter, in any other country is there so much intellectual communication.

Columbia is quietly becoming two institutions. One owns the buildings, pays the professors, gives academic credit, arranges for the instruction in disciplines grouped in departments; the other provides stimulation, criticism, new ideas, and continuing evaluation by an immersion in an intellectual community. That is where the "real university is," the "spiritual side of the university," as Professor I. I. Rabi once expressed it. In time, these two institutions—the formal one, having legal powers and responsibilities, and the informal one providing enthusiasm and intellectual communication— will approximate each other in numbers. The vast majority of the faculty will be participants in both universities. When that happens these two institutions will somehow merge, and when they do, the University will become a Community of Scholars made up of many small scholarly communities, each autonomous, self-governing in an "independent universe" inside the University.

Without anyone noticing, the merging is partly underway. When I was a student and later a member of the faculty, each course and seminar was taught by a single professor. It would have been unheard of for a number of faculty members from different disciplines to teach the same course and be in the classroom together. When in 1937 I suggested to Professor Lynn Westerman that we give a joint seminar on slavery, involving four members of the History Department, I was advised to ask permission from the head of the Department. He gave his consent with considerable reluctance. A glance at recent graduate and undergraduate catalogues will show evident changes in the instructional pattern. Many courses and Seminars are now given involving several members of the faculty, frequently from different departments. Certainly the traditional one teacher to a classroom is gradually changing and will continue to do so. Some day this new pattern and the departments will have to come to terms. When this comes about, the University will become a holding company for many autonomous collegia with their junior scholars. Many of them will set their own standards for the degree and provide for their own research.

In a measure this change is already on the way. It has arisen quietly and unwittingly in the developing relationship between some Seminars and research institutes. This symbiotic bond exists, for example, in the relations between the Seminar on Communism and the Institute on Communist Affairs. The collegium antedates the Institute. When the

Institute was established, the Seminar was able to place
before it the rich resources on communism available in New
York City. It brought ideas, experience, criticism, personnel.
The Institute found people who had a book in them among
members and guests of the Seminar. When it hired new staff,
it introduced them into the Seminar as a way of broadening
their view of the area within which they were working. A
new idea for research could be laid before the Seminar for
criticism, review, and suggestions. The Institute and the University Seminar acquired an interrelated life; their officers
became interchangeable. One had money and directors, and
hired people to write books and monographs; the other supplied ideas, insight, information, contacts, stimulus, and an
intellectual environment for members of the Institute.

A comparable relationship exists between the University
Seminar on Japan and the East Asian Institute; this is also
true of the Seminar on China; in different ways it is true of
the Institute of Social Research and a number of Seminars,
including the one on Basic and Applied Social Research. The
director of the Institute of Science and Society has said that
the Institute was deeply indebted to the collegium on technology and social change. The Seminar on Southern Asia
antedates the Institute of the same name, and just recently
the director of this Institute was elected chairman of the
Seminar. These developments were unplanned and unforeseen, except possibly in the last instance. They just came to
be because they fitted the logic of an expanding movement.

One can foresee that the introduction of graduate students into one of these Seminars would satisfy needs of the
Institute and probably of the collegium. Although not all of
the University Seminars will accept students, a number of
Seminars do have a few students; for example, The Atlantic
Community, The Renaissance, and Genetics and The Evolution of Man. The junior scholars working for their degree
could be hired by the Institute through a fellowship to work
on subjects that had arisen in the Seminar. The collegium
could see some of its ideas examined, researched, and made

part of the scholarly record. This seems a natural and logical by-product of the Seminar movement: a collegium, an associated research institute, and a group of junior scholars learning their craft and receiving their broader training from association with a group of masters. Here you have what seems like a natural model of the small scholarly community, autonomous and self-governing. Professor Paul Kristeller expressed this once by saying that the Seminar on The Renaissance provided a natural interdisciplinary faculty for the doctorate. If a student got his degree and had a place in a neighboring university, they invited him to become a member of the Seminar. The apprentice was now received by his masters as one of them.

The developing situation is, however, broader than here outlined. The collegia are composed of participants from many disciplines and numerous colleges and universities. These professors from off the campus, if the Seminar is to have junior scholars, will want to bring their students to the meetings. In fact, one of the Seminars has voted to allow each professor to bring his best student to the gatherings of the Seminar, and we have agreed to pay his fare. The junior scholars would therefore be from more than one institution. They would, in fact, be an interuniversity and interdisciplinary body of junior scholars. They would work on theses that had mainly originated from the program of the collegium. The research institute associated with the collegium would provide the fellowship (a salary) to make the needed research and writing possible. The Seminar would then act as critic, adviser, stimulant, and, in the end, judge. In the final examination members of the Seminar would participate, regardless of where the student received his degree. The logic of the situation makes such an interdisciplinary, interuniversity graduate school not only possible but inevitable. The new kind of graduate school merely waits upon financing. The administrative structure for this new institution is already in being and functioning in an incipient fashion. It is not a question of first inventing and creating the machinery

for an interuniversity program. That is already here, waiting
to be used. This Graduate University that has its basis in the
Seminars is interdisciplinary, interuniversity, drawing students and professors from many institutions. It should, however, be repeated that not all University Seminars would
accept students.

As a cross-disciplinary and cross-community fellowship
the collegium possesses the knowledge and experience to
become a key agency in unraveling perennial as well as contemporary issues confronting our time. If unraveling is an
unrealistic aim, then it is ideally fitted to analyze and examine the most complex of our difficulties and bring to bear
upon the issue in hand the best available expertise in a way
that is not now possible in the University or beyond it. In
fact, one of the chief merits of the collegia is their ability to
bring the knowledge and experience possessed by many men
in many places and focus it on a given question. This way of
attacking a problem can go on inside or outside of the academy, provided there exists a basis of objectivity, scientific
competence, and a search for the full incidence of the issue
at hand. It is really one way of saying that the University will
be taking in the community or that the community will for
the purpose in hand behave like the University. The collegia
provide a means for bridging the gap between Town and
Gown, and if the bridge is narrow and frail it will in time
become wide and solid. The traditional isolation between
Town and Gown is not only no longer desirable but no longer
tolerable.

Among the unforeseen by-products of this movement has
been the occasional voluntary conversion of the collegia into
a self-imposed *ad hoc* committee on the University. This has
now occurred in the collegia on Higher Education, on Mathematical Methods in the Social Sciences, on The State, and on
the Ancient Mediterranean and Near Eastern Studies. The
collegium on Higher Education converted itself into "Her
Majesty's Commission" on the granting of the Ph.D. degree
at Columbia University. It called in witnesses and took evi-

dence. It invited heads of departments, chairmen of *ad hoc* committees empowered to give degrees in fields for which there are no departments, heads of schools and faculties and asked them to describe the requirements in their special field for granting of the higher degree. After the testimony, the invited "witnesses" were cross-examined to bring out the details and implications of the different ways a higher degree may be acquired in the separate branches of the university. No such close study of this phase of university life has probably been made before. The record went into the minutes but unfortunately was never published.

Under the leadership of Professor Paul Lazarsfeld the University Seminar on Mathematical Methods in the Social Sciences, within a special committee, examined the teaching of this subject in the various parts of the university where the social sciences were taught. After a full survey the Seminar suggested a separate degree to meet this need. Its proposal, which with some modifications has since been adopted by the University, provided that an *ad hoc* committee of thirteen participants of the Seminar who were professors in that many separate departments administer the new degree. In 1965–1966, the University Seminar on The State, under the leadership of Professor Wallace Sayre, turned itself into a commission on the teaching of comparative politics at Columbia University. The members of the Department of Political Science were asked in turn to describe what they were doing and lay themselves open to questions and comment so natural at these gatherings. Professor Sayre has said that the year's self-examination by the Department influenced its staffing policy and led to changes in course offerings.

Finally, the Seminar on Ancient Mediterranean and Near Eastern Studies under the leadership of Professor Morton Smith—a Seminar that so far has remained an intramural group representing Columbia, Barnard, and Union Theological Seminary—undertook an examination of the offerings in these fields, the library holdings, the requirements surrounding the higher degree, and the manner in which the library

300 cared for the relevant material. It has appointed committees to meet with members of the administration regarding special needs in the various fields of ancient history, has recommended an arrangement with the Metropolitan Museum of Art for participation by Columbia students in a course given at that institution, recommended bringing specialists to the University to fill in certain gaps, and allowed its own members on occasion to bring their graduate students to present a preliminary version of their thesis for comment and criticism. In addition to all this, the Seminar has interspersed substantive meetings of professional concern to its members. This Seminar has gathered together professors of Greek and Latin, Jewish History, Hebrew Language and Literature, Ancient History, Religion, Arabic Studies, Art History and Archaeology, Biblical Theology, Linguistics, Sacred Literature, Armenian Studies, Philosophy, Turkish Studies, Middle East Languages and Culture, Latin Language and Literature, German History, Old Testament, Art History, Church History, Arabic and Islamics, Law, Biblical Interpretation, Hebrew and Cognate Languages, Curator of Greek Coins and Iranian Studies.

I am not suggesting that the function of these developing small scholarly communities is to act as *ad hoc* committees on the university. The fact is that some have temporarily taken on this role and others will probably do so in the future. What these groups make possible is self-criticism of the University by insiders. They are led to the task in pursuit of their own professional involvement. It reveals a hitherto unknown voluntary feedback within the University that has potentially great value to the institutions of higher learning; it also opens up a hitherto unsought avenue of innovation and reform generated by voluntary organized activities of members of the faculty in pursuit of higher professional standards.

These are rare examples of the built-in mechanism for dealing with needed change by the only people who really understand the need and are capable of bringing the improvement to fruition. In each instance the proposals came as a result of self-examination, self-criticism, and mutual agreement of what needed to be done. What we have here is a mechanism for internal adjustment and reform as a by-product of a continuing dialogue by those involved. It certainly adds something new to ways of dealing with questions of institutional and professional rigidities, with repeated failures within large institutions to recognize developing needs, and to the distribution of power within organized bodies. Change brought about this way could only occur as a result of cross-disciplinary interplay by professionals in a given complex to which they are all related. It casts light upon the question of how to secure the good functioning of a decentralized institution and suggests how a centralized administration could probably be safely decentralized. Within the University it provides a new basis of cooperation with the collegia on behalf of the very ends for which the Academy exists. For in each instance the aim was to inform the University of the present situation, of proposing ways of dealing with relevant flaws where possible by the groups themselves or by cooperation with the central administration.

In closing, it may be useful to emphasize that the main purpose of the University Seminars is the Seminars; every other thing that may be said about them is secondary. Whether we speak of students, self-criticism, publications, impact on centralization, the prospects of broad changes in the structure of the University, changes in the pattern of instruction, increased communication between the University and the community, and possibly new relations between student and teacher—these are all by-products, secondary effects of an ongoing movement. The University Seminar, the collegium, is primary; it comes first in fact and in importance. The primary aim of the University Seminar is the attempt to see things whole, to merge the disciplines for the purpose of getting a unified view; the aim is synthesis, insight, wisdom, the understanding of the full incidence of the ongoing phenomenon to which any collegium is devoted. The attempt to

302   do this by a group of scholars, joined together for life and devoting their best energies to the unraveling of the mystery to which they are attached is the essence of the University Seminar. The influence of this endeavor upon the individual scholar, upon the institution where he has his professorship, upon the relations between the academy and the community are the natural by-products of grouping together the scholar, the practitioner, and the policy maker in the joint enterprise of seeking fuller understanding of the particular complex that is the reason why the group came into being in the first place. A great deal lies hidden in this single effort. If it prevails, it will have provided this generation with a new tool with which to confront the difficulties that threaten to overwhelm it and the next generation with the foundations for a new kind of University.

the professional criminal: *15*

an inquiry
into the making of criminals

. . . THE PROFESSIONAL CRIMINAL is a human being and a professional. That . . . may seem strange, but it isn't. A professional is one who practices a skilled and elaborate technic of a specialized character. People learn their professions after a painful apprenticeship. It takes a long time to make a good criminal, many years of specialized training and much elaborate preparation. But training is something that is given to people. People learn in a community where the materials and the knowledge are to be had. A craft needs an atmosphere saturated with purpose and promise. The community provides the attitudes, the point of view, the philosphy of life, the example, the motive, the contacts, the friendships, the incentives. No child brings those into the world. He finds them here and available for use and elaboration. The community gives the criminal his materials and habits, just as it gives the doctor, the lawyer, the teacher, and the candlestick-maker theirs.

All criminals were children once. The murderers, the thieves, the gangsters, the sneaks, the cutthroats, those who

This essay first appeared in *Century Magazine*, CX (September 1925), pp. 577–588. It grew some years later into *Crime and the Community* (New York: Columbia University Press, 1951; first published, 1938).

fill the world they live in with hate and fear, were little children once. . . . The child grew up, and somewhere along the way, somewhere in his childhood, between his infancy and his embittered and degraded manhood, a beginning was made that envisaged the end, a shadow was cast ahead that led to crime, to theft, to murder, to the gallows. There was a beginning somewhere; that too is important. There is no sudden criminality. There is even no sudden insanity. People who go suddenly insane have been going insane for a long time. It is physically, emotionally, psychologically impossible for people to go insane all of a sudden. A conflict was started along the path of life somewhere, a disease was contracted, a gap was made sometime before, long before, so long ago that it is often outside present memory and often escapes even careful scrutiny. But there was a beginning. So too in crime. There is no such thing as a sudden criminal, a sudden murderer, a sudden thief. Somewhere a start was made, and it is in the story of the growth of this small beginning that the tale must be told.

There is much passionate controversy in the discussion of behavior. People are so insistent that they know the why of it all, especially of bad people, that it might be a useful thing to inquire into the behavior of good people. We take "good" behavior so much for granted as not even to ask questions about it. Why are you good, if you are? What do you mean by being good? I am not urging the philosophical problem of evil versus virtue, of ultimate goodness and ultimate evil. . . .

What seems obvious is that people are judged by their behavior—by their public behavior, by what they do, by how they do it. What kind of a man is he, means what kind of things does he do, how does he do them, what are his habitual modes of response. The good man . . . fits in so well with our way of doing and living, of talking and reacting, that we barely notice him. If he stands out from the crowd, it is because he differs from it, is conspicuous by some deviation. If he differs in degree only, we forgive him, sometimes we acclaim him. But if he differs in kind, in the value he gives to things, if he does the things we condemn, then he is bad, a sinner, a dangerous crank, a criminal. But it is by his behavior that we judge him, just as our neighbors judge us by ours.

. . . [T]he way [a man uses his capacities] is determined by the tools, the habits, the molding, the slant, the attitude, the values, the recognition of environmental situations as worthwhile that have been kneaded into him. . . . The habits a human being [forms] are the most important things that he has to live with and to live by: they ultimately become the person. His very values are habitual. How does the "bad" man get his bad habits? How does the "good" man get his good habits? What do we mean by habits? What do we mean by forming a habit? Upon the clearness of the answer to these questions depends our understanding of the criminal and our understanding of the saint. . . .

A habit is a slow growth. It takes a long time for a mode of behavior to become so organized as to be automatic and propulsive. It is not a habit until it projects itself, until one is carried by it, and until one resists it with the greatest difficulty only after many failures and after a long struggle by gradually substituting another habit. To watch the growth of a way of living there is no place like the family. That is where habits are first formed, first organized, first acquired, and at the most plastic period in one's life.

How does a child learn to be polite, learn to say "please"? How many thousand times does a mother say to her little son, "What do you say now, Billy?" And with a rising accent if there is no response, "Billy, what do you say now?" Ten thousand times is an understatement. She says it until there is no more need for saying it, and age does not matter. Again the technic may change, the temper may change; but the persistence goes on, the watchfulness knows no relenting. The other members of the family join in. In a friend's house the other day, I gave a little girl of five a gift. Her sister, a little girl of eight, said, "Mary, what do you say now?" Mary did not respond, and the older child repeated the variation: "Say 'Thank you,' Mary." There was to be no mishap, no break in the practice; the family mode must be carried on even by the younger members of the family.

It is interesting and important to observe the physical response that such pressure to conform imposes. Watch a child say "please." Notice the outstretched hand, the submissive tone, the slightly stooping attitude, bent a little forward, a supplicating, a begging attitude. Apparently, if you are going to say "please," you are going to do it that way, in a submissive, respectful, courteous manner, with a slightly bowed head and slightly stooping body. That is the habit. It is not merely the word "please." It is the physical accompaniment of the word, it is a way of looking at people and a way of approach to companionship and acceptance. The habit is thus more than the mere sound—it is a whole pattern, a mode of behavior, an expression of personality. What needs to be observed also is that once you learn how to say "please" to people that way, then for all your life and even under the most trying circumstances the word "please" will call forth that attitude of supplication, the slightly bowed head, the slightly stooping body. The habit is thus an organized physical posture which expresses itself in a word, "please"; the word "please" is the vocalized summary of the physical attitude. That is the habit. And a human being has thousands of such habits, each an organized physical pattern, each slowly acquired, each accompanied by a sound, a word, that expresses it. A human being is a bundle of such habits; they are the organized personality, the effective human being expressing himself in relations with other human beings. His habits are his way of living. He could not live without them, and different habits would give him different relations with his fellows.

For the sake of clarity, let us take another example of the way a family group organizes and molds a child's behavior. Have you ever watched a family gather itself to do battle against a few new and strange and disapproved words that the child brings home from the street? What happens when the family discovers that the child has acquired a string of words, vulgar, disrespectful, coarse? Have you watched the family flutter and stretch its wings the way a fowl does to protect its young? Have you watched the family swoop down upon the words and do battle, unceasing battle, even if the child barely understands what the words mean? There is a curious artifice, a whole technic, a full catalogue of practices that come into play almost automatically.

Why this sudden rousing of the family to campaign against a few innocent words? There is reason enough. A new word is a new way of looking at life; it is a new way of having a good time; it is a new way of making friends; it is a new way of living; it is a vehicle for a new set of habits, for a new set of interests in life. It is the opening up for a new personality development. The family strives to keep the mold solid, to keep the form straight, to make the pattern as nearly like its own as possible. The family group is important in the making of the child's character because it is the earliest, the most persistent, the longest in time and the widest in range of any of the influences that touch the child's life. It begins with the cradle and extends to maturity. It is relentless in the sense that it notices every deviation, observes every difference, condemns or approves every attitude.

The child, like every older person, lives not in one environment, but in many. Every contact is a new environment. Every friend, every group—the school, the church, the street gang—all these are environments for the growing child. Each gives attitudes, words, experiences, beliefs, behavior; but the family is the most continuous, the most unrelenting. If the family influences are sufficiently strong and effective, the other experiences are trivial, passing, and slight deviations. They slip off the child as water does off a duck's back. The family pattern remains. That, however, is true only provided that the family iself is a unit, that there is a common attitude, a ready reaction, a single standard, an adequate organization of life and relations in the family. The sufficiency of the family is largely determined by its unity, its continuity, its positive standards, its lack of internal conflict. Things are wrong and right, good and bad, acceptable or unacceptable, without much question, without hesitancy. Given that setting, and the child's range of interests outside the family group tend to remain in the form of experiences which are passing things, glimpses upon life that vanish readily, and attitudes that come to no fruition. Especially is this true if the family mode fits in with the community interests and habits, so that there is no conflict between family values and community values. Under those conditions habit formation is easy, ready, and inevitable; conflicts are few and passing. . . .

It is significant that the professional criminal comes from an insufficient home. It is frequently a broken home. Frequently there is a [deceased parent], sickness, disease, drunkenness, poor moral standards, internal conflict, lack of family discipline, lack of family interest. Where the home is insufficient, the child takes the street as a substitute for the home. The street gang becomes the place for more than adventure; it becomes the place of escape from the home, it becomes a substitute for the home. The beliefs, attitudes, interests, and ideals of the gang remain; they are not straightened out by a hostile and watchful family. The gang itself tends to be made up of boys whose homes are insufficient. Not that all children do not share the common experiences of the gang; but while they share them as occasional experiences, the others take them as a means of life. The older children, already adjusted to a life outside of proper and sufficient family control, set the fashion, organize the pursuits, give meaning to the activities. They are already acquainted with the new world and initiate the novice into the ways of the street. The inadequate control at home means that the gang experiences persist and are organized into habits. They become the way of living. The older boys, and not the parents, set the fashion. A child learns how to smoke because older boys smoke, to spit because older boys spit, to swear because older boys swear. They seek for types of adventure which are forbidden; they learn to look at the policeman with suspicion, at school with disdain. They talk about strange things, about criminals. They become interested in and learn to know the doubtful and condemned facts in their neighborhood; they live in a different world from the adequately protected and guarded child, and become different children.

The child's association with the gang leads to a new point of departure. It becomes the source of new interests, attitudes, habits, beliefs, acquaintances, joys, and values. There grows up a sense of unity in the gang, a feeling of difference from other gangs. There comes a sense of conflict, sometimes actual fighting with other gangs in the neighborhood, depredations, pilferings, trouble-making; they become a noisy, reckless, mischievous group of youngsters in conflict with the community. The boy is arrested. Here starts a new series of experiences. The boy ultimately goes to an institution, and that when he is a youngster of ten, eleven, or twelve, and sometimes even younger. Interesting to notice is the fact that the professional criminal begins his institutional career at a very early age. The two outstanding facts about him seem to be the broken, insufficient home and the institution.

The story of the influence of the juvenile institution upon the children sent to it is yet to be told. Here and there one gets a glimpse of the meaning of institutional life, and an occasional scandal breaks the surface of things and lets in a flood of light, only to pass away again and leave the institutional life, as delicate as that of the family influence, unchanged. Its inmates are young, children of nine, ten, eleven, twelve, up to sixteen. It is under the control of a superintendent and a number of guards. The guards are underpaid, comparatively illiterate men who work for wages, who need peace and quiet and self-assertion, and freedom for living their own lives. The children come from badly organized homes, from poorly organized neighborhoods. They bring to the school all of the problems of a family multiplied a hundredfold in number and a thousandfold in complexity.

Their arrival is the culmination of a series of exasperating and fretting experiences. They have been talked to and talked about, examined and scolded, chased and caught; strangers have manipulated and condemned them; every bit of finesse and delicacy that was left has been strained to the breaking point. They are stripped and raw and fearful, little unfortunate children herded in a group, under unsympathetic control—kindly and well meaning if you will, but with the kindness of a job where kindness is a strained virtue and an open weakness, and with sympathy for one's own driven hours and lack of peace. Let me put these general terms into a concrete example. Have you brought up a family of five boys between the ages of six and sixteen at the same time? If not, watch your neighbor's family. The children come down the stairs head first and pull one another's hair. They bully, fight, tease, and playfully roll about the ground or the floor, and occasionally tear their clothes and hurt one another; they do these things as a matter of growth.

Think of the trouble one child may give, think of the trouble five hundred can give, and that to a stranger who is taxed beyond mercy. A little unhappy child in an industrial school complained to me that he had been whipped because he climbed a tree. If you have trees and if you have children, the children will climb the trees just the way kittens do. But if you have five hundred children, and if one child climbs a tree, all of the children want to do it. If you have a limited budget for clothes, you cannot take the chance; the clothes are likely to be torn. One must not climb a tree in an institution.

So every morning will find a dozen boys standing against the wall and with their hands folded awaiting the hour of judgment. One child climbed a tree, one climbed a fence, one pulled another's hair, and two boys had a fight. Apparently, if you are going to run an institution of five hundred children under disciplinary control for twenty-four hours, the mere problem of organization and administration imposes a rigid program. You gradually find yourself in a state of mind where the method of procedure is repression, and where the instrument of punishment is physical pain. Bitterness, tears, and sullen fervor for "getting even" on one side and flushed indignation and appetizing self-righteousness on the other result. Oh, I know that men mean well, that they are kindly and good-natured, that they like to boast of their achievements and exhibit a well-disciplined and well-groomed group of quiet youngsters to a visitor, that they are convinced of doing the best they know how. But the inevitable happens, and you must do something. What can you do? You cannot permit a lot of wild youngsters who fear neither God nor man to run loose. And that is true, too; you cannot. And you don't. That is the tragedy of it. It is bad either way, and it is worse, apparently, the more conscientious you are, because you are likely to lose your temper and shed your sense of humor and be almost too good for the job—too good for the world, so to speak. All the while twisted lives of children are being embittered and hardened. The fact that they are children, that they need to frolic and play and fight, to climb trees and pull one another's hair, and to have buddies and tell secrets and run away—all of that is the thing that must be remembered, and is generally forgotten in the attempt to get efficiency, save money, cut expenses, and have rule and order and symmetry and cleanliness.

The children get what they need—love, companionship, and understanding. They must. They get it under cover, furtively, secretly. They learn to look upon every older person as a natural-born enemy. The older boys teach them bad personal habits, vice. They take out in secret things the joy that comes from open freedom. They become sullen, stubborn, peevish; they have a grudge against the world; they develop inferiority complexes. They develop unhealthy slants upon life and queer attitudes; they are spoiled children. Their release signifies merely that the bad habits which they brought to the institution are now more untenable because of the additions that have been made to them.

Two or three years pass. The boy is now fourteen, fifteen, or sixteen. He returns home. The home has not improved. It has often grown worse. To overcome the handicaps that the boy had acquired by his absence it would have to be even better than it was. The street is still there, but not all of the children that he knew. Some have moved away, some are now going to school or are at work, regular children with regular habits and regular interests. And everybody says: "Don't play with Billy. Billy is a bad boy. He has been up at the juvenile." And he has, that is true, and he is bad; he does bad things. But despite all that, he is just a boy; he needs companionship and love. He finds them. There are a few such boys in the neighborhood, who like himself, have had a similar career. They are outcasts in the world. They know one another as such. They have perhaps met in the "juvenile." They cling together. They carry on in terms of their interests and habits as these have been shaped by the world's destinies. They do the old things better, more skillfully, and with greater deftness; they have learned how. The boy is arrested again. He is now sixteen or seventeen. Reckless, bold, devilish, fearless, suspicious, and highly sophisticated, he thinks the world belongs to him. What can the community do with him now? It sends him to a reformatory.

A reformatory is like a juvenile institution, only it is worse. It generally is a prison, differing little from the ordinary prison either in organization, building, work, influence, or even age. The age of persons in the reformatory in New York State was under thirty years for 99 per cent of those admitted in 1921, while in the prison it was 69 per cent for the same year. The same thing happens to the boy that took place before, but with less pretense, with harsher, more undiscriminating results. After two years the boy is released again.

He returns to the gang. There is no other place of welcome, no other place to go. By habit, friendship contacts, interests, associations, all the threads that bind life to its sources, he is destined to return to the gang. He returned to his gang because that was his world. He knew no other; for him there was no other. He returned for the same reason that leads you to your old haunts—your office, your club, your associates, your world.

But to return to the gang is to live the life of the gang. He returns hungry for new experience, for new adventure, for new satisfaction. The gang is the instrument, the vehicle, the opportunity, the loyalty, the comradeship that make common effort possible, and crime is a common effort. He is arrested again. He is now eighteen, nineteen, or twenty, and calloused, hardened, embittered. His life has been dour and unkindly; he has been behind prison bars many times. His contacts with the whole world were persistently at wrong times and in the wrong moods. He has been hounded, hated, persecuted, abused; all the world has been against him excepting a little gang, five or six intimate friends who have shared their common lot with him, have risked their lives for him, have been loyal and true. The rest of the world has been dishonest. In his experiences he has known only people who were dishonest or afraid to trust him.

To understand fully the meaning of the gang in the life of the criminal is to understand much about him and much about ourselves. The group one inevitably, naturally, associates with is perhaps the most important factor in the shaping of a person's life attitudes and the reason for their persistent practice. One needs and finds succor and defense, recognition and approval, in one's gang, and one needs approval so much that what the gang approves of is the legitimate and right thing to do. The gang approves because carrying on the accepted mode of behavior is merely a corroboration of its own attitudes and activities. The gang approves the criminal, and then let the world condemn if it will. Its condemnation is but a proof of the heroism of the actor. The papers may condemn the fact and blaze it forth, but the greater the disapproval, the more honor for the culprit. . . .

What happens in your own "good" gang? If your gang smokes, you smoke, and the ladies do too when it is the fashion. That is true of jazz, of card parties, and of golf and church and sociables. If your gang approves of you, you are right in your own opinion because you are right in theirs, and their opinion is yours.

The bad man gets his approval for a bad thing, and the basic difference between you and the bad man is that you are a member of a good gang while he is a member of a bad gang. You have a group about you that approves your social behavior, that approves of your carrying on their way of doing and living. And the criminal has a group about him that approves of his carrying on in an unsocial way. Let me illustrate: A crime has been committed; the community is agog with the scandal; the papers are full of it; everyone is talking about it, and no one knows who did it. The boy tells his tale, and the tale grows in the telling, as all tales do. Someone says that it was "great." He is acclaimed; he becomes the hero, perhaps the leader of the gang. And the larger the condemning headlines, the greater the worth and value of the thing the man has done. That, of course, is merely an explanation of the why of the behavior. It does not involve a justification of it.

It is useless to talk about the criminal in terms which are different from those we use about other human beings. [He does] different things because [he has] different habits and different interests in life; [he does] them in terms of common human needs—habit, approval, love, friendship, loyalty. And then the boy is arrested again. His sentence to prison is a repetition of an old experience. After a few years he will be out again to carry on the old game. Then again the same story. Or he is shot in some gang feud or dies of some disease contracted in his irregular life. He becomes a narcotic, a derelict, a broken body in a rickety world. Or he may be sentenced to prison for twenty years, for life, or to be hanged. His career comes to an end when he is a young man, usually under thirty, and sometimes under twenty-one. Recently Warden Lawes of Sing Sing Prison pointed to the fact that out of twenty-one men he had in the death house, nineteen were under twenty-one years of age. And that is the typical career of the average professional criminal.

All he knows about life, about people, about the world, is limited and circumscribed by this curious contact with the world in this circular relationship. After a while he accepts it as a matter of course. He bargains upon the amount of freedom he may have, hopes for escape, for total freedom from arrest, but bargains with fate and gives hostages to freedom, calculates his chances, and accepts the inevitable with stoicism. He turns with bitter revenge upon the traitor, builds up a code of honor and rules of the game; he must be fairly caught and fairly dealt with—a recognized punishment for a recognized deed of evil. He bargains with the district attorney, "cops a plea," calculates the amount of "good time" that he can save by good behavior, uses his friends to secure leniency in judgment, bribes the policeman to change his charge, frightens the witnesses, or buys them or pleads with them to forget or to change their charge or to fail to appear in court, accepts imprisonment as a part of the game, and hungrily returns to the gang and to his career of crime again for another indulgence.

A world of contacts and friendships is built up, and a code of honor. A good criminal and a "square guy" is known and respected; a famous one is lauded and sought after; a clever one is admired; a "snitch" is hounded, persecuted, and even killed. Treason to the gang, to the rules of the game, is unforgivable. So strong is the tradition that strangers may execute a common judgment even if they have not been hurt personally. In between are great emotional strains and fears. The exciting life leads to the need for excitement, stimulants are needed, perversions are acquired and practiced, and the best foot is put forward, and the best face is turned upon misfortune. A man takes his "bit" just as a soldier takes his wound, decently and without whining. The community itself has developed a certain admiration for the ["heroic"] criminal. . . . Think of the admiration involved in the columns of news given to O'Banion in Chicago, who was known to be guilty of some thirty murders. Or to Chapman; he is almost a hero. The police themselves speak with admiration of these men and boast of their friendship with them and the wardens and guards will often tell you proudly how they handled them and got along with them.

The part the institutional career plays in keeping the man bound to his world of crime, to his experiences as a criminal, to his hungering for a return to the field from which he came —that part is misunderstood and overlooked. The prison term is looked upon as punishment and as a separation from the world of crime. The prison was first built in the hope of isolating and gradually cleansing the criminal of his sins by giving him time for communion with God, for pondering upon his failures in life, to resolve to do better, to forget the old, and to lay the foundation for the turning over of a new page in life. As a matter of fact, it has the opposite result. It is perhaps not too much to say that the prison is the chief reason for the continuance of the criminal career, for the return of the criminal to his previous haunt. The fact that approximately 75 per cent of the professional criminals are known to be recidivists (have been in prison before) is sufficient proof that confinement does not keep them from returning. The object of the prison is not fulfilled in practice. The reason for that is not always clear and needs to be explained in some detail.

People—you and I, everyone—live in terms of experience. We are embedded in a stream of experience and are carried along by it. Our habits and our physical needs, which are served by these habits, are but contacts, relations, interests. They are loves, hates, friendships, acts; they are a satiation of the things we need and the way we have learned to feed the needs we have. We live by doing the things we do in the way we do them with people as part of the process. We practice upon other people as part of the materials of the very life we live. We carry on in a stream of experience which is both our limiting relation as well as our opportunity, but, what is perhaps most important of all, our emotional contact with the world. When arrested, the criminal leaves the stream of life experience outside the prison wall, and nothing takes its place. But man must live in terms of experience; he cannot live outside of it. After a few days, when the physical side of the prison has become a recognized and identified existence, the man slips back to the world outside. He lies on his cot and thinks, or rather indulges in day-dreams, of the things he did, the friends he had, his loves, his hates, his adventures, his world. He goes over the thing emotionally. He lives, that is, feels, over again and again the things he felt before. Experience must either be present—the thing that happens and absorbs now, that occupies attention, interest, and brings self-forgetfulness now, or it is lived in terms of the past, in what brought forgetfulness of self before. The very future that men build is rooted in the past. The castles in the air are but projections of past experiences, with past failures out of the way. They may be up in the air, but they have foundations in the ground of past behavior, past experiences, past glory and shame.

Day-dreaming for the criminal becomes a substitution for living: he lives in the past because he is not living in the present. Day-dreaming is but chewing the cud of the past, and being denied the very things that made life go. The criminal returns to them emotionally because he can feel again the past, though he cannot live it. That is in the nature of an emotional fixation. The little things drop out with time, and the keen, vivid emotional interests remain. The love, the hate, the fear, the anger, the chase, the stirring things, remain. The days pass into weeks, and weeks into months and years. The farther away the world slips in reality, the keener and the more insistent become the emotional substitutes for it. He day-dreams at his work—it is mechanical and uninteresting—and his glance is backward, turned upon the past. At night he lies on his cot and lives over again the battles and loves of yesteryears and builds new programs like unto the past. He can do nothing else; he must carry on the stream of the past because there is no present.

And so the world becomes more and more unreal, more and more emotionalized, more and more tense and vivid. Sometimes the dream world becomes a complete substitute for the real prison world, and the man goes insane; he may even become violent. That is the reason why there is comparatively more insanity in prison than in freedom; there is more day-dreaming; there is less real check upon life, less real substitutes for the dream. If he does not go insane, he always overemphasizes the feeling of content of the past. Upon release, he returns to the world from which he came; he is more inevitably bound to it than ever before.

What shall we do about it? Our present system of dealing with the criminal and the problem of crime is a futile exercise in despair and bad humor. It seemingly has no relation to the problem involved—that of changing the habits, the life interests of the people whose behavior is unsocial—or at least of intelligently *trying* to achieve such a metamorphosis in character. For it is in its residue in behavior, habit, that the system must express itself.

A short discussion of the court technic will complete the picture of the process the community employs in making the criminal. The court is confined by its organization to an examination of the act that the man is charged with. The definition is an artificial one made by a legislature apart from the specific person who actually is under trial. The lawyers and the district attorney engage in a dialectical game of trying to prove or disprove that the man did the thing involved. There is passionate contention and appeal to the emotions of the jury, and then the conviction of the criminal and the sentence. The question, Why did he do it; what kind of man is he? is slurred over. The sentence is for an arbitrary time, a few years or months, depending on the caprice of the judge and the latitude of the law. The whole thing has its origin in the definition of crime as a malicious, deliberate choosing to do evil. Hence a need for compensating punishment. It goes back to the notion that a man who does evil is possessed of evil, and that you can "exorcise the devil," drive him out by pain. It is based on the assumption that men act in terms of a calculation of pain and pleasure, and that you can remake a man by balancing the pain he gives to the community by the pain he receives from the community; that if you treat a man badly enough, you will ultimately make a saint out of him; that if you sear and scar a man for evil, he will mellow and soften and be saved. None of these assumptions is true, and none of them is acceptable as a basis for the development of a legitimate penal system.

The scheme is breaking down; the juvenile court is a breach in the prerogative of the criminal law. And even there we are going from defining the child who gets into trouble as a "delinquent" to defining him as a "problem child." When we have done that, the juvenile court will give place to the medical and psychological technic for the handling of the boy, and we shall dispense with the court procedure, just as we do in a hospital. The scheme is also breaking down with a broadening of the definition of the term "irresponsibility." We are going from insanity to admitting notions of psychopathic personality. But as long as we are organized to scrutinize the individual act of the man rather than the man himself, and as long as our court procedure is in terms of adjusting penalty to an evil act, just so long will a rational consideration of the problem be very difficult, if not impossible. Until we concern ourselves with the problem of reconstruction, center our attention there rather than upon the individual act, with legally and arbitrarily defined judgments, just so long shall we be playing an innocent game of hide-and-seek with antiquated notions, while leaving the problem of crime very much the way it was yesterday and is today.

16 two towns that are one:
a picturesque bit of americana

I WAS TALKING TO THE TEACHER, a nice, friendly, smiling, and gracious teacher, who gently, as a matter of pride, almost of indulgence, strove to point the many things of interest in the community. It was more than professional exhibitionism. There was a tone of honest boasting and friendly initiation into the excellence of Terre Haute. This is no mere city. It is no mere collection of drab structures, with a main street, a cigar store, a drug store, a "movie," and a church. Terre Haute is an old center of civilization in Indiana. It began long ago and has heroic traditions. It was settled by a sturdy, liberty-loving, adventurous folk, who found the Wabash attractive and pleasing and cast their fortunes along its beautiful banks and turbulent current. The city is one of wide streets, of old impressive residences, of neatly kept lawns, of stately trees, of long, clean thoroughfares and a busy populace. There is a little of flourishing self-conscious display about Terre Haute. Its citizens know that they live in the "Capital of the Wabash Valley Empire, one of the richest agricultural districts in America."

Terre Haute is a virtuous, God-fearing city. It is church-going and dutiful. There is the simple fact of its seventy-five

320

This essay first appeared in *Century Magazine,* III (November 1925), pp. 19–26.

churches. Each church has its Sunday-schools, endeavor
societies, men's clubs, women's socials. Not only that but at
least three of these churches are liberal and forward-looking,
progressive and abreast of the newer things in the world. It
is a city of much public spirit. There are three country clubs
in Terre Haute, a Protestant country club, a Catholic country
club, and a Jewish country club. Each country club has its
own golf-links. These are havens of rest and enjoyment, of
play and friendly rivalry for the prosperous and well-to-do
citizens of Terre Haute—places of refuge from the weightier
and more burdensome affairs of life. In addition there are
municipal golf-links for those who do not "belong."

This stress of civic interest and civic pride is fundamental
to Terre Haute. It has the largest women's club in the State
of Indiana—more than a thousand members. They are serious,
socially minded, and busy with plans and programs to do the
better and the more useful thing for Terre Haute. They
spend much time and money, they bring out-of-town lec-
turers, they participate actively in the life of the community,
they are a power to be reckoned with. To this force for the
making of public opinion is to be added the Forum, one of
the few public forums in the Middle West. It invites distinguished men from varied spheres of society, and the citizens in considerable number avail themselves of the
opportunities for information and inspiration that the Forum
provides; and it is worth registering that it is one of the very
few of such public rostrums in that part of the country.

One must of course add to the above the simple statement
that Terre Haute has a Chamber of Commerce, a busy and
wide-awake Chamber of Commerce that does its proper duty
by the city. And then too there is the Rotary Club, the Kiwanis Club, the Lions' Club, the Exchange Club, and the
Business Women's Club. A thousand other social clubs add
their varied and colorful shades of popular life and activity,
of busy conjecture and happy program. One can only mention
a few of these—the more is the pity—for a mere naming of
them all would be an impressive thing. We shall have to be

content, however, with the Blazing Stump Club, the Montrose Club, the College Hill Club, etc. But even so we are not through with the varied and organized social groupings of Terre Haute. One cannot omit the fact that Terre Haute is a strong center of the Knights of the Ku Klux Klan, who as in other places make themselves felt in a weird and mysterious fashion, always adding a bit of glamour, a bit of romance, a bit of thrill, a bit of the promise of freedom for the imagination, a bit of terror and folly, a bit of nonsense to even so sensible a city as Terre Haute. And then, last but not least, there are one hundred branches of the more prominent of the sacred and secret orders, there is a sufficiency of mystery and adventure, a sufficiency of titles and honors, of colored robes and elaborate whispers, there is a sufficiency of pretense and self-conceit to startle the dullard and satiate the mystic.

Terre Haute is an educational center of no mean importance. It possesses a school system that compares favorably with any city of its size in the Middle West. There is a cultural flavor, an interest in things intellectual, a love of books and learning, an eagerness for adventure in things of the spirit, that is strangely full of conscious striving toward a higher level—strangely because it stands out from other cities in its own environment. One of its Thursday evening clubs is an important and recognized institution. For many years there has accumulated a tradition of intellectual achievement in connection with this organization that is a creditable record and might well be emulated by other communities. The papers read at this club are preserved in the public library, and the range of interests exhibited as well as the thorough scholarship which some of these literary undertakings display would do credit to doctoral dissertations in our ordinary universities, and stand well above a large percentage of the masters' theses that are usually found acceptable in institutions of higher learning. This undertaking singled out for mention here is but one of the many aspects of Terre Haute's intellectual life. It has two schools for higher education. It is the proud home of the Indiana State Normal School, an establishment of fine reputation, and the Rose Polytechnic Institute. Then there is St. Mary of the Woods and the King Classical School. Two business colleges contribute scholarly interests to the general atmosphere, and of course there is the public school system, one that any city might well boast of. Three high schools, three junior high schools, twenty-six grade schools, and five parochial schools, all together making an impressive list of houses dedicated to schooling. To complete the record one must add a finely organized, well equipped, and much used modern library, with more than seventy-two thousand volumes. This library is like a busy workshop for the serious-minded and earnest souls that inhabit Terre Haute, not to mention the fact that the lighter spirits, those that read the less arduous fiction and the more entertaining modern magazines, find there the things that fill idle hours with fancy and dreams.

Terre Haute is not only intellectual. It is charitable. Its activities for the worthy poor are wide and varied, it gives itself without stint, it gives until it hurts and even beyond that. There is an atmosphere of kindly supervision, of generous interest, of courteous indulgence with the weaker in spirit, with the poorer in health, with the lesser in ability, with those who have either failed to arrive or have fallen by the wayside, that fills Terre Haute with activities of a charitable character which last from one year to another. It would be impossible to enumerate all the balls, dances, card-parties, sociables, country-club affairs, Kiwanis and Rotary activities, church festivities which are organized for the purpose of charity, for the purpose of brightening the hours, the days, the years, the very lives of the needy and the poor. There are classes for under-privileged children; there are Y.M.C.A. activities, Y.W.C.A. activities; there is a day nursery, a Welfare League, a Light House Mission, a Salvation Army to add its ready tune in the name of charity and salvation. Terre Haute has many things worthy of mention, but the following will be enough: the Friendly Inn, the Florence Crittenden Home, the Gibault Home, Glenn Orphans' Home, Rose Or-

324 phans' Home, and the Fairbanks Home for Aged Women. There are, in addition, two well organized and equipped hospitals.

I nearly overlooked the city's bathing-pool. "The best people in town" are using it. There have been innumerable parties at the pool. Thursday there were two couples from Chicago, and they said that the pool "beat anything which Chicago had." Then of course there are the city's athletic activities, sports for the old and the young, for the rich and the poor. As one of the editors of Terre Haute gracefully puts it, "As we look backward through the winter and allow our thoughts to dwell on the many interesting entertainments which we have enjoyed, we fail to find any reason why we should be sorry that our home is in Terre Haute, a city of clean amusement and sport . . and invite those who are less fortunate than ourselves, in that they do not live amongst us, to come to Terre Haute with their industries, their business interests, and their families."

Important and significant also is the fact that Terre Haute has a strong and well led trade-union movement. This is especially true among the miners. Here is a force for social-mindedness and creative interest in community life that helps give Terre Haute much of its liberalism. Terre Haute has in addition been the home of Eugene V. Debs, a veteran in the cause of social justice, a man who has done yeomanly service in stirring America to a sense of social deficiency and to awaken the imaginative interest in a better-ordered world.

Terre Haute is prosperous, even rich. It is fortunate in its natural resources. Not only has it a world-famous river (and Terre Haute is fully conscious of all it owes to the Wabash), a rich agricultural valley, but it has coal, three billion tons of workable coal.

Terre Haute is not only prosperous, but, as already suggested, it is rich. The ten banks in Terre Haute have combined resources of thirty-seven million dollars and deposits of more than twenty-seven millions. Its people are a saving, careful, industrious people. There are fifteen building and loan associations in the city serving the needs of the citizens, and they alone have assets valued at fifteen million dollars. One hundred and seventy different industries give employment to fourteen thousand workers who receive an annual income of fourteen million dollars. There are a hundred miles of sewerage within the city limits, a five-cent fare and thirty miles of street-car tracks, as well as eighty miles of interurban railroads that tie the city to its rich and picturesque neighborhood. The city has fifteen parks, which added together make five hundred and twenty acres; and adding to its beauty, cleanliness, and pride are sixty miles of paved streets within the city limits as well as two hundred and fifty miles of concrete sidewalks. These are but a few of the many things about Terre Haute; they are taken from a modest list sent out by the Terre Haute Chamber of Commerce.

Nor is this all. Terre Haute is at the very core of things American. It is only forty miles from the center of population. It combines the older, duller East and the lighter, fresher, more picturesque West. Two national highways, the National Old Trail and the Dixie Bee Highway, cross on its main street; what the people of Terre Haute fondly call the "Cross-roads of the World" are at the crossing of Seventh and Wabash streets. "The Tall Sycamore," who runs a column in the leading paper of Terre Haute under the caption of "On the Banks of the Wabash," notes that "10,000 people drive through this crossing per day and the cars come from all the States of the Union, one day alone having seen license-plates from 38 different States," and insists that "the need of the Cross-roads of the World marker is imperative. It will bring more fame to Terre Haute." This central location of Terre Haute makes a very well served railroad point. It is entered by four railroad trunk-lines, and seventy passenger trains per day leave Terre Haute for all points of the compass. It is at the very heart of America and is striving to be worthy of its fortunate position. A stadium to the soldier dead is now going up, at a cost of four hundred thousand dollars, and even while this civic project is still incomplete a new one on a more ambitious scale is being planned. To properly commemorate the name of Paul Dresser, the author of "On the Banks of the Wabash," a Dresser memorial is to be constructed which will make the entrance to the city "the most beautiful of any in the country." Terre Haute is prepared to welcome all comers; the entrance to the city is the beginning of a reception that lasts while you linger and which is inviting for a return. Twenty-five hotels are there at your disposal—good and bad, costly and cheap, for the rich and the poor; a welcome is extended to every passer-by and to every prospective settler.

In a measure also the new American religion is as well under way here as in almost any city of the country. This new American religion, which is foreshadowed flamboyantly, arrogantly, self-assertively, and with advertising display, that this is the best little town in the world, finds discipleship and followers in Terre Haute. I mean not only the arrogance of the boast that this is the best little town—or rather the greatest little town of the world—but the new version that we are going to make this the greatest little town is also to be found. The new note of civic interest, of real civic pride, of honest endeavor to plan, to build, to beautify, to prune, and to varnish, to make a home, to build a city, to make the place of one's birth and growth a place of honest endeavor for the nurture of good fruit and gentle spirit—I mean the interest which the social worker has cultivated, the philanthropist contributed to, the politician rendered lip service to, the revolutionist challenged the world on, the old bitter cry, that is, that we are our brothers' keepers—this note, even in spite of ourselves, has its disciples here. We must make Terre Haute a place where the under-privileged child will be given special privileges, where the under-nourished will be given special food, where the poor will be fed—or better still where there will be no poor, where the community will organize itself to protect and nurture life and give genius and faith the means wherewith to challenge the evils of the world; the dream of a city beautiful is not entirely absent from Terre Haute. All these aspects of the new religion are to be found here, and there is a liberalism and decency to it all that is well worth detailed enumeration. Terre Haute is a home that expresses much of the beautiful and the true.

I WAS talking to the teacher, a nice, friendly, smiling, and gracious teacher, who gently, as a matter of pride, almost of indulgence, strove to point the many things of interest in the community. It was more than professional exhibitionism. There was a tone of honest boasting and friendly initiation into the excellence of Terre Haute.

"What," asked I, "is the scapegoat of Terre Haute?"

"What do you mean?"

"Well, what's the city down on?"

"Oh! Taylorsville."

"Then lead me to Taylorsville."

Taylorsville is on the banks of the beautiful, turbulent Wabash. Its inhabitants are pure Anglo-Saxon stock. The Negro is driven from its doors, and the foreigner is frowned out of countenance. There is something exclusive, self-sufficient, and selective about this community. It is old, as old as Terre Haute. Its inhabitants count their descent from the pioneers; its persistent struggle against the turbulent current of the beautiful Wabash bespeaks a heroic strain. For many long years the Wabash has risen and washed the community away—carried off its belongings, wrecked its habitations, endangered its life. Soaked, muddy, cold, stripped of their worldly goods, with nothing but suffering and hope to avail them, they always and inevitably returned to their chosen plot and resurrected such fortune out of the debris of their scattered possessions as the receding current left behind it. They rebuilt their homes—homes made out of reeds, tin cans, old sacks, and odd pieces of wood. It is a squatters' community. It does no work, at least not regularly. It has no streets, no lights, no sewerage, no proper water system; it is neglected and frowned upon—but bravely persists in its slender hold upon the shores of the Wabash. Its people are

328 often dirty, unkempt, shaggy, dressed in odd styles. It makes
its living in dubious, doubtful ways. One travels its length
and breadth and finds little industry. Men, big and strong,
are found lying on their backs, their trousers rolled up above
their knees, smoking corn-cob pipes. Its main occupation
seems to be collecting. It collects everything collectable—tin
cans, rags, bottles, pieces of wood, cast-offs, ashes, dirt; its
business is to act as the scavenger of Terre Haute. Its greatest point of activity is in the evening when the garbage, dirt,
and filth of Terre Haute are cast out on the dumpings. Then
Taylorsville gets busy and begins collecting—little things—a
reed, a piece of leather, a torn dress, an edible morsel, a
relishing left-over, a thing of beauty no longer serviceable
in the proud city but here useful and coveted. It collects
broken dishes and strands of hair, accidental pieces of coal
and cracked looking-glasses. Taylorsville is the worst, the
poorest, the least attractive community I have seen in the
United States. It is worse than the poorest Negro sections
of some of our Southern cities; it is poorer and more neglected
than the Mexican section of San Antonio. It is a part of Terre
Haute and votes in Terre Haute—and I understand heavily
and with a will.

In talking to the people of Terre Haute about Taylorsville
I noticed a most curious and at first mystifying reaction.
People shrugged their shoulders and then smiled—rather
foolishly—a sort of idiotic grin of sheepish glee and blushing
bashfulness. It was disconcerting. Gradually it dawned on
me that Terre Haute was proud of Taylorsville, that it liked
to talk about it, to tell tales about it, to weep over it, to tell
funny stories about it, to make a mystery of it, a comedy, an
emotional exercise. If Taylorsville were to move away. Terre
Haute would really feel that it had lost something, something indefinite but real enough. All of the jokes in Terre
Haute are about Taylorsville, jokes of varied and numerous
incidence; the tragedies of Taylorsville are half a joke to Terre
Haute, a sort of indulgence in emotional exasperation, half
hysterical, half jocular. All the tragedy of Terre Haute has its

origins in Taylorsville. Let something happen in Terre Haute, and Taylorsville did it. Not some particular person in Taylorsville,—oh, no,—but Taylorsville. Terre Haute likes to tell of the terrible things that happen in Taylorsville, or, as one man called it, "Our Little Hollywood."

I heard from a dozen different sources that recently a mother and a daughter gave birth to a child each, within one week, and that the father of the daughter was the male parent of both children. Some told it as if it were funny and some as if it were a great scandal and some with a little peevishness, but none so far as I could see with real indignation or with real sorrow. The point is that it is hard to take Taylorsville in a normal mood; it is either melodramatic or humorous. Another tale was of a daughter and a mother quarreling over a piece of the shroud purchased for the mother's prospective funeral; and the quarrel was over the fact that the daughter wanted a piece of the shroud for a dress so that she could attend the funeral of her mother. Now that "bootlegging" has become a fairly respectable and comparatively safe enterprise, Terre Haute believes that Taylorsville has become fabulously wealthy; it is supposed to roll in wealth. People talk about it in wonder. Every little thing grows to great extremes. A fire takes place in Taylorsville, and the paper reports the following incident: "The fire had just been extinguished . . . when some man unknown to the firemen ran into the ruins, grabbed up a copper kettle, a coil, and a few other miscellaneous parts of the still and fled into the fields at the south of the village as fast as he could go." Everything about Taylorsville is exaggerated. A reporter goes to Taylorsville, and this is what appears on the front page of the leading newspaper for May 1, 1924:

"POOR TAYLORSVILLE!"

"Poor Taylorsville!

"Home of the down and out—the under dog; last stand of the unfortunate paupers whom the grinding heel of the city has forced into a poverty as ugly as it is wretched.

"And now it faces oblivion at the hands of the Paul Dresser

Memorial association. With a view to beautifying the district, it proposes to wipe out the 'Little Hollywood' of Terre Haute!

"With these heart-rending thoughts in mind a reporter for the Post fared forth to commiserate with the over-the-river oppressed. He traveled the length of the village.

"He got an awful shock.

"Evidence of poverty there was to be sure. Squalor abounded. But lo, there also was evidence of wealth than which the downtown district itself affords no better!

"Here are some of the things he saw:

"Twelve large, new, high priced motor cars, parked before various pseudoresidences of the suburb. They were not just 'autos'; they were 'motor cars' with an approximate total value of 25 or 30 thousand dollars. There were two Cadillacs, two Buicks, a Stutz, a Marmon, a Packard, and others of like makes.

"He saw taxi-cabs coming and going with brisk frequency. During his 90-minute survey, no less than five taxis bustled into and out of the village, discharging or picking up cargoes of passengers.

       o   o   o

"Well-dressed men, and in one or two instances, expensively gowned women, went into and out of the houses. At one place the reporter saw a woman emerge from a house and approach a limousine at the street, drinking from a bottle as she went.

"It was surely a revelation to the reporter.

"Poor Taylorsville!"

It must be obvious that this appearance on the front page of such an unusual article takes for granted both a common knowledge as well as a half-hilarious, half-tragic attitude toward Taylorsville on the part of the citizens of Terre Haute. The reader will note some of the references to Taylorsville.

The reporter fared forth to commiserate.

He got an awful shock.

Evidence of wealth which even the down-town district affords no better.

Motor-cars (not automobiles).

Pseudo residences (he could not say shacks, hovels).

The taxis came with brisk frequency.

Cargoes of passengers.

Expensively gowned women.

It surely was a revelation to the reporter.

Terre Haute is much exercised over Taylorsville; at least it indulges itself at the expense of Taylorsville. Many of its social functions, much of its emotional and society life, is organized about Taylorsville. A large number of the balls, card-parties, country-club affairs, dinners, teas, meetings, resolutions, committees, are about Taylorsville. Terre Haute collects money in the summer-time to keep Taylorsville from freezing in the winter-time; it occupies its winters in preparing for the emergencies of the spring floods. It is concerned over the health, the morals, the well-being of Taylorsville, and Taylorsville is not at all grateful. A friend reports the following conversation with one of the substantial citizens of Taylorsville: "Terre Haute ain't done nothin' fer Taylorsville —why should they ask anything of us? We didn't git none of that money we was supposed to git after the cyclone in 1913. Did you see what the papers called us? They called us dogs! They wus ten dollars' worth of them papers sold in Taylorsville every week, and now they don't sell one." So much for gratitude.

This relationship between these two American cities was hard to understand until one day it all became clear and obvious. Taylorsville lives physically on Terre Haute, and Terre Haute lives spiritually on Taylorsville. Taylorsville acts as the scavenger for Terre Haute; Terre Haute finds inspiration in Taylorsville. Taylorsville feeds on the left-overs from Terre Haute, and Terre Haute feeds on the sorrows, the misery, the shortcomings of Taylorsville; they supplement each other and enrich each other's existence. Taylorsville would starve if Terre Haute were to move away; Terre Haute would be stripped of much of its emotional interests if Taylorsville were to be swept away by the beautiful and turbulent Wabash.

This essay was written to raise a question rather than to

332   point a moral. It was not written to defame Terre Haute. I
       have said all the nice things that Terre Haute says about
       itself, and I am willing to take Terre Haute at its word. Does
       every American town have a Taylorsville? Does every Amer-
       ican town need a Taylorsville? What does such a relationship
       mean in American religion, politics, philosophy? Must every
       town in the United States have a scapegoat, and what would
       it do if it suddenly found itself without one? I am merely
       asking a question. It is for others to answer it.

the miracle school 17

THE WHOLE EDUCATIONAL SITUATION in Mexico is exceedingly interesting, probably the most interesting thing in Mexico. At the head of the Department of Education is Señor José Vasconcelos, whose great ambition it is to give Mexico a public-school system. The difficulties are so numerous and the lack of material equipment and educational personnel so great that he is prepared to accept any assistance from any source. He is reported to have said that if the devil were to come and offer to establish a school to teach the children to read and write, he would be cordially welcomed. The problem of standardization, of method, of curriculum—all that will come afterward; the first need is schools where the children can learn to read and write.

One day a man walked into Mr. Vasconcelos' office and said:

"Señor, I should like to establish a school."

Reprinted from *Century Magazine*, CVI (August 1923), pp. 499–506.

"Go ahead; we are delighted," said Mr. Vasconcelos.

"I should like to establish a school in the Colonia de la Bolsa," said the man. Mr. Vasconcelos looked at him inquiringly.

"In the Colonia de la Bolsa?" repeated Mr. Vasconcelos in a surprised tone. "You know what the Colonia de la Bolsa is?"

"Yes, I know," interrupted the visitor, Mr. Oropeza, quietly. Mr. Vasconcelos smiled and said:

"We give you our blessing. Go and establish a school."

Everybody knows that the Colonia de la Bolsa is a thief's paradise. It is not suggested that paradise is like the Colonia de la Bolsa. It is the haven for the outcasts of Mexico City. The bums, tramps, thieves, pickpockets, burglars, and disreputable women congregate in the Colonia de la Bolsa. No policeman is kept there; first, because it would not be safe, and, secondly, because the people are too poor to steal from one another, anyway. The place has no streets. No garbage is ever collected in the district. It has no water system, and the Department of Health does not know of its existence. I know people who own property in the Colonia de la Bolsa, but who never go to collect rent. It would not be safe, and the people have no money. The district has never had a school. It was just left alone to its destiny, and forgotten except for the delinquent children. One half of all those of Mexico City came from that district.

One day Mr. Oropeza appeared in the district. An ordinary man of a little over medium height, dark complexion, small, round black eyes, and a quiet voice that was hardly more than a whisper; rather retiring, bashful, unobtrusive, slim, and slightly stooping, no one paid any attention to him. He found a place to live in one of the houses of the district, and for two months just took in his environment and his new acquaintances.

One Sunday morning he startled his neighbors by appearing on the streets with a wheelbarrow of books. He knocked at the first door. The master of the house came out, and Mr. Oropeza said:

"Good morning. What would you like to read this morning?" Everybody in Mexico is polite, even the thieves are polite. The man took off his hat, bowed, and said:

"Good morning, señor." Then, not knowing what to do, he called his wife, and the wife called the children. To be offered something and not to accept is outside the ethical code, and so, after much discussion and examination, they picked a book, and Mr. Oropeza told them that he would be back the next Sunday morning, and if they had finished the book, he would bring them another one. He went to the next door, and to the next, until all his books were gone. He returned next Sunday with more books, and found that some of the men had covered the books with newspapers to keep them from being soiled. Others had built little shelves for them, and still others, not being able to read themselves, had formed a little group and hired a ragged beggar to read to them, paying him by contributing a few centavos each.

Mr. Oropeza kept this up for nine months. He built up a library of seven hundred volumes. In all that time he never lost a book. The people waited for him at their doorsteps in the early dawn. The children came and helped him push the wheelbarrow. He became the friend and confidant of the neighborhood. The children took off their hats as he went by. One fine morning some of the elders of the neighborhood came and said:

"Señor, it would be nice if we could have a school for our children."

"Yes," said Mr. Oropeza.

"Well, can't we have one?"

"Let us find out," said Mr. Oropeza.

"Yes, let us find out," they said.

So one morning a delegation of the Colonia de la Bolsa appeared at the office of the commissioner of education and startled the department by asking for a school. Mr. Vasconcelos said:

"I have nothing to give you just now except an old beer-garden in the Colonia de la Bolsa. Take that and make a school."

The old beer-garden was the last house in the district. During the revolution it had been wrecked; the walls and the ceilings were on the floor. The teacher called the children together and said, "Let us make a school." They did. The first thing to do was to clean the place up and reconstruct it The teacher showed them how to do it. He picked up a stone and began to carry it out. The children did the same. There was no organization. There was no telling this child to do this and this child to do that. The children knew the place had to be reconstructed, and every child did what he could or would. Some did one thing and others did another, and some did half a dozen things during the day. They sat down when they were tired and worked when they felt like it. The children gradually divided into groups. Some children pulled grass with their hands, some carried stones, and some pushed wheelbarrows, and all had a joyous time. Each little group found its own leader, and the children naturally called him a commissioner. And being called a commissioner made him feel like one, and gave him a sense of responsibility and new ideas. There was a commissioner of a wheelbarrow and a commissioner of a stone pile. There were as many commissioners as there were jobs, and as many groups as concentrated about a particular thing. One day one child would be a commissioner of one thing, and another day a commissioner of something else; thus the work progressed gradually. Out of one room alone the children carted four hundred wheelbarrows of stone and dirt, and all to the tune of much joy. All the children in the neighborhood heard of the great enterprise, and many came to share in it, because it was a happy one.

In a little while they had the place cleaned, and the ceilings and walls began to be reconstructed, and the children came to the teacher and said:

"Teacher, shall we do this?" and the teacher said:

"Yes." The teacher added: "I do not know anything about teaching. All I know is that I love the children and that they teach me."

And so the children reconstructed the walls and fixed up the ceilings. When all the dirt had been taken out of the inside of the school, they began to clean up the outside of the school, and gradually followed the dirt into the streets of the neighborhood.

Those streets had never seen a broom from the days of creation, and the first appearance of little children sweeping them startled the neighborhood. Occasionally, one might now see an older man sweeping the streets with the children, attempting to discover the secret that made the children so playful and happy at their task.

The pigs in the neighborhood enjoyed the privilege of scattering the dirt the children collected. But one day the children came and said:

"Teacher, why don't the big wagons come and collect the piles of dirt we sweep together with our brooms?" And the teacher said, "I do not know." So one of the children said, "Let us find out," and the teacher said, "Yes; let us find out."

One of the children who had seen a parade of workers in the streets of Mexico City said, "Let us have a parade." The teacher said, "Yes, let us have a parade." And Mexico City was soon startled by the appearance of nine hundred ragamuffins, but with clean bare feet, with many little signs demanding that the big wagons come and collect the dirt in the Colonia de la Bolsa. And so now at nine o'clock every morning the big wagons come and collect the dirt that the children sweep together in the early dawn. The children come at five o'clock in the morning, and stay until it gets dark. They don't have to come until half-past eight. The teachers don't come until half-past eight. The children come as soon as they get out of bed. And as soon as they arrive they get busy. Some sweep, some push wheelbarrows, and some go out in groups to sweep the streets, and some set the table for breakfast. Everybody is busy.

After they had cleaned out the yard and pulled out the weeds, one of the children who had come from the country and had seen his mother plant vegetables said to the teacher, "Can I have a piece of land to plant vegetables?" And the teacher said, "Yes." Soon another child wanted a piece of land, and another and another. In fact, they all wanted a piece of land. That raised many new problems. The land had to be divided. It had to be distributed in some form of order to the children who asked for it. And so there gradually grew up a commissioner of agriculture, and he now has nine assistants. The commissioner is twelve years old, barefooted and black-eyed.

To get the land the children had to ask for it. To do so formally they had to make a written request. They suddenly developed a craving for writing. They went to Señor Oropeza, and Señor Oropeza went to the department of education and secured a teacher to teach the children how to write. As soon as a child could, he wrote to the "Most Honorable Commissioner of Agriculture," asking that he might have a piece of land to work in the mornings and grow vegetables.

There was no standard form, and each child wrote on such a piece of paper and in such poetic language as he discovered. Each applicant received from the commissioner of agriculture a piece of official-looking paper. The paper had a big red stamp and a number. The stamp made it official. It was the deed for the child's piece of land. The children became landowners. The children planted vegetables. They dug, scratched, hoed, pulled weeds, asked innumerable questions, had long disputes and deliberations about the things to plant. Some of the children planted one thing, some an-

other, a few experimented with different things at the same
time, and all the while there was much joy. The commissioner
of agriculture became an important personage. He not only
distributed the land, but he and his assistants supervised
operations. The agricultural commission was taxed for tools,
for seeds, for advice. There were many applications for land.
Those who neglected to work their little holdings were asked
to surrender them to children who had no land. Disputes
arose. This brought a judicial commission into being: it just
grew up.

The commission of agriculture needed money. It had to
purchase tools and seed. Some one suggested that the children ought to pay a regular tax. Now each child pays five
centavos a month for each piece of land, and they can have
as many pieces as they work well.

The ripening vegetables brought new problems. They had
to be disposed of. Some of the children knew more about
market than others. They became the marketing commission.
This commission has three members. They go to market every
Friday morning and acquaint themselves with the prices of
beets, carrots, onions, radishes, cabbages, and other things
grown at the school. Each child brings to the commission of
markets all the things he can sell at that time. A common
price is set for each kind of vegetable, a little lower than the
regular market price. After the products have been disposed
of, the money is divided into three parts. One third goes to
the agricultural commission to buy more seeds and tools,
one third goes to the bank, for by this time a bank had been
developed, and one third goes to the child that raised the
vegetables. Ten per cent of the total sum is given over to the
school for the lunch which is provided free to some two
hundred homeless children.

All of this imposed elaborate mathematical problems upon
the children. Arithmetic became a pressing matter. They
wanted to know just where they stood financially. What was
a child worth when he had twenty beets, fifty radishes, three

hundred onions, and a dozen cabbages, when the price of each was different from the other, and when they had to give one-third to the commission of agriculture, one-third to the bank, and ten per cent of the whole sum to the school luncheon fund? They went to the teacher of arithmetic. The teacher of arithmetic has a big room with a large blackboard. The children come and present their problems. The arithmetic teacher puts it all on the blackboard and simplifies things. Occasionally the children become interested in one another's problems and stay in the room while the other children's problems are being worked out. If not, they say, "With your permission, may I leave the room?" Everybody in Mexico says "with your permission," and permission is always granted. So the children go and busy themselves with other more pressing things, because they are more interesting.

As soon as the children began to get money, the problem of saving arose. To keep from losing it, they elected a commissioner of banks. The banker keeps the money of all the children in a big paper bag. He was the only child that had shoes. Each little child has a record of the amount due him. If a child wants to buy a pair of trousers, for instance, as one of the youngsters told me he wanted to do, he goes to the bank and borrows some money, giving the bank a note, with a promise to pay interest and return it at a certain time. If he does not keep his word, the case goes before the judicial commission. A judicial commission has gradually developed. This commission becomes the center of an elaborate legal battle. The judgment it renders is very serious because if the child loses his land, he really loses something. One child had four pieces of five Mexican dollars. The boy had twenty Mexican dollars, and that for a grown peon, not a child, is almost a million. And so, if the court decides against him, it is not mere play. The poor child has really lost a fortune.

The Department of Education serves nine thousand children with breakfast every morning. Nine hundred of those

are in this school. The children know that the breakfast-table
has to be set, and so they set it. Nobody tells them to set it.
When they come, if they do not go out to sweep, push a
wheelbarrow, or pull weeds, they are doing something else,
and that something else may happen to be setting the table.
When it is set, they are ready for breakfast.

While they have been setting the table, some of the other
children have been filling a great big tub of water. I remember one morning seeing two little tots not more than five
years old dragging a pail and, in a little while, coming back
with it, literally dragging it along the ground, spilling the
water, as it was too heavy for them to lift. They got the water
into the tub and then they brought another pail and emptied
that into the tub, and sat down, panting for breath. Then a
large boy went for water. He saw the tub and the pail. He
knew that the tub would have to have water, and the pail
was there to bring water to the tub, and so he took it and
went for the water.

When everybody is ready for breakfast and everybody is
standing in line, just ready to step up to the table, where
there are hot milk and rolls, they have to pass this tub of
water. Before it stands a little commissioner of hands and
faces, with a big towel. He scrutinizes each one. After they
pass him, there is another little commissioner standing near
him, the commissioner of noses, who is armed with a big pile
of small handkerchiefs. If a child is really too young to perform the public operation himself, or doesn't know enough,
the commissioner does it for him.

Then they are ready for breakfast.

After breakfast the three hundred children wash and clean
the dishes and set the table for the other children.

There is also a small commission of woolly heads that
occupies itself with shearing about twenty crops a day. They
capture a little midget whose hair seems to be dangerously
long. If he begrudges them the privilege of making an operation on his hair, he can appeal to the judicial commission,

and then the judicial commission, after a careful survey, decides the fate of the child's hair.

The children who are most quarrelsome have, by a curious instinct and common consent, been elected as judges, the philosophy, I suppose, being that those who quarrel most should themselves best understand the quarrels of others. And the fighting boys are made commissioners of law and order.

The older children in the neighborhood who have to work for a living could not resist the temptation of going to the school, so they came and said, "Teacher, we should like to come to school," and the teacher said, "Come." But they couldn't. They had to earn some money. So one of the older boys suggested that he would work his way through school by teaching the younger children his craft, and then they would work for him while he was going to school. Now all the older children of the neighborhood who want to go to school come and find some of the younger children who want to learn their particular trade. The little ones spend part of their time working for the older ones while they are going to school. The teacher smiles and says, "Yes," and teaches them goodness. He doesn't teach them honesty. I asked him why not, and he said:

"They learn to be honest by having honest relations with one another."

But he does teach them goodness.

I don't quite know what "goodness" is, but it is something like this: he points out that if you do not plant the soil, it grows weeds. If you do plant it, there are also weeds growing up beside the plants, and those are bad habits that you have to pull out. Then he has a little silkworm establishment, and the children come and watch the little worm spinning its threads. Of course there is a commissioner of silkworms, and that is a child most interested in the silkworm. Then the teacher points out that the silkworm never breaks its thread. If it did, it would die. And he says, "We Mexicans always begin things and never finish them. We break our threads, and that is why we die." That he calls "goodness."

The children's problems are increasing as the activities of the school continue. For instance, for a time the remains from the breakfast were wasted, until one day a child suggested that they ought to have some chickens to eat the crumbs that were left over. Now there are a few chickens about the school, and there is a chicken commission, and the children take much joy in feeding the chickens and looking after them. They want to know all about them, so now the teacher is worrying about somebody to teach the children about chickens.

Another child has been asking for permission to bring a little pig to school, because, he says, "Pigs can eat the bread the same as the chickens can," and he would like to be commissioner of pigs.

The children in the school have spread out into the community so that the community is becoming the school and the school is becoming the community. Soon it will be hard to tell which is which. The children have assumed the responsibility of older people, they clean the streets, they have planted trees, and they refuse to go for liquor for their parents, and the parents don't get drunk so frequently.

The children insist on being kept clean; so they are teaching their parents the habits of cleanliness. The children bring their parents to a moving-picture show or a lecture on a Saturday night, and keep them from going to the drinking-shop, and so save their weekly income.

As soon as the children began to clean the streets they became interested in the habits of their parents, who, because of lack of proper toilets, used to perform the excreting functions of the body in the highways and byways. Now the children are leading their parents off the streets. The children came to their teacher and said, "Why don't we have public places, as they have in Mexico?" and the teacher said, "I don't know." They said, "Let's find out." The reason was very simple: that district had never paid any taxes, and therefore did not get any benefits. Thus it was the children who began to collect centavos and half-pesos, and it was they who were responsible for the demand that public toilets be built in the district. Ten are now being constructed.

The school has now grown so that it has nine hundred children. That is, all the little ones in the neighborhood, as soon as they can crawl, come into the school. They cannot stay away. They have something like a dozen teachers. The teachers teach the children what they want to know, and if the children love them, the children want to know everything, especially things that are related to their own problems. As the children's problems become more complex, the information they want is more specialized. Thus it is interesting to recall that when the big patio was broken up into little patches of garden there was a walk around it. Next to the walk, against the wall, was about one and a half feet of land that lay idle for a year. It never occurred to anyone to do anything with it until one day a child who had seen flowers against a wall came to the teacher and said, "Teacher, can I plant some flowers?" The teacher said, "Yes." So the child began to plant flowers, and pretty soon other children wanted to do the same thing, and there gradually grew up a commissioner of flowers, and now every inch of land against the wall is planted with flowers. When they finished planting flowers inside, they wanted to know why they couldn't plant flowers against the wall outside of the school. Thus the outside has bowers planted there, too.

Now the children want to know about flowers, their kind, seasons, names, etc., and thus they have to have somebody at the school who knows something about flowers, not to teach the children, but to tell them what they want to know about flowers when they want to know it.

This impetus on the part of the children for going to school has affected the parents and the elders in the neighborhood, and now there are three hundred of them going to night school. They, too, are broken up into groups according to their interests. They do not go to school to learn reading, writing, and arithmetic. They go to school to find out something about what they want to know. Some go to school to find out whether they are being cheated when they get so much per meter for a piece of cloth of a certain length and width, and how can they tell how much they ought to get. Those who want to become conductors come to learn something about arithmetic and the map of Mexico City—about how to read the streets. And the mothers come and want to find out how to take care of their children. Some mothers bring their children to school and stay and watch them study, and they themselves learn. Thus the school and the community are becoming one.

When a child comes to the school, nobody pays any attention to him. He is not told to do this or to do that or to do some other thing. He is just left alone, and pretty soon he makes friends. As soon as he makes friends, he wants to do what the friends are doing, and he does it, and nobody tells him not to. Gradually he finds himself, and pretty soon he wants to get a piece of land on which to grow vegetables. Then he has to learn how to write to make the request. In a little while he wants to get some seeds, and he has to borrow some money, and then he has to keep a record of his debts and a record of his income, and he has to learn something about arithmetic. Then pretty soon he has to go to court over a dispute, and then in a little while he may become a commissioner. All the time he is having a wonderful, joyous, busy time. So what has happened is that delinquent children have disappeared, and the chief of police has written Mr. Oropeza, telling him that virtually all the delinquent children of that neighborhood have disappeared in the last two years. The children are so busy they have no time to be bad, and it is much more fun, anyway. Even the little unadjusted children, in the variety and complexity of the life in the school, soon find something to do, and as nobody pays any attention to them, they do something for one while and something else for another while, and learn what they can, and the school is growing.

Mr. Oropeza says, "I love the children, and they teach me." One time he added, "If only more people would come and let the children teach them, Mexico would soon stop breaking its threads and live." And so the miracle of miracles —a child shall lead them—is working.

SUPPLEMENTARY NOTE 1923

The little school is growing. That was one of the first things I learned upon my return to Mexico City this year. There have been new developments and expansions. New problems have arisen and new discoveries have been made and still greater difficulties are being struggled with. The teacher is hopeful. So much has been done—so much more needs doing—and it will, somehow, get itself accomplished.

The organized activities of the children reach more fully into the life of the Colonia de la Bolsa than they did last year. That is probably the most noticeable development of the school since I first visited it. The people of the neighborhood have become greater participants in the school and feel its influence at more points.

The cleaning of the streets still goes on. The children with their little brooms invade the community every morning and sweep the dirt into piles. The cleaning of the streets has become a point of competition with the elders in the neighborhood. The children began by cleaning the blocks nearest the school. The older folks were teased into participation and as they joined the children in the work the little ones gradually drifted to the neighboring streets, where such love

of cleanliness had not been stimulated. And so it has gone.
The children invade a street. The older folks shamed out of
their laziness flock into the street with brooms and crowd
the children into exploring new fields while a spirit of rivalry
manifests itself between the older folks in the different
corners. The children have thus become the initiators of an
enterprise which their parents carry on.

Last year's program for the construction of public comfort
houses in the neighborhood broke down on account of many
political and financial difficulties—especially because it was
discovered that it would involve far-reaching reconstruction
in the water works system of Mexico City to give the Colonia
de la Bolsa proper drainage—and so a new method—that of
building deep pits and using lime—the type used in the American Army cantonments, was developed and the children dug
the first one—and then supervised the digging of the others.
More than one hundred of these pits have now been built
and in each case it was the children who supervised and instructed their elders in the doing of it.

The school has constructed a bath for itself—and the
colony has given land for a public bath—but they have no
money for the materials. The ways of the school are strange.
The night school where the elders gather has become a kind
of local government. The needs of the community are discussed and settled there. The night school keeps the neighborhood clean by cooperative enterprise, a cooperative dis-
pensary has been organized—five centavos a week—and a
doctor, medicine and funeral expenses are provided while
the night school pupils do the nursing by turn. The night
school has developed a commission for mothers—and
more than a hundred children are looked after and instruction in hygiene is given on Tuesday and Thursday at
11 A.M.

Their newly discovered interest in cleanliness has its
varied manifestations. On Saturday, the children distribute
little printed cards in the neighborhood giving instructions

about cleanliness in some specific thing as, "How to kill flies," "How to clean mattresses," "How to rid dogs of fleas." The people wait for these instructions on Saturday morning and then make a rush to apply them. One Saturday every dog in the neighborhood was waylaid and given a scrubbing. The dogs howled for mercy at this new affliction and appeared skeptical and a little abashed at their unexpected washing.

The children's influence has reduced drunkenness and some of the pulque shops in the neighborhood have closed their doors while others have begged and tried to bribe the teacher into abandoning the education against drink.

The night school elects, for each patio in which there are a number of families, a kind of superviser who watches over them and who reports to the night school anything out of the way. One day a Captain and a band of robbers settled in one of these patios and the night school sent a commission to the Captain asking him to go somewhere else to live. "Why should I and my men not stay here?" he asked. "Because you will do harm to our children," they replied. "Where are your children?" They answered, "In our school." The Captain of the bandits came and looked over the children working on their pieces of land and busy with their cooperatives and said, "Yes, I think you are right. I and my men will not be good for your children." So he took himself and his followers out of the neighborhood. This is but one illustration of the curious influence of the school on the neighborhood. The children are teaching their parents not to swear—at least not so much. And recently they printed and distributed a little card on "Why Parents Should Not Scold Their Children." To protect the young children who in the crowded poverty stricken houses have always slept in one room with the older members of the family, the night school has succeeded in getting in each patio one room set aside for the children to sleep in and the children have instructed their elders in the use of trousers—a habit which many of the older inhabitants had never acquired—a robosa being used instead.

In a hundred ways that one cannot describe the school has developed and is growing. Probably the most interesting feature of the last year's growth has been the development of children's cooperatives in the school. That is, a number of children organize a cooperative association for some specific purpose. There were five when I was there last—a bakers' cooperative, a soap makers' cooperative, a dressmakers' cooperative, a tanners' cooperative and a printers' cooperative. A number of children sign an agreement to carry on some common enterprise—select officers—a commissioner, a purchaser, a machinist, a bookkeeper, a treasurer, etc. They borrow some money from the bank (they have a real little bank with 500 pesos loaned to them by Ramon P. de Negri, Secretary of Agriculture and a little banker, fourteen years old, who keeps the accounts of all the cooperatives and private depositors— he is so small that one has to lean over the counting table to see him)—make their purchases of raw material, manufacture it, sell it in the market and after paying their debt to the bank divide the income—part goes to the school and the remainder is evenly divided amongst the children. The cooperatives are designed to meet the needs of the community. The bakers' cooperative has an oven which was given to it by the Department of Commerce and Labor—and they actually bake fine rolls and sell them to the neighborhood at such a price that many of the people who have always lived on tortillas are finding it cheaper and better to purchase these rolls, incidentally raising their standards of living. The teacher told me that in the recent months of straitened finances it was the bakers' cooperative that enabled them to look after the orphans of the school who would otherwise have had to go on the streets. The same is true with the soap makers and printers. The only interference with the cooperatives is in the supplying them with technical instructors—until they learn their trade.

These cooperatives are already fruitful in the obvious

350 pride, initiative and independence of the children. I have never seen brighter, more self-reliant and promising children anywhere in Mexico than in this outcast district. There is an obvious seriousness and joy of enterprise that if allowed to develop—and the present difficulty is lack of sufficient finance to carry on—will prove one of the greatest single influences for a better Mexico—and one of the most remarkable educational institutions anywhere in the world.

on play and *18*
meaning in society

PLAY IS UNIVERSAL. It is like worship and like learning. Men everywhere have invented games, dances, physical contests. The Aztecs with their ball games, the Yaquis with their wild deer dance, the Tarahumara running like deer while playing football over endless miles, are expressing the universal impulse that led the Greeks to initiate the Olympics. At its best, play is a social enterprise. For full enjoyment the game needs to become an expression of fellowship, an immersion within the game that gives the players a sense of common rhythm and purpose that welds the body and the spirit.

When institutionalized—as in organized bull fighting, horse racing, baseball, football, soccer—play is more than games. It is in fact popular drama, socialized symbols of heroism and skill, speed and achievement, victory and defeat. Such games involve popular emotion and sometimes popular hero worship. They are symbolic forms of conflict, expressions of cultural values, and definitions of the ideal of manhood. They become public ways of exhibiting cultural values

351

This paper was read at a conference arranged by the *Comite Organizador de Los Juegos de la XIX Olimpiada,* held in Mexico City during June 1968.

and national pride. It is a way for an individual, a group, or a people to define its character in public, in the face of the world. A team of athletes known for their skill, endurance, strength, and speed describes not only themselves but the community that nourished them, the culture that applauded and sent them out to meet the world in friendly combat, to prove themselves worthy of those they represent, winning for themselves honors and for their fellows pride and distinction.

The way of man with nature and with his fellows is tentative, experimental, playful. Anyone who has watched a group of farmers, each armed with a scythe, mow a field of hay, or a group of men armed with machetes cutting down a field of corn, will have recognized that work and play go together in the less-mechanized society. It is no accident when the Indians in Bolivia dress in their holiday clothes and sing their folk songs while working the land for the church as their forefathers did in the ancient days of the Inca Empire. The work men do jointly, voluntarily, takes the form of a rhythmic dance, where the body and spirit are in unison and where work and play are the same. When the community tills the land together, and the women, dressed in the gala dresses, prepare the food to refresh the body, they sing the songs that express the emotional satisfaction of physical well-being, and the rhythmic pace with which the task in hand is being carried forward is akin to play. Throughout the ages, the people working the land have both played and worked, or worked and played in a kind of ongoing rhythm. That is how man mastered the physical world about him. Play is almost the essence of life itself for it identifies man with nature. It is a symbolic expression that he belongs to the earth and is part of it. It symbolizes a gladness of being alive and part of a known and identifiable environment. People are blessed who have not lost this identity between themselves and the physical setting within which they find their sustenance, their mates, their companionship, and their community. When play, rhythm, song, and work go together and where they are all rolled into the daily rhythm of an ongoing community, its members are blessed indeed. Life here is meaningful and its hardships and sorrows become absorbed in a total symbolism. In such a world there is no alienation, no sense of defeat, no lack of will to be part of the group, for that is where the meaning, the essence of life is to be had. Rhythm, companionship, work, play, and community identity go together, and the individual stands inside the group, not outside of it. Self-consciousness and personal ambition are almost meaningless, almost nonexistent. That is how the great cathedrals of medieval Europe were built, by the hands of anonymous architects and plastic sculptors. That is how the great monuments of Indian America were created. It was the work of men absorbed in their love of the supernatural and doing the work in common harmony and rhythm as a symbolic game—or it could never have been done at all.

It is difficult to write about play because it is all-embracing and timeless. It begins at the very beginning of human life—or, better perhaps, of animal life. For it seems as if life and play go together. It is earlier than what the anthropologists call "culture" and has vast outlets long before "civilization." All one needs to do is watch a couple of kittens, or puppies tumbling about, nipping and scratching at each other, chasing each other, knocking each other down, and tumbling all over each other. And anyone who has watched groups of children at random amusement will have glimpsed its significance. They invent games, dances, running matches, hide and seek, wrestling, climbing, standing on their heads, yelling, shouting, jumping, fooling, and, above all, laughing. The whole body is involved, every muscle, every organ. Energy pours out unstinted and uncontrolled. Every child has fallen fifty times, picked himself up and rejoined the game. This is how they make friends, develop companionship, grow in strength and self-assurance, become members of groups or gangs that have an identity, sometimes a name and a leader. And the whole thing is play. It is fun, excitement, companionship, loyalty, identity. It is the beginning of society, of culture, of civilization—for here they take their basic values from each other in play. They acquire honor and pride, standards and ambition from each other. They acquire their discipline and their character from the games they play with their companions and from their companions in the games they play.

Without play there would be no society—no personality, no loyalty, no honor, and no life with one's kind. These basic values are not taught really in school, or by lectures, or by admonitions. They are passed on from children to children, from youngsters to youngsters. When the boy or girl is ready to go to school, his character has already been shaped by the spontaneous free-flowing group activities of the children in the yard, the street, and town square, the field. Without play, man would grow—if he grew at all—to be a stiff, unsocial, uncommunicative creature who would have no friends, no security, and would be incapable of distinguishing between right and wrong. The family and the school merely reinforce what youngsters learn from each other at play, and men continue to play all the time even if half-consciously when they are at work. Play is the essence of life for the young and the old—boxing, swimming, wrestling, running, football, baseball, soccer, checkers, darts, chess, horseshoe throwing—any game, all games.

The free flow of associated relationship, the companionship in a difficult contest, the natural discipline that a game like football or soccer imposes upon the group, defines their relations to each other and jointly against the opposing team. It provides a special quality of social integrity and nurtures a regard for others which helps define man's place among men.

The essence of the difference that lies between a good society and a less desirable one is the degree of spontaneity that the individual and the group are permitted to retain in their daily lives. The demands of society can be stifling and destructive, humiliating and excessive, taking from the individual the spark of inner joy that can only be had in spontaneity, in the freedom of the body and the spirit to respond as the rules of the game require. And all of life is a game which terminates only at its end.

Societies in some ways can be divided or measured in the degree of spontaneity. I am not speaking primarily of political freedom but of the freedom of the spirit that can only go hand in hand with the freedom of the body, of associated groups, of the self-imposed rule, or better still of the rules natural to the game. And the game really becomes life itself— all of it, not just the children's game of marbles or the boys' play at basketball. It really becomes the game of living at ease with your neighbors, of being comfortable in your work, of playing the part of an active and good citizen.

Play is many things. It is harmony. It is rhythm. It contains its own logic. Every game of children or grownups has an inner logic that sets the rules. It is only a game if the rules are followed and lived by. This is even true of animals at play. Dogs nip at each other though pretending to be furious and look ferocious. Kittens only pretend to scratch while tousling over each other. Play carries its own sense of permissiveness, propriety, and rule which may never be broken.

Play is a voluntary activity set within rules known to all players. The order is spontaneous, the law part of the game itself. From a certain angle play educates, disciplines, and prepares for life but does so without plan or purpose because it is a part of life—perhaps the major ingredient in making the social order acceptable and tolerable, and this only as long as the element of play is not suppressed. The slave gang and the prison is where play has been driven underground and denied. But a close observer will note that even in a slave gang, even in a prison, the spontaneous urge for play, frolic, uninhibited games and the expression of fun finds its way to the surface. Here is something as strong as life itself, stronger than the bars of a prison or the state of slavery. Play, however, lies beyond moral valuation. It has nothing to do with folly, with truth, wisdom, goodness. It is a category by itself.

356   Though it permeates all of life and all ages and all cultures,
it cannot be identified or classified with anything else. It is
unique to life. It exists, and as long as life exists, it prevails.
It appears and by appearing changes the situation, making
it lighter, easier, allowing for fun, mirth, hilarity, frolic. Play
can bring buoyancy and joy, but it is none of these. It is an
activity that manifests itself with the living being and must
be considered part of it. It flourishes most easily where there
is room for spontaneity, where the life of man is enveloped
in a many-sided cultural milieu, where play goes hand in
hand with art, religion, architecture, music, drama, philosophy, and literature. The Greek games, the Olympic, Pythian,
Nemean, and Isthmian were all part of a total culture, where
the people were both the spectators and the actors, and where
the city-state provided for a face-to-face community.

The humanistic culture of man flourished in the city-
states of Greece—Athens, Corinth, the city-states of Italy—
in Genoa, Florence, Venice, and the small German states
before the days of Bismarck and Hitler. Be that as it may, the
world of spontaneity and freedom for the human spirit, the
world of myth, wonder, surprise, and belief where man
turned faith into a symbolic drama and worship into a game
that would appease the gods has almost passed away in those
parts of the world that call themselves modern. It has in these
parts of the world been substituted by other views of the
nature of the world and of man's relation to it. It has become
a world in which there is only room for reason, science,
accuracy, speed, productivity. This is a situation where man
aims to control the world rather than abide in it, where he
interferes with nature in pursuit of his short-term interests
and does not really know what it does to the total ecological
environment. There is, in fact, accumulating evidence that
what man is now doing to nature may in the end prove more
inexorably fatal than the atomic bomb itself. In this world
spontaneity, gaiety, freedom, laughter are substituted for by
diligence, ambition, anxiety, fear, and insecurity. The spirit
of play is challenged by the society that science has created

and it remains a question whether many can survive in a world where every moment has to have its logical explanation, where every step is regulated by the computer, and every utterance recorded by some hidden, "snooping" mechanism in the hand of those who would guide and control and direct everyone's life. The challenge is a real one and the stakes are human sanity, for sanity and play are handmaidens and can only live together. The challenge to the spirit that brought the Olympics into being is also a challenge to a society of regimentation and the obsession of endless material possessions.

What characterizes our world is enhanced regulations. The rules that govern the life of man in our industrial society are innumerable and are daily being multiplied. Each rule and regulation so seemingly necessary acts to restrict the area of spontaneity and play. And man is caught in a bind where he seemingly has no choice. He cannot go back and he can only go forward at the known risk that the present direction leads to a kind of self-strangulation. How otherwise explain the revolt of the youth of our time—from Warsaw to Prague, to Belgrade, Paris, London, New York, and Los Angeles. They are rebelling because the elements of spontaneity and play have been siphoned out of their lives, and without spontaneity and play life has no meaning, no values, and no direction.

This present state of increasing logic and specialization has been of slow growth and its effects but little noticed. Our "civilization" has tried to meet the challenge to play in our culture, but not sufficiently and not effectively. It may perhaps be incapable of meeting it.

The last hundred and fifty years have been characterized by increasing industrialism, mechanism, urbanism, centralism, by uniformity, efficiency, productivity, and ever-larger bureaucracy. This list is incomplete, for there is also increased literacy, communication, travel, a longer life span, and many good things too numerous to mention. Certainly they seem or seemed at the beginning good and desirable. And so they were. But perhaps there is a limit. Perhaps we can see a point when any further growth of these elements in contemporary society will prove harmful or even fatal to human well-being and possibly to human survival.

It is clear that the work-and-play theme that characterized agricultural societies through the ages is not possible in the large mechanized factories, mines, and mills. They are governed by rule of speed and efficiency, cost and productivity, and are completely indifferent to the essential needs of human spontaneity and play. So in the large city, the larger it becomes, the more crowded and noisy, the less habitable. Those who can, flee from it permanently or for a few days a week to get back to nature, to the green grass, the birds, the frogs, and the grasshoppers; away from the time clock and from efficiency. But only a few can escape. This is true of all the large cities of the world and they are increasing in size. Where a hundred years ago only about 5 per cent of the people of the world lived in urban centers, now in the United States only 10 per cent make their living on the land. This trend is universal, and the growing urban center is of necessity crowded and noisy, often dark and sunless, often regimented, bureaucratic, anonymous. It provides no room for a face-to-face society, for the companionship and the comradeship required for social cohesion and identity out of which the game grows and the team is organized. The mass in the city can no longer play or participate in playing. It can only stand in long lines to find admission to a movie or a theater, a boxing match—to watch others play, to cheer and shout at other people throwing a ball or winning a fight. Or they can only sit at home and watch television. These are not adequate substitutes for what our "civilized" world has lost. Play is something we all need to participate in personally, and a life of vicarious participation will not do.

It is true, of course, that in more recent years the large cities have begun to attempt to meet the challenge of regimentation. Cities have tried to develop parks and playgrounds, stadiums and amphitheaters where the people can go on Sundays or at night. However except for the park and the playgrounds these facilities do not allow the individual to play; they only make it possible for him to watch other people, if he has the money to pay for the ticket. It is also true that most schools have gymnasiums and playgrounds. But again, they are no substitute for the hilarity of a field where all the village children ran wild and played, or the village green where the entire community turned out to dance in the open under the sky.

There are many cities and universities in the world that have stadiums that will hold fifty thousand people—but of course this is the difficulty. The fifty thousand people have to go through the frustration of securing a ticket, standing in line, traveling to the place, and to sit for hours watching others play—instead of playing themselves.

The professionalization and the institutionalization of games of sport inevitable in our society merely add to the difficulty because they provide a substitute for personal participation rather than an opportunity. In some measure this has happened to music. In a country like the United States there are now over fifty well-known orchestras, such as the Philadelphia, New York, Boston Symphonies, but there are fewer people who play themselves. Piano playing has almost gone out of existence except as a professional matter —the city apartment has no room for a piano, and the noise made by a person learning how to play an instrument would be unacceptable to the other tenants in the same building. Only if you can go to school and take music lessons and have time to practice, and the money to pay teachers, can you become proficient as a musician—and that means a professional route, rather than just fiddling for pleasure. The radio, the portable record player, the television will amuse you. You need only sit and listen or watch; why exercise initiative, why possess spontaneity, why should you play yourself? It may even be against the law one of these days. Only in painting and in sculpture, but especially in painting, has there been a visible growth of personal initiative. The sale of paints, brushes, and paper has become a major commercial enterprise in most modern cities.

Taken as a whole our industrial society has regimented and isolated the individual through regularity, system, clock punching, responding to the whistle, working a given number of hours each day, spending a given number of hours traveling to and from work, living in an environment with a physical relation to the world which allows for little initiative and little spontaneity. The play element in life is stifled or disturbed. The restlessness in the world is the by-product of the lack of the kind of relaxation and joy that an unregimented society makes possible. Play belongs with poetry, art, philosophy, architecture, the dance, drama and music. It requires a spiritual freedom and a spontaneous outpouring that men who live in a mechanical universe attuned to material productivity cannot really achieve.

The pressure of mechanism, efficiency, and regularity is so great that in most industrial societies the hours of labor have been markedly reduced to eight, to seven, and in some cases even to six per day. But this is not the answer. The people freed from the factory and the office or the shop do not know what to do with their leisure. The city has little place for the use of their free time except as spectators. The urban setting has not permitted the growth of the innumerable small "societies" and fellowships that would be required for the spontaneous play-games involving most of the people released from their labor after a shortened work day. And, unfortunately, in most cities the population has now lost the innumerable folk songs, dances, plays, and games that once occupied the leisure hours of the mass of people—from hand carving and knitting to local football and horseshoe throwing.

When I first visited Yucatan in 1923, I watched Governor Felipe Corrillo Puerto playing baseball with some Indians to whom he talked in Maya. And when I asked him why he was so interested in the game, he replied "people that play will not be slaves and slaves do not play." This was exactly forty-five years ago. In these years Mexico has been taken possession of by a cultural, social, economic and political renaissance. In fact, it is the only country in the world of which this can now be said. The renaissance was made possible by the humane spirit of its revolution. I do not know of a single person killed for ideological reasons—though the revolution cost a million lives and lasted many bloody years. The revolution united the people of Mexico with their past. It gave them an identity with the tradition of their Indian forefathers and a sense of continuity. The Mexicans who built the Ciudad Universitaria could only have been those who had in the past constructed the pyramids of Teotehuacan, and the new Museum of Anthropology could only have been designed by the heirs of the artists who contrived the palaces of Bonampak. I am not trying to praise Mexico or glorify its people. But when I first saw Mexico City forty-five years ago it could not have housed the Olympic Games that will be here this year. The changes have not been physical only; they have been social, economic, political, cultural, and moral. They have given the people of this land a true pride in themselves and in their achievements; like the ancient Greeks they could say of those who are not Mexicans that they are barbarians. For the interesting feature of these profound changes visible to the eye in architecture, art, music, literature, and poetry, and in the social and political life is that they have not been at the cost of the elements of spontaneity, of play, of freedom. There is a richness in the cultural variety in this land—not just in the frescos that you see on the walls or the buildings in the large cities, but in folk arts that differ from village to village, where dress, custom, tradition, and even the language may be local and unique, that have remained free and unregimented.

One can only hope that this modern miracle of a cultural renaissance where men are free to play with colors, themes, forms, concepts, and ideas in as many ways as the human imagination will allow, can go on its way to increased eco-

362   nomic well-being without losing its spontaneity, its freedom, the elements of play and fun so visible in the popular arts and in the work of its great artists. The spirit of the Olympic Games requires freedom for both the body and the soul and an environment where the creative play element in human life manifests itself in all facets of men's relations with each other and with nature, and the people of Mexico are closer to that ideal than any others in our day.

index